Much recent fiction from the American South has spotlighted the American ordeal in Vietnam, and a generation of southern writers has been imaginatively preoccupied with ironic parallels that rise out of the Vietnam experience and their own region's tragic past.

This stimulating study of American cultural history discovers the powerful and intriguing links. It shows how profoundly the Vietnam experience has penetrated the imaginations of some of America's most acclaimed writers and how their compulsive sense of southern history unites their vision with the history of the Vietnam war. Set against the backdrop of their homeland Vietnam reveals striking parallels.

Works by a profusion of southern writers have disclosed this astonishing connection in their heritage. James Webb, Bobbie Ann Mason, Jayne Anne Phillips, Clyde Edgerton, Madison Smartt Bell, Barry Hannah, Winston Groom, Gustav Hasford, Harry Crews, Larry Brown, Sydney Blair, Pat Conroy, David Huddle, Yusef Komunyakaa, and Walter McDonald have found in Vietnam many provocative echoes of fundamental issues that first came to a head in the American Civil War. Out of the past the issue of race and the dedication to the land remain distinct themes in contemporary southern fiction about Vietnam.

This absorbing study of cultural echoes that have charged the creative imaginations of fifteen southern writers unites shades of the southern past with the reality of the American present. Both periods have evinced an alarming impulse toward violence.

In this context James Dickey's *Deliverance*, although not a novel about Vietnam, becomes a paradigm of force and southern violence. It serves to reveal the modern southern storyteller's imaginative vision of violence both past and present.

Whether writing of soldiers at war or of the tumult at home, whether expressing the persisting anxiety about race relations or sustaining the community through storytelling, southern writers have found in Vietnam a weirdly revelatory mirror of their own cultural heritage.

Vietnam and the Southern Imagination

Vietnam and the Southern Imagination

by

OWEN W. GILMAN, JR.

UNIVERSITY PRESS OF MISSISSIPPI
Jackson & London

93-1070

The University Press of Mississippi thanks the following copyright holders for granting permission to reprint their material.

"Going, 1960–1970." Reprinted from *Paper Boy,* by David Huddle by permission of the University of Pittsburg Press and David Huddle. © by David Huddle; "Nerves," "Work," "The Air Rifle," "Croquet," and "Icicle." Reprinted from *Stopping by Home,* copyright © 1988 by David Huddle, by permission of Gibbs M. Smith, Inc. and David Huddle; "Nearing the End of a Century." Reprinted from *After the Noise of Saigon,* by Walter McDonald (Amherst: University of Massachusetts Press, 1988). Copyright © 1988 by Walter McDonald; "Caliban in Blue" and "Interview with a Guy Named Fawkes, U.S. Army." Reprinted from *Caliban in Blue and Other Works,* by permission of Texas Tech University Press, copyright © 1976 by Walter McDonald; "Settling the Plains," "The Songs We Fought For," and "The Middle Years." From *Night Landings* by Walter McDonald. Copyright © 1989 by Walter McDonald. Reprinted by permission of HarperCollins Publishers; "Tu Do Street," "Communique," "Report from the Skull's Diorama," "Dui Boi, Dust of Life," and "Facing It." Reprinted from *Dien Cai Dau,* copyright © 1988 by Yusef Komunyakaa, Wesleyan University Press by permission of University Press of New England; "The Firebombing." Reprinted from *James Dickey Poems 1957–1967,* copyright © by James Dickey, Wesleyan University Press by permission of University Press of New England; "Success is counted sweetest." Reprinted from *Final Harvest: Emily Dickinson's Poems,* edited by Thomas H. Johnson, copyright © 1961 by Little, Brown and Company; "To the Lacedomonians" and "Ode to the Confederate Dead." Reprinted from *Poems* (Denver: Swallow Paperbooks, 1961), copyright © 1960 by Allen Tate, by permission of Helen H. Tate and Farrar, Straus, and Giroux (*Collected Poems, 1919–1976,* copyright © 1989); Small sections of my chapter "Regenerative Violence: Or, Grab Your Saber, Ray," were originally developed for another essay, "Barry Hannah." This material is reprinted, as revised and expanded, by permission of Greenwood Publishing Group, Inc., Westport, CT, from *Southern Writers of the Second Renascence—the Fiction,* edited by Joseph M. Flora and Robert Bain, copyright © 1992 by Greenwood Press.

Library of Congress Cataloging-in-Publication Data

Gilman, Owen W.
    Vietnam and the Southern Imagination / Owen W. Gilman, Jr.
       p.   cm.
    Includes bibliographical references (p.   ) and index.
    ISBN 0-87805-591-6 (alk. paper)
    1. Vietnamese Conflict, 1961–1975—Literature and the conflict. 2. United States—History—Civil War, 1861–1865—Literature and the war. 3. American literature—Southern States—History and criticism. 4. American literature—20th century—History and criticism. 5. War stories, American—History and criticism. 6. War poetry, American—History and criticism. 7. Southern States in literature. I. Title.
PS228.V5G55 1992
813'.5409358—dc20   92-18324
                                                                                   CIP

British Library Cataloging-in-Publication data available

For
Joseph M. Flora,
Carolina's Finest,
and for
Mary

What shall we say who have knowledge
        Carried to the heart?
                —*Allen Tate*
                "*Ode to the Confederate Dead*"

Contents

Acknowledgments

This study began to take shape following "Vietnam and the South," an essay that I had the good fortune to write for the *Encyclopedia of Southern Culture*. Over the past five years, my debt to others has grown substantially, for many people and several institutions have been generous in assisting my labors.

My appreciation and understanding of southern culture deepened directly as a consequence of an NEH Summer Institute on "The Southern Novel and the Southern Community," held at the University of North Carolina in Chapel Hill, 12 June–20 July 1989. The program of the institute, a rich mixture of lectures and readings by some of the South's best scholars and writers, was positively inspirational, and the small-group discussions of well-known southern texts proved equally valuable to my efforts to establish a proper background for literature about Vietnam. The discussion group that I joined was led by Bob Bain, Joe Flora, and Fred Hobson, each of whom illuminated the texts we were reading; but I am just as grateful for the spirited comments contributed by the other participants in that group, a fine collection of talented teacher/scholars: Tim Adams, Ann Alejandro, Tom Callison, Tam Carlson, Chuck Hanson, Joyce Jenkins, John Lang, Jennifer Randisi, and Mary Louise Weeks. I am deeply grateful to them all.

The final research and writing required for this project would never have been possible if Saint Joseph's University had not provided me with a sabbatical leave in 1990–91; further support for the last stage of manuscript preparation was also forthcoming from my home institution through a course reduction in the spring 1992 semester. Regarding this assistance, I am particularly grateful to Frank Morris and Eileen Cohen, who provided steady encouragement and backing from the position of departmental chair, which each of them has held while my project moved from inception to conclusion.

Quite a number of colleagues have been generous in efforts to refine my approach to the material in this study. I would like to thank first the students who have been part of my "Southern Literature" classes; in their diverse reactions to assigned texts and to my remarks, they have led me to see things about the South that I would otherwise have missed. Paul Aspan, a member of the Saint Joseph's theology department, listened to my reading of the manuscript in draft form; his forbearance with me is deeply appreciated, and his reactions were always helpful. Whenever I needed quick access to texts from the Vietnam War, I was able to turn to John Baky and the extraordinary collection he manages so skillfully at the Connelly Library of LaSalle University in Philadelphia. John is familiar with just about everything concerning the imaginative responses to Vietnam. W. D. Ehrhart was equally helpful in my efforts to settle upon the group of poets from the South to be included. Jim Webb honored me with a timely and thorough response to my inquiry regarding his own family background vis-à-vis war and the portrait of Robert E. Lee Hodges, Jr., in *Fields of Fire*. Later on, Philip Beidler and Peter Rollins scrutinized the entire manuscript; each of them brought to light matters that needed adjustment in order for the study to be more accurate and satisfying. I appreciate the care evident in their responses. I am grateful, too, for Gwen Duffey's masterful efforts in the copyediting phase of manuscript development. Finally, at every stage of development, this project has benefited from the warm, kind guidance of Seetha A-Srinivasan, who liked the idea of linking Vietnam and the South from the outset and who prodded me gently at key points to keep the work going forward. No one could be served better by an editor than I have been. It has been so pleasant that I am sorry to see the project end.

For encouragement and help of a more transcendent nature, I wish to express my deepest gratitude to my wife, Mary, who has sacrificed much so that I would have time to do this work. She has taken the lead in raising our two boys, Andrew and John, and her talents are everywhere evident in the life we have together. Without her, none of this would have been possible, and none of it would have been, from my perspective, worth doing.

Vietnam and the Southern Imagination

I

The Vietnam War
in Southern Time

FOR A LITTLE OVER A CENTURY, the South had ready access to knowledge not common to Americans at large: indelibly in the southern past stood a defeat in war. Southerners had this particular loss—the Civil War— stamped on their record as a mark of uniqueness. The following study tracks the implications of this sense of southern uniqueness through the experience of the Vietnam War; but before getting to that matter, it must be recognized that other Americans, in some rather large demographic groups, have known their own kinds of defeat, in many ways equal to the experience of the South in the Civil War.

First on the list of American subgroups to know the impact of collective defeat would be the native Americans, who over the course of several centuries suffered the regular removal of both their dignity and their land—by trickery or by armed aggression—as a consequence of the west- ward movement of European settlers in the new world. While the settle- ment of the West was known widely to Americans and contributed power- fully to the mythic foundation of the United States, for many years the story was known exclusively from the perspective of the victor. Only recently have Americans paid attention to this story from the perspective of the defeated, a process perhaps abetted by consequences of the Vietnam experience. It is hard to imagine that Dee Brown's celebrated (hardcover bestseller, with nearly 4 million copies sold) *Bury My Heart at Wounded Knee* (1970), an accounting of the native American's encounter with the "other," would have been nearly so well received even a decade earlier, before the Vietnam debacle had oriented Americans to consider battle outcomes from the side of loss, before the giant nation of the new world had reason to appreciate the gravity of Emily Dickinson's "Success is counted sweetest" poem:

> Not one of all the purple Host
> Who took the Flag today
> Can tell the definition
> So clear of Victory
>
> As he defeated—dying—
> On whose forbidden ear
> The distant strains of triumph
> Burst agonized and clear!
>
> (*Final Harvest* 7)

Dickinson's poem was probably written in 1859, before the Civil War, and she had no war experience in her background. She was certainly not thinking of the plight of the native Americans when she composed the poem. She had, presumably, only intensely personal reasons to be preoccupied with the knowledge that profound loss or defeat brings. In a matter of a few years, it would have been possible for southerners to comprehend Dickinson's message on a large scale, if only the poem, published in a Massachusetts newspaper, had been available to them in the South. It was not, of course, and Americans generally would not have cause to read her poem in light of national experience until the Vietnam War era. By then, there was a readiness to listen to a variety of anthems of defeat, including those of the native Americans, a process that seems to have endured remarkably, as underscored by the box-office success of Kevin Costner's *Dances with Wolves* in 1990, twenty years after Brown, who happens to be from the South (a native of Arkansas), brought out his "Indian History of the American West."

A second subgroup with long-standing historical awareness of defeat would be the African-Americans. Their story was not suppressed in public awareness as long as that of the native Americans, yet their search for a sympathetic and large American audience was not without complications and frustration. The African-American angle on defeat soon doubled, as represented in the split between Booker T. Washington and W. E. B. DuBois in the early years of the twentieth century, a split that appeared to shimmer at least marginally in the choice of Clarence Thomas to replace Thurgood Marshall as a Supreme Court associate justice. The literary record of the African-American knowledge of defeat is distinguished, with a line of powerful writers running from Charles Waddell Chesnutt through Richard Wright and Ralph Ellison. At any point in the literature of the African-American, we are not far from the condition of defeat, haunting specter that it is.

James Weldon Johnson illuminated this condition particularly well in his classic text, *The Autobiography of an Ex-Colored Man* (1912), which recounts the internal struggles of a male protagonist who is so light-skinned that he could pass as white—if he should choose to take that opportunity. Three-quarters of the way through the narrative, the pro-tagonist is made explicitly aware of the probable fate waiting him—and any person of color—as a simple consequence of his racial identity. He has been traveling in Europe with a wealthy patron, but he has determined to return to America and connect himself with black people. In shock, the patron poses a challenging question: "My boy, you are by blood, by appearance, by education, and by tastes a white man. Now, why do you want to throw your life away amidst the poverty and ignorance, in the hopeless struggle, of the black people of the United States? Then look at the terrible handicap you are placing on yourself by going home and working as Negro composer; you can never be able to get the hearing for your work which it might deserve" (105).

The protagonist eventually finds it necessary to take a path that will not be bound to the certain defeat outlined by his former patron, and yet at the end of the story, he finds himself envying those who have accepted the challenge of struggling for racial equality. He is unable "to repress the thought that, after all, I have chosen the lesser part, that I have sold my birthright for a mess of potage" (154).

The African-American struggle has been particularly well represented in the post-Vietnam era with a host of contemporary figures—Alice Walker and Toni Morrison, for example—who couple the African-American sense of loss with the experiences of yet another significant subgroup: women. In Walker's *The Color Purple* (1982), Celie must contend with repression within the world of the African-American; tyranny is known to her first and foremost in the way the men in her life treat her. The whole women's liberation movement, now a phenomenon of several decades, has helped bring to light imaginative works by women, white as well as black, with stories to tell about the knowledge of defeat.

Hence it is clear that defeat cannot be considered a stranger in America, certainly not when all of these various subgroups are considered. Against such a backdrop, the case of the South stands just slightly apart. The southern defeat was a glitch in historical time, ostensibly more finite than the experiences of defeat noted above, more easily locatable in place and time, although its repercussions certainly headed quickly toward the infinite. The loss by the South in the Civil War was something that—from the southern point of view—should not have happened, something conceivably avoidable, a cruel work of fate that cast a proud people into the shock of loss. Once it had happened, however, history owned the defeat, and the South was bound to history.

While the Southern experience of defeat, situated historically between prewar anticipation and postwar reconstruction, has given rise to titles such as *The Burden of Southern History*, C. Vann Woodward's provocative study of the definitive southern identity, it may well be that the ferocious possession of history by southerners has been more beneficial than burdensome. Anyone attempting to explain the extraordinary richness of southern imaginative writing in the last century would certainly be tempted to posit the resonance of history in the South as an enabling factor for the writers of that region, and many scholars have noted the affinity of southern writers for history—their history.[1]

Donald Davidson captured the centrality of history in the South especially well in his *I'll Take My Stand* essay, "A Mirror For Artists": "Its people share a common past, which they are not likely to forget; for aside from having Civil War battlefields at their doorsteps, the Southern people have long cultivated a historical consciousness that permeates manners, localities, institutions, the very words and cadence of social intercourse".[2] (53).

Southerners are programmed to gaze into the past. It is their destiny. The past upon which they gaze is murky, full of enigmatic figures and moments, the very sort of enigma that makes powerful literature. While it is often assumed that the chief benefit of memory is to allow people the possibility of avoiding past mistakes, such an assumption is incorrect. The major asset in remembrance is that it deepens and enriches the stories that might emerge. Stories from a culture with a well-known past have a natural echo chamber, which serves to add greatly to the weight of the storytelling art and tradition.

It might seem, given the events of April 1975, when the collapse of South Vietnam gave Americans as a whole their first taste of defeat in war, that the entire nation had now been given cause to assume the obligations to the past long paid by South, and so it has been, to an extent. The literature of the Vietnam War is extensive, and it is driven by the furies of loss, and anxiety, and enigma.

The winter of 1991 seemed, to some, to offer an experience that would bring the Vietnam angst to an end. American-led forces organized a month-long decimation of the forces of Iraq, whose leader and belligerent policies toward Middle Eastern neighbors, particularly Kuwait, were held to be dangerous for the economic health of many nations, threatening to world peace, and grievously in violation of basic human rights. Even the memory of the last F-15 streaking to its home base across the desert sands of Saudi Arabia has faded quickly, however, and long after President George Bush, exulting in the Operation Desert Storm "victory" of 1991, declared that the "Vietnam Syndrome" (presumably the whole impulse to dwell on defeat) was buried, Vietnam will not be forgotten. Writers for decades will concern themselves with the moral and social consequences of America's lost war, just as innumerable southern writers looked beyond the horizons of the great world wars to see the dust still swirling around Confederate soldiers' statues.

Benjamin Barber's recent reflections on "The Importance of Remembering" in *The Legacy: The Vietnam War in the American Imagination*, edited by D. Michael Shafer (1990), eloquently highlight the addition that memory makes to one's culture: "One of America's troubles now is its inability to read and remember its own past, and so to converse with its future. Memory is how we confront ourselves and legitimize our citizenship. . . . To remember is finally to accept, to possess, and to acquire—to make of memories a force for living" (5).

Because southerners have been working under the spell of history for such a long time, they are ideally suited to the task of placing Vietnam within lasting time. In fact, quite a few southern writers have already engaged themselves in this enterprise. It is the purpose of this study to examine the engagement of the southern imagination with the Vietnam

War—to show how southern writers have brought the unsettling war in Southeast Asia home to their own land, how that war has been fitted into the larger history that is always present for southerners, and how the literature concerning the Vietnam War which came from the American South has a unique character.

Since this study involves the role of history in the life of the imagination, it is fitting and proper to begin with a backward look, searching for a paradigmatic text and a moment in time when the southern propensity for carrying the past into the present was ideally realized. Such a moment and text occurred roughly sixty years ago, when Allen Tate first made public his "Ode to the Confederate Dead."

"Ode to the Confederate Dead" dates to the mid-1920s in terms of composition. Not long after it appeared in *Poems* in 1932, it began to serve as a convenient benchmark of southernness in Tate's growing reputation as a poet; the poem is frequently taken as a handy index to the central concerns of Tate and the group of critics, poets, and essayists (Ransom, Davidson, Warren, and others) with whom he is regularly linked. In *Southern Renascence: The Literature of the Modern South* (1953), for instance, Louis Rubin's discussion of Tate, "The Serpent in the Mulberry Bush," is cued to the "Ode," finding it to be the door that best opens up Tate's acute sense of his region and its past. Rubin has always taken Tate as an important figure for understanding both the South and its literature, and I am inclined to follow his lead. Naturally, though, Tate's "Ode" has not been without its detractors. Ernest Hemingway, for one, disparaged the subject matter of the poem, declaring in a 1945 letter to Malcolm Cowley that Archibald MacLeish had some competition in terms of writing about dead soldiers: "I thought good old Allen Tate could write the lifeless-est lines to Dead Soldiers ever read but Archie is going good."[3]

Tate's "Ode" and its companion poem, "To the Lacedemonians," which was situated before the "Ode" by Tate in *Poems*, with the two poems serving to close the first part of that collection,[4] bring together a host of matters that are indelibly southern. Both of these poems show a southern writer fully engaged with the manifestation of historical events in the present consciousness. While most of my points dealing with this concern for history are linked to "Ode to the Confederate Dead," a few words are first warranted about the posture Tate assumed in "To the Lacedemonians," a work that was originally composed to be part of the forty-second annual reunion of the Confederate veterans in 1932.

With the title of the first poem, Tate angled far back into history, as was his wont throughout his career. Tate was the most effective conservative, in the best sense, of his generation, always looking for a way to pay his respects to the past, and as he organized his imaginative faculties to address the issue of remembering the past, he reached as far back as he could. Be seizing upon an ancient parallel, the commemorative epigraph offered by Simonides for the Spartans who gave their lives defending the pass at Thermopylae in the assault of Persian forces against Greece in 480 B.C., Tate embedded his own region's history in deeper time, a pattern of linkage that demarcates much of southern literature, whether in such masterpieces as Faulkner's *Absalom, Absalom!*, Warren's *All the King's Men*, or the host of more recent narratives dealing with Vietnam.

Tate's speaker in "To the Lacedemonians" seems to be a personage of a time gone by, caught in a moment of memory, at a time when those memories do not fit the present circumstances. Thus Tate acknowledged the problem that he and his fellow radicals in the southern temper of that time—a set of well-educated men who came to be known as the Agrarians—had taken on as an adversary. To a person, they feared that the South was being lost to the modern world and modern ways in a fashion that virtually precluded history.

The land itself had to be their solution, for the land is both life sustaining and long lasting. Whether one hunts or farms, the land must be known intimately, and through this engagement comes continuity through time. That was the constant goal for Tate and his confreres, although in varying degrees they managed to differentiate the segments of the past to which they maintained fixed allegiance. Warren, for instance, eventually retreated from the defense of segregation that was at the center of his "The Briar Patch" piece in *I'll Take My Stand*. While Tate did not follow the path of Warren, whose *Segregation* (1956) explicitly rejected efforts in the modern South to stand in the way of racial integration, thus freeing Warren from charges of racism—we can nevertheless profitably engage ourselves with Tate's poetry, including that linked directly with the South's position in the Civil War, without affirming all that the South once stood for in the historical record. The essential point regarding Tate which must be noted here involves a concern for responding to times gone by. Tate and his colleagues wanted to preserve a linkage with the past. They wanted to resist the rage to change, the forces that were so abundantly evident in the American landscape of their time and that collectively threatened to make all history irrelevant. Lacking a past, the American (or for Tate and others in his circle, the southerner) would be a creature only of the present moment, chasing an ever-accelerating future filled with all sorts of things—televisions, interstate highways, fast-food restaurants, suburban tract developments, computers, laser-guided smart bombs—that have no respect for the land and that coerce the people joined to them to be alienated from land-based values.[5]

According to Tate, the Civil War had been fought, ultimately, about such matters. At the end of his biography of Jefferson Davis, a book published a year before the appearance of the Agrarian Manifesto, *I'll Take My Stand*, and written in the same general period that yielded "To the Lacedemonians" and "Ode To The Confederate Dead," Tate went on record—in absolutely clear terms—regarding his view of the import of the South's loss:

> The South was the last stronghold of European civilization in the west-ern hemisphere, a conservative check upon the restless expansiveness of the industrial North, and the South had to go. The South was permanently old-fashioned, backward-looking, slow, contented to live upon a modest conquest of nature, unwilling to conquer the earth's resources for the fun of the conquest; contented, in short, to take only what man needs; unwilling to juggle the needs of man in the illusory pursuit of abstract wealth. (301)

Thus did Allen Tate align himself with a host of cultural critics, quite a few before him and many since, who have voiced regret concerning the worship of progress in America, a process that tends toward rapacious interest in acquisition of material objects, generally at the expense of the natural environment.

Not long ago, in *The Dispossessed Garden: Pastoral and History in South-ern Literature* (1975), Lewis Simpson provocatively reconsidered the di-verse reactions of northerners and southerners to the place of the garden myth in the American mindscape. Even before the Civil War, northern writers had bewailed the loss of a close and special relationship to the land. Thoreau's *Walden*, the quintessential Agrarian Manifesto of the nineteenth century, turns most directly on that particular point. After the war, southerners had cause to join in this complaint. Tate's position is central to a major concern of his generation that the South's agrarian roots were in danger of being lost, and on a number of occasions, he linked the decisiveness of this loss to the outcome of the Civil War.

As "To the Lacedemonians" rages to its bleak conclusion, the central consciousness of the poem, a personage with some memory of distantly past circumstances, speaks plaintively about the conditions of the present:

> Soldiers, march! we shall not fight again
> The Yankees with our guns well-aimed and rammed—
> All are born Yankees of the race of men
> And this, too, now the country of the damned:
>
> (*Poems* 18)

The last two stanzas of the poem flesh out the consequences of change and loss which attended the signal event of the preceding century, culminating in a final image of defeat: "Damned souls, running the way of sand/Into the destination of the wind!" With damnation echoing all around, Tate used "To the Lacedemonians" to vent his frustration with all that he felt had been lost to the wind.

In contrast, "Ode to the Confederate Dead" serves to resurrect—at least in the realm of possibility—an idea of preserving linkage with the past. This time, the image of the wind that "whirrs without recollection" (*Poems* 19) appears in the first stanza. In the midst of falling leaves, a traditional image of death's sweeping presence, there stand "Row after row" of headstones in a cemetery for the Confederate dead. Additionally, there is a witness to the scene in which "the headstones yield their names to the element," but as Tate himself made clear in "Narcissus as Narcissus," an essay devoted to explicating "Ode To the Confederate Dead," the poem is "'about' solipsism . . . or about Narcissism" (*Selected Essays' 1928–1955* 334). Thus the central persona of the poem, the witness, is an unstable figure, unable to commit absolutely to the spirit of the past. This figure clearly feels the tug of the past, of others, but is caught in the uncertainty that attends "self-love" or "preoccupation with self," Tate's two quick, layman glosses on the meaning of Narcissism (335).

Preoccupation with self occurs in the domain of the present; it precludes effective union with others, whether in the present or in the past. Such is the central dilemma of Tate's "Ode." He offers his readers a figure who is able to respond only partially to the call of the past. This figure has a certain openness to things long gone by and is naturally disposed to accept the following directions from Tate:

Turn your eyes to the immoderate past,
Turn to the inscrutable infantry rising
Demons out of the earth—they will not last.
Stonewall, Stonewall, and the sunken fields of hemp,
Shiloh, Antietam, Malvern Hill, Bull Run.

                                                                (*Poems* 21)

Certain facts about the poem should be recognized at this point. First, that the figure in the poem has access to a graveyard of the dead from a war fought many years before—generations before—and that in many places in the country outside the South, such a moment would be improbable at best. The fact that the graveyard is encircled by a stone wall is hardly peculiar to the South. In my native Maine, I can recall many cemeteries bounded by stone, but nowhere outside the South does the image of a stone wall (and one that is being threatened by the ravages of time and weather) immediately call to mind the loss of a key Confederate general, that loss being accented by a dirge-like repetition ("Stonewall, Stonewall") in the lines quoted above. Nowhere outside the South would the Stonewall figure prompt a rush of place names from the distant past: Shiloh, Antietam, Malvern Hill, Bull Run. Finally, the fact that the consciousness of the figure in this poem can be so readily filled with emotion-laden specifics (persons/places) from the past is crucial to understanding the nature of southerners and their concern for history. In any other region, a writer could not hope to set in motion such reverberations from a graveyard, a stone wall, and names from long ago, but most significant of all is the impulse to respond to the call of the graveyard, not out of morbidity but out of respect for the past. The witness is clearly not Tate himself, but his openness to the past is taken straight from the heart of a southern writer, one abundantly supplied with the inscrutable by birthright.

True, the witness is immediately "Lost in that orient of the thick-and-fast," Tate's explosive image of the almighty American present with its fixation on hustling profits, but at least there has been an opening to the past—immoderate, no less. There exists a sense of events gone by. Sight soon yields to the sense of hearing—"You hear the shout"—and then to the sense of taste—"Now that the salt of their blood/Stiffens the saltier oblivion of the sea," all serving to add to the weight of the past in the receiving consciousness. Shortly thereafter comes the iteration of one of the major themes of the poem, rising to listening ears through the figure of a night creature:

> In a tangle of willows without light
> The singular screech-owls's tight
> Invisible lyric seeds the mind
> With the furious murmur of their chivalry.

(Poems, 22)

Tate explained in "Narcissus as Narcissus" that his "Ode" deals with the "theme of heroism" (*The Man of Letters in the Modern World*, 337), which he clarifies by citing Hart Crane's description of the theme as the: "theme of chivalry, a tradition of excess (not literally excess, rather active faith) which cannot be perpetuated in the fragmentary cosmos of today—'those desires which should be yours tomorrow,' but which, you know, will not persist nor find any way into action" (337).

Chivalry—tradition of excess—in active faith. "To the Lacedemonians" did not rise toward "active faith." Instead it fell finally into the despair of "fragmentary cosmos" as the damnation lines clearly imply. In the "Ode," Tate is somewhat more hopeful, although the ending of the poem leaves the witness in a quandary as to what to do with the past. However, before reaching the haunting enigmas of the poem's conclusion, Tate added two lines that he noted in the Narcissus essay could be taken as providing "the gathering up of the two themes, now fused, into a final statement" (345): "What shall we say who have knowledge / Carried to the heart?" (*Poems*, 23). I take these two lines as being the heart of the matter for Tate and for most of the southern writers of the twentieth century, including those who have worked to place the Vietnam War in the history of their region.

Tate used the comprehensive and gathering pronoun "we" through the last three major sections of the "Ode." "We" broadens the call of the past beyond the consciousness of the particular graveyard witness noted at the poem's outset. Tate also observed in his own commentary on the poem that "knowledge carried to the heart" was "Pascal's war between heart and head, between *finesse* and *geometrie*"(*The Man of Letters in the Modern World*, 344), and so it is, but in the logic of Tate's argument, these words come to represent the essential charge for any and all writers who would ever hope to deal successfully with the commitment of linking past and present—a charge that few southern writers of the century have not accepted willingly and enthusiastically.

Given the movement of reasoning and images in the "Ode," for anyone lacking openness to the past, there is no knowledge carried to the heart. There might be facts, but no valued connection between what had been and what is. Knowledge would be divorced from feeling. There would be surfaces, but no depth. There would be "fragmentary cosmos," but no "active faith." In essence, a historical consciousness creates the conditions for knowledge carried to the heart, and Tate's finest gift to the southerners who would follow in his path finds expression in this phrase that shows where the process embedded in the whole poem leads.

Even though the "Ode" proceeds to a set of open questions—"Shall we, more hopeful, set up the / grave / In the house? The ravenous grave?"—and then on to leave-taking from the "shut gate and the decomposing wall," with all finally left to "The gentle serpent, green in the mulberry bush, / Riots with his tongue through the hush— / Sentinel of the grave who counts us all!"—Allen Tate provided his readers with an explicit definition of both purpose and practice for writers in the South. Continuity was all—linkage of time—and such a process was truly knowledge carried to the heart. Once that phenomenon had been recognized and given its due, one could yield without fear to the "gentle serpent," the figure standing as "sentinel" to our passage back into the land from which we come.

Recent scholarship has shown that Tate may have been wrong in some of his interpretations of the past. Simpson argues successfully in *The Dispossessed Garden* that the old South, before the Civil War, was not the quaint feudal world that Tate imagined but a society transfixed by the fact of chattel slavery, a fact that effectively manacled the imaginations of writers from the prewar South. Louis Rubin, in *The Edge of the Swamp* (1989), generally agrees with the main points of Simpson's analysis. Nevertheless, even as Tate misconstrued certain matters of grave import regarding the makeup of the South, there can be no question about his acute concern for history. In a well-known essay, "The Profession of Letters in the South" (1935), another work from the same time period as the "Ode," Tate identified the strengths of southern writers with history, noting, "From the peculiarly historical consciousness of the Southern writer has come good work of a special order; but the focus of this consciousness is quite temporary? (*The Man of Letters in the Modern World* 319). In the final section of *The Dispossessed Garden*, Simpson wrestles with Tate's anxious concern for the temporariness of historical consciousness and shows how it went through some trying permutations in the writings of Warren and Styron and a few others in the late 1960s. In *The Confessions of Nat Turner*, for example, Simpson finds Styron attempting to ratify "a covenant with the existential self" (*The Dispossessed Garden* 99), a covenant that took "the idea of the self as the constitutive realm of being." Such a position was meant to supersede the efforts of an earlier generation (Tate, Faulkner, and company) that had firmly asserted "the primacy of memory and history" (99).

Yet if we turn to a host of southern writers who have been challenged by the Vietnam War, we can see abundant evidence that historical consciousness is a sweeping phenomenon in the South to the present moment. To a person, these writers seem to have accepted the paradigm of necessity for the past as it is shown in "The Ode to the Confederate Dead." They have been called to deal with knowledge carried to the heart, and as it did for Tate, it rises out of a past both long and richly moving.

The study that follows will concern itself with a dozen or so contemporary writers, all of whom have southern roots, some better recognized than others. The feature of their writing that most tellingly marks it as southern involves the use of history. We can think of the body of literature to be studied here as a large and growing tree. At the top, there are spreading branches, which show the differentiating tendencies of individual writers. At the bottom, there are diverse roots, reaching down into a wide variety of social and cultural conditions in the South. The trunk is history, the common denominator in the play of the southern imagination upon the Vietnam conflict. The southern writer typically does not approach Vietnam as an anomaly—a weird mutation on the otherwise spotlessly good American record in war. The southerner knows better. He or she knows that Vietnam is part of deeper time and that dispiriting losses like the Vietnam War have at least one prior analogue already lodged in the nation's past. As a consequence, the southerner is not likely to write about Vietnam as a narrowly defined experience, one that commences with the formative moments of a fictional protagonist's life (including perhaps some recognition of obligation to carry on the legacy of victory in World War II) and proceeds along to combat and then—in some cases—to consideration of the problems of the veteran in rejoining American culture after Vietnam combat. The southerner's sense of time extends backward, far beyond Vietnam.

In contrast, novels about the Vietnam War by people not from the South generally deal with a time frame fixed on the present. It often seems that Vietnam constitutes the beginning of time in these texts, and in some, the end of time is foreshadowed as well. To illustrate this pattern, we can turn to two well-known novels of the Vietnam War by nonsoutherners: *Dog Soldiers* by Robert Stone (1973) and *Paco's Story* (1986) by Larry Heinemann.

Robert Stone is one of America's finest novelists. From *A Hall of Mirrors* (Faulkner award for first novel in 1967), through *Dog Soldiers* (National Book Award), *A Flag for Sunrise* (1981), *Children of Light* (1986) and *Outerbridge Reach* (1992), Stone has probed anxiously at the nature of American culture; his explorations of the limits of man (and America) are unsettling. Despite occasional flashes of recognition on the part of his characters that there might have been a time worth knowing before their own, they never respond deeply or successfully to the past. They are universally creatures of the present moment, rushing along often enough to an end that is at best pathetic. Stone's novels are awash in nihilism. The most hopeful statement offered by a Stone character occurs near the end of *Children of Light* when Gordon Walker, a movie scriptwriter with plenty of turbulent clutter in his past, personal and professional, declares: "I thought that at my present age I might stop going with the flow" (353). "Going with the flow" is the dominant habit of being for the Americans in Stone's fictional world; they inhabit the present, with no anchors to the past. Memory is an unwanted feature of life, painful at best.

Consequently, *Dog Soldiers* takes up the Vietnam War as a point of departure—for drugs, as it turns out, not just for the flow to the future of America—although Stone weaves a sense into the narrative that America-to-come does indeed flow from the innocence that led to Vietnam, innocence that finally collapsed on itself in a cataclysmic way. Stone builds his Vietnam novel on the principle of analogy: as Vietnam was, so shall America be. Vietnam eventually became a moral cesspool, and in such an environment, Stone places an American opportunist, a man named John Converse, who plans to capitalize on his deliverance from Vietnam by shepherding a big load of heroin back to the states. His plan runs afoul of circumstances beyond his control (in the tradition of Vietnam), but the drugs get to America anyway, where another man, Ray Hicks, tries to carry forward the dream of cashing in on the American yen for narcotics. His plan also goes awry. It seems that there are plenty of mean and ugly entrepreneurs who are interested in distributing the Converse drug haul. In the loving company of Marge Converse, John's wife, Hicks perseveres for some time, traveling a few steps ahead of organized thugs, but he eventually dies as a consequence of an apocalyptic mountaintop shoot-out. All of the stateside action takes place in California, used symbolically by Stone in this novel and in *Children of Light* to indicate the future in America.

To the extent that any kind of tradition is recognized in relation to Hicks's action, it comes through the analysis of Dieter, a cosmopolitan citizen of the universe who is widely traveled and full of both Zen mysticism and drugs. Just before the battle precipitated by the intrusion of Antheil and Angel, two corrupt law enforcement officers—one from the United States, one from Mexico—who see a chance to strike it rich in busting Hicks, Dieter says to Marge: "Look at Ray. . . . He's trapped in a samurai fantasy—an American one. He has to be the Lone Ranger, the great desperado—he has to win all the epic battles single-handed" (270).

Thus Hicks embodies something a little larger than himself, not surprisingly since Stone is so completely a symbolist, but Hicks does not seem directly connected to any particular past. He hails from Chicago (Converse is a New Yorker, a former Catholic), but he could be from Anywhere America, the America that is endlessly mobile in pursuit of the American dream.

Hicks dies by himself, a lone ranger, beside railroad tracks running through the desert of southern California. His expiring thoughts are scattered, running the gamut of his cultural experience, from a large dose of *semper fi* Marine Corps slogans to a tad of Nietzsche. He aspires to simplicity of thought ("Let's just say I carry what I carry and leave it at that"), but he knows that: "It's not so simple because there are as many illusions as there are grains of sand in the goofy mountains and every one of them is lovable. The mind is a monkey" (327). Eventually he passes into nothingness ("I am not my five senses. . . I am not this thought"), connected to the world in his final moment only by his grasp on the "blazing rail" (327) of the tracks across the desert.

Converse and Marge find Hicks's body. They leave the dope for Antheil and make their escape in a jeep that sends up a giant column of dust, to which Marge yells, "Fuck you. . . . Fuck you—fuck you" (335). Converse closes this part of the narrative with an ironic echo of the Beatles: "Let it be" (335), words lifted from an anthem of hope and placed as a conclusive note to a tale of hopelessness. It then falls to Antheil to offer the final words to summarize the desert world at the end of the novel, a bit of wisdom that he carries along from somewhere in his enigmatic past: " 'Someone told me once,' he said, 'something that I've always remembered. This fellow said to me—if you think someone's doing you wrong, it's not for you to judge. Kill them first and then God can do the judging' " (338–39).

Stone's novel is about such amorality, and it is replete with figures who come from "somewhere" and are destined to land eventually "nowhere." They are certainly not anchored to any particular place in their past, and Stone presents them as quintessentially American.

The situation in Heinemann's *Paco's Story* (winner of the 1986 National Book Award) is similar, although Heinemann more than Stone presents the Vietnam War as a radically new point of departure for America. His narrative begins self-reflexively with "Let's begin with the first clean fact, James. This ain't no war story. War stories are out—one, two, three, and a heave-ho, into the lake you go with all the other alewife scuz and foamy harbor scum" (3).

By such a declaration Heinemann stakes out the total newness of his territory—one so unlike any preceding that it mandates a new genre, departing distinctly in every way from existing "war stories." It is a bold stroke, and it signals the arrival of a postapocalyptic world.

The ultraironic jive talk of the narrative voice at the novel's outset derives straight from Vietnam, and to complete the Vietnam idiomatic matrix, Heinemann adds the necessarily hypothetical—even ubiquitous—receiving audience: James. James is not "in the know," is not privy to the secrets of Vietnam, and so must be informed—with a new idiom in a new form. The old ways of telling will no longer suffice. So much for the past!

Paco, of course, has something of a past, but mainly it involves a particular moment in Vietnam when his entire company was overrun in an enemy attack, leaving Paco as the sole survivor. Paco as we come to know him dates only from that experience.

The days following the near annihilation of Fire Base Harriette are not happy ones for the survivor. Paco is a wandering alien as he returns to his homeland, and he is forever destined to be an outsider. Life goes on apace for the people he encounters, caught up as they are in their present affairs, but Paco finds no grounds for community with them.

Much of the narrative concerns Paco's time in a small town in the middle of the country, a town to which he travels without plan, just leaving the Greyhound bus at that point, finding a place to live (the Geronimo Hotel) and a place to work (washing dishes at the Texas Lunch). All the while, Paco remains a distant figure to those he meets. He is close only to the dead from whom he parted in the horror of Vietnam combat; they visit him regularly in dreams; they are present in his waking thoughts; they watch over him constantly like guardian angels, but they can offer him no real assistance as he contends with the business of living. As it eventually becomes apparent, the dead are in fact responsible for telling Paco's story. Instead of stories about the dead, the regular pattern, here readers meet a story by the dead about the living. True, Paco is in possession of the past, but the past is intensely personal, woefully private. Paco's story is a tale born of pathos, and the ravaging effects of Vietnam are shown without compromise.

The closest that Paco can come to the intensity of life represented by sexual union occurs only through Paco's senses of sight and hearing. He watches a woman in an apartment near his, and he hears her engaged in sex with "Marty-boy," her college-student, future-accountant lover. When she is not so occupied, she watches Paco in his room—even makes some notes about him in her personal journal—but when Paco visits her room surreptitiously and reads from her diary, he learns the true distance between them. It seems that she has had a dream about making love with Paco, but her diary entry shows Paco how his Vietnam scars have forever barred him from acceptance. Cathy, the girl, has seen Paco's scars; her dream turns into nightmare as her subconscious fixates on them:

> . . . and I think I hear screams, as if each scar is a scream, and I look up at him again and he's peeling the scars down his arm, like long peels of sunburned skin, brown and oniony. Then he's kneeling on my shoulders, like we used to when we'd give a kid pink belly and he's laying strings of those scars on my face, and I'm beginning to suffocate. Then he reaches both hands behind him, as if he's going to pull of a T-shirt, grabbing and pulling the scars off his back. And I could hear the stitches ripping. And he lays

them across my breasts and belly—tingling and burning—lays them in my
hair, wrapping them around my head, like a skull cap. And when each scar
touches me, I feel the suffocating burn, hear the scream.
    And then I woke up. I just shuddered. . . . It made my skin crawl.
(208–9)

Reading of this rejection, privately inscribed though it is, Paco knows
that it is time to travel on. Within moments, he is headed out to the
service station to catch "the westbound bus. There's less bullshit the
farther west you go" (209–10).

Heinemann provides a Huck Finn ending ("I reckon I got to light out
for the territory ahead of the rest") for *Paco's Story*, but Paco is no Huck
Finn, and readers of this Vietnam story are not about to be seduced back
into innocence by thinking that there is any hope for innocence in the
West. When the bus pulls out and Paco is gone, he is long gone, just
biding his time until he joins the dead who constitute the best part of his
waking world.

Dog Soldiers (by a nonveteran) and *Paco's Story* (by a Vietnam veteran)
are fairly representative of Vietnam literature by writers who are not from
the South. As extensive and impressive as this body of literature is, it
reflects scant concern for deep history—time in America before the Vietnam era—and the protagonists are not deeply rooted in any one place in
America. Of course, writers outside the south have told stories of veterans
going home and attempting to reconnect with the people they knew
before Vietnam. Tim O'Brien's *Northern Lights* nicely illustrates the pattern of the veteran who tries to find his former place in his homeland, but
in Minnesota, where O'Brien's narrative unfolds, there does not seem to
be much of the past that can be reclaimed.

Southern writers who have dealt with Vietnam, however, seem preoccupied with placing the whole experience deep in the context of their
region. Again and again, southern writers have shown a fascination for
the call of history, and this sense of the long reach of time has mandated
placing Vietnam against the backdrop of earlier events in the national
record. Thus the pattern of concern for the past in the South—as reality
or as myth—which C. Hugh Holman carefully scrutinized in *The Immoderate Past: The Southern Writer and History* (1977), has been extended into
another generation. Holman borrowed his title from Tate's "Ode," and he
built his analysis upon the consideration of writers ranging from William
Gilmore Simms through Ellen Glasgow, William Faulkner, and Robert

Penn Warren, drawing upon a host of earlier studies of the South (including William R. Taylor's *Cavalier and Yankee: The Old South and American
National Character*, C. Vann Woodward's *Origins of the New South, 1877–
1913* and *The Burden of Southern History*, W. J. Cash's *The Mind of the South*,
works by Clement Eaton, and many others). Several other studies in the
past fifteen years have fleshed out this pattern, but none to date has
addressed the group of contemporary writers from the South who have
imaginatively engaged the Vietnam experience. The general studies of
Vietnam War literature have dealt, to varying degrees of success, with
matters of myth and reality on a national scope.[6] As this study unfolds, it
should become clear that the "historical consciousness" alleged by Donald
Davidson as a natural part of southern life has survived both modernity
and postmodernity, finding its way—almost inevitably, it seems—into the
southern writer's representation of Vietnam.

Often southerners have found in the Vietnam War provocative echoes
of fundamental issues that came to the surface in the Civil War. The whole
issue of race, for instance, is developed rather differently by southern
writers, and writers of the South have frequently found in the Vietnam
War traces of an earlier generation's passionate concern for the land and its
values. Similarly, the turmoil of the Vietnam era brought the southern
tradition of honor into prominence and, with it, the related spirit of
violence. In short, southern writers find in Vietnam a weirdly revelatory
mirror of their own particular cultural heritage. From the mustering of
soldiers for war to the propensity for violence at home, from the persistent
anxiety about race relations to the sustenance of community through
storytelling—when the southern writer surveys the Vietnam War and its
impact, he or she sees the South. Thus this study begins with *Fields of
Fire*, a novel that solidly presents the southern warrior tradition and
vividly portrays combat action in Vietnam, and it concludes with *Deliverance*, a novel that does not mention Vietnam but contains all the essential forces brought to light by the war—in essence, Vietnam fought in the
South.

2

Vietnam and the Warrior South

This study began some six years ago with an unexpected telephone call. Peter Rollins, one of the pioneers in exploring the aftermath of Vietnam from an American studies perspective, phoned me to inquire whether I would be interested in writing an essay on "Vietnam and the South" for the *Encyclopedia of Southern Culture*, a project that he himself could not undertake because of prior commitments. Up until that moment, my analysis of Vietnam literature had been concentrated on purely formal matters, looking at narrative forms for signs of revelation about the meaning behind the war experience for Americans. From the imaginative texts—both fiction and nonfiction—that I was reading then, it seemed that the essential message of Vietnam was radical discontinuity, a break in time, signaled by the fragmentation of language and formal structure in many of the major narratives dealing with the war. The exploration that went into "Vietnam and the South" opened my eyes to the whole issue of cultural continuity as it might be witnessed in certain aspects of the South's heritage. What most immediately surfaced in that regard was the warrior tradition.

Tate's "Ode" contains a tantalizing hint of the South's impetuosity with regard to the call to battle. We need only remember how the "screech-owls's tight / Invisible lyric seeds the mind / With the furious murmur of their chivalry." Clues to the South's warrior tradition are abundant here. An "invisible" but penetrating "lyric" comes out of nature itself—out of the place and its creatures—and "seeds the mind," thus assuring continuity of harvest, generation after generation, each generation caught in fascination with the "furious murmur of their chivalry." The call to war quickens the human imagination everywhere to some degree, a point driven home by the enthusiasm of Americans all across the nation for the Operation Desert Storm military action in the winter of 1991, which lasted just long enough for there to be scant flagging of support for the operation as it whirled and churned to its conclusion. We would have to turn to an event of much longer duration—and involving much greater duress—than the month-long devastation of Iraq to measure more comprehensively and truly the various levels of war readiness (perhaps even fervor) that might be discerned in Americans. Given such a long look, diverse kinds of evidence—in oral histories, in memoirs, in literary texts, in statistics—signal the unusual magnitude of this phenomenon in the South.

As noted above, Tate's "Ode" opens the door to the matter of chivalry, a code of behavior long linked to the South. Surveying the Louisiana Capitol building in Baton Rouge, one of many stops along the meandering way of *Life on the Mississippi* (1883), Mark Twain tied the South's enduring fascination with the chivalric to the steady influence of Sir Walter Scott:

> Sir Walter Scott is probably responsible for the Capitol building; for it is not conceivable that this little sham castle would ever have been built if he had not run the people mad, a couple of generations ago, with his medieval romances. The South has not yet recovered from the debilitating influence of his books. Admiration of his fantastic heroes and their grotesque "chivalry" doings and romantic juvenilities still survives here . . . and traces of its inflated language and other windy humbuggeries survive along with it. (237)

A bit later in the same work, Twain took on Scott's influence in an even more hostile manner, culminating with the well-known assertion about Scott's role in pushing the South into the Civil War: "Sir Walter had so large a hand in making Southern character, as it existed before the war, that he is in great measure responsible for the war" (266). Although

Twain quickly labeled this suggestion a "wild proposition," allowing readers to take it as just another of his impetuous jests, we know that Twain's jests were usually in earnest. He was certainly serious a few sentences later when he wished for a time when southern writing might emerge from Scott's long shadow: "Instead of three of four widely known literary names, the South ought to have a dozen or two—and will have them when Sir Walter's time is out" (267).

Twain's hope for a bountiful crop of southern writers has been amply realized in the twentieth century, and on the surface of most of the great modern literary texts of the South, there certainly seems to be little of Scott's influence. However, at a deeper level, the chivalric impulse decried by Twain in Scott's work has survived. Chivalry involves a code of honor, and the South has not shaken itself free of a deep and abiding sense of responsibility to the standard of honor. To grasp the full import of this phenomenon, we must turn to more deliberate and systematic evaluations of the south than Twain ever claimed to offer.[1]

Although Bertram Wyatt-Brown's *Southern Honor: Ethics and Behavior in the Old South* (1982) does not attempt to show fully the evolution of Old South honor into contemporary forms, it provides an illuminating background for consideration of the southern warrior in the modern era. In Wyatt-Brown's analysis, the origins and implications of honor in the South are rather complex, emerging from Celtic traditions (with roots extending into antiquity) and soon blending into issues of patriarchy, gentility, and social hierarchy, but when he lists the elements "crucial in the formulation of Southern evaluations of character," honor stands at the top of the list "as immortalizing valor, particularly in the character of revenge against familial and community enemies" (34). Wyatt-Brown demonstrates convincingly how fully a code of honor served southern social, economic, and political needs in the eighteenth and nineteenth centuries. Once southern culture embraced the concept of honor in one generation, its associations with family and with the individual's position of respect in the larger community made it almost impossible to abandon.

The twentieth century gradually brought changes in southern life, first in the gradual shift from agriculture, then in a wrenching turn away from blatant racism, and finally in a sweeping realignment of political power. Through all of these transformations, each of which naturally created a degree of anxiety, there was an urgent need for continuity, and of those things that stayed constant, southern honor became perhaps the most potent, and nowhere else than in responding to the call to battle has southern honor been more salient. In the South, serving one's country in war became the highest obligation of honor that one could hope to realize; by such an act, an individual paid clear and unambiguous respect to the family of one's birth, to the community, and to the past.

In the Vietnam War years, southerners were more than proportionately represented in the American armed forces—at all levels. In the early 1970s, four out of five army generals came from southern towns. The best known of these generals, William C. Westmoreland, who commanded the U.S. forces in Vietnam from 1964 to 1968, was from Beaufort County, South Carolina. When Westmoreland retired from military service in 1972, after four years of service as chief of staff, he returned to South Carolina to live near the battery in Charleston. Westmoreland comes close to embodying the perfect image of the southern warrior, a stance of honor demonstrated by virtue of service to country, although by the time he completed his military service in 1972, he felt obliged to tell his own story because, in the minds of many Americans, his honor had been severely questioned, most fully in a CBS news documentary concerning his role in managing information about enemy troop strength in the year preceding the 1968 Tet offensive. The title of his story, *A Soldier Reports* (1976), shows how fully Westmoreland accepted the warrior image, and his preface candidly notes his desire to "tell it like it was" (xi) so as to remove any possible stains from that image.

Westmoreland used the first chapter of his "report" to establish his early background vis-à-vis honor. First to receive tribute was the general's father, "a man of strong character, industrious, thrifty, scrupulously honest, intolerant of unreliability and immorality" (10), who "tried to instill in me respect for those virtues for which I later learned West Point stands" (10). After a year at The Citadel in Charleston, Westmoreland received an appointment to the Military Academy, which brought both challenges and rewards: "Most rewarding of all was the appreciation and respect I gained for the code of ethics for which the Military Academy stands and which its honor system exemplified" (11). In Westmoreland's retrospective, "an officer corp . . . must have a code of ethics that tolerates no lying, no cheating, no stealing, no immorality, no killing other than that recognized under international rules of war and essential for the military victory" (11). When the army chief of staff, General Douglas MacArthur, addressed the West Point graduating class of 1933, his remarks on the honor code impressed young plebe Westmoreland: "The military code that you perpetuate . . . has come down to us from even before the age of knighthood and chivalry" (11). Thus did Westmoreland line up his formative experiences in the military, taking pains at every turn to show how fundamental was the place of honor.

Westmoreland also makes his southern heritage clear in the first chapter. He observes, for instance, how taken he was with Lieutenant Colonel Simon Bolivar Buckner, the commandant of cadets, who was "proud of a reputation as an outdoorsman and of the father for whom he was named, Kentucky's Confederate General Buckner, who had surrendered at Fort Donelson, Tennessee, to his old friend Ulysses S. Grant" (11–12). With such a detail early in his memoir, Westmoreland accentuates the fact that, even in military defeat, persons of honor can maintain the stance of pride, a point of wisdom only southerners could take to heart before Vietnam.

Another early anecdote points to the same general conclusion—that honor and valor rise above other considerations, including military loss. Back in South Carolina after his second year at West Point, Westmoreland paid a call on a great-uncle "who had joined the Confederate Army at the age of sixteen and had fought in a number of major Civil War battles, including Gettysburg, and had been with Robert E. Lee at Appomattox" (12), a man who hated "Yankees and Republicans, not necessarily in that order, and talked derisively about both." Uncle White asked Westmoreland what he was doing with his life. When Westmoreland answered, "I'm going to that same school that Grant and Sherman went to, the Military Academy at West Point, New York" (12), the old veteran reflected silently for long moments, then responded, "That's all right, son . . . Robert E. Lee and Stonewall Jackson went there too" (12). History placed its stamp upon Westmoreland through his own family, and as a consequence, he was able to pursue his career, with honor, as a southerner.

Recently, when interviewed by James R. Wilson for *Landing Zones: Southern Veterans Remember Vietnam* (1990), Westmoreland once again voiced the particular lessons of history that go with being a southerner. He was able to assert, naturally and without hesitation, that the past contained a parallel to the Vietnam War. Though not a perfect counterpart to Vietnam, "the Civil War comes close in some respects. The Civil War was not a static war, but one of movement; it was not a war one could follow very well on a map" (18). Through a number of provocative points, Westmoreland traced the similarities of the two wars, leaving the final point—about how the conclusion of each conflict would be registered upon a native southerner—unstated, but forcefully implied.

The perspective of the best-known general from the Vietnam era carries obvious weight, but there were numerous southerners involved in the war at lower levels of service as well, and while their stories are not widely known, they show the broad dispersion of the warrior tradition in the South. For example, John S. Candler, Jr., from Atlanta, Georgia, was an army platoon leader in 1968 and 1969. In his interview with Wilson, Candler confided, "I come from a conservative, flag-waving family. . . . My grandfather was a commander of the Georgia National Guard, and my father served in the Army Air Corps in the Pacific during World War II" (147). Richard C. Ensminger came from a military family, too, so it was natural for him to join the Marine Corps, a move that took him to Vietnam as a forward observer in 1966–67 and in 1969. Ensminger's cultural preparation for military service was clearly sufficient to make him happy enough to go to Vietnam, but it did not prepare him for "what a nasty situation Vietnam was" (*Landing Zones* 23). Still, even after having discovered the realities of Vietnam, Ensminger volunteered to return for a second tour, because, as he told Wilson, "I believe in God and country. When I went to Vietnam, I believed it was my duty to go over there and fight for my country" (28), and furthermore, by 1969, "Somehow, I felt I wasn't wanted in American society" (29), largely because of drift away from fervent patriotism in much of the country outside the South.

In the South, of course, there was some evidence of protest against the Vietnam War, but support for the war remained stronger in the South than elsewhere. One reason for the steadfastness of the South involves the extensive presence of the military in the eleven states of the Confederacy. In 1967, for instance, 42 percent of the stateside payroll for military personnel went to the South. Linked with these payroll dollars were whole communities dependent in large part on the military.[2] The South's economic well-being was intricately tied to the war, and beyond that, southern recruits could also expect the natural support that went with military training conducted in their own region. Army trainees were sent to Fort Benning, Fort Gordon, and Fort Stewart in Georgia; Fort Rucker in Alabama; Fort Bragg in North Carolina; and Fort Polk in Louisiana. The marines had Parris Island in South Carolina and Camp Lejune and Cherry Point Naval Air Station in North Carolina.[3] In short, the vitalizing presence of the armed services in the South simply added to the already existing ethos of the patriot warrior, thus making it possible for popular support of the war effort to remain fairly high in the South until the end—and even in the years after the fall of South Vietnam.

It was the patriotic angle that served to motivate George D. Riels, a Mississippian, who volunteered for the marines in 1967: "We felt it was the patriotic thing to do" (*Landing Zones* 111). Certainly there were patriots throughout the nation, but the spirit of patriotism seemed to have greater impact where the history of military service within families was known to potential young soldiers. J. Houston Matthews observed to Wilson, "Like a lot of other southern families, mine has a military tradition that goes back to the Civil War" (102), and although Matthews's father, who had served with Patton's Third Army, did not want his son to risk his life in Vietnam, Matthews felt that the call of service was a time-and-family-honored way to give his life direction; he subsequently joined the marines. For some who served in Vietnam, the identification of southern heritage became even stronger as a consequence of the war. Twenty years after his time in Vietnam as a machinegunner with the 82nd Airborne, Donald L. Whitfield, of Eutaw, Alabama, lives in a mobile home with "a huge, fading Confederate battle flag tacked over the front door" (202). During his talk with Wilson, Whitfield made clear his need for the Confederate flag: "I fly the Rebel flag because this is the South, Bubba. The American flag represents the whole fifty states. That flag represents the southern part. I'm a Confederate, I'm a Southerner" (209). Despite having rendered service to the nation as a soldier in Vietnam, Whitfield has chosen to align himself only with his native region. Only that identity makes sense given his experience, for only in the South does he feel the devotion to freedom that outlasts military setbacks like the one in Vietnam.

Of course, some of the soldiers who came into the army during the Vietnam era were not motivated by a sense of honor or a call to serve a family tradition. Instead, military service was just a way to escape the poverty that still was profound in much of the South in the 1960s. Robert McNamara's Project 100,000, a program designed to open up military service to "marginally qualified" youths as a means to extract them from impoverished conditions, eventually brought more than 240,000 men into the armed services. Many southern African-Americans joined the army through this project. All too often, of course, the route to a better life involved service in Vietnam, and as this pattern became apparent, there were significant numbers of desertions, and with so many recruits from the South coming through Project 100,000, the South is overrepresented in the cases of military desertion.

Despite the desertion statistics, the South's image of honor in military service is reinforced by the fact that, with only 22 percent of the nation's population, 29 percent of the Medal of Honor recipients for Vietnam service went to southern soldiers. This detail confirms the enduring nature of a passion for valor, a trait that rises out of southern history and seems to strengthen in the adversity of defeat. James Webb's first novel, *Fields of Fire* (1978), rages defiantly against anyone who would question the value of valorous service to the nation, even when that service took place in the moral nightmare that was Vietnam. In Webb's development, the warrior tradition becomes mythic, something that stands high above the ugly political contortions that were evident in the conduct of the war until its sad conclusion.

James Webb found his life's work recast in the labors of bringing *Fields of Fire* into print. The final chapter of the novel represents the confrontation that motivated Webb to turn his efforts to the making of books. That chapter recounts the experience in law school of a character named Goodrich. As a liberal graduate of Harvard and as a weak-spirited soldier, Goodrich is initially the direct antithesis of the native character of Webb the author, but Goodrich has been transformed by his war experience. He has lost a leg (Webb's own combat wounds primarily affected the use of one of his legs), and he feels more affinity with his soldier associates from Vietnam—most of them dead, a few casualties even coming as a consequence of Goodrich's soldierly ineptness—than he does with his fellow law students or with the law faculty.

After Webb left military service in 1972, he went to law school at Georgetown University, where he earned his J.D. degree in 1975. He felt like a total anomaly in the world of the Georgetown law school, the one person with combat experience, the one person who had loyalty to the soldiers who had served their country in Vietnam. Whenever Webb recalls that experience, as he did for the students in a Vietnam war novel course I taught in 1982, he boils with anger. His outrage at the sweeping rejection of both the war and its American combat participants grew to the point where he desperately needed an outlet. The answer came in a work of fiction.

Webb wrote *Fields of Fire* in a frenzy of creativity, driven by the compulsion to tell a story that would restore a sense of honor to the record of servicemen in Vietnam. It is not a simple story, however, and it does not whitewash the moral wretchedness that combat conditions in Vietnam created. Yet the story unabashedly celebrates the warrior tradition. In the mid-1970s, that tradition was not popular, and rejection of Webb's manuscript by nine publishers might even signify that the tradition was not deemed marketable.

Delivering the keynote address for the May 1985 Asia Society Conference on "The Vietnam Experience in American Literature," the program that Timothy Lomperis summarized and disseminated in *"Reading the Wind"* (1987), Webb assailed the "Academic-Intellectual Complex" (18) that had resulted in a monolithic, antigovernment, antisoldier stance in the literary world. Such a stance, Webb argued, was in need of balancing, with the balance to be provided by books like *Fields of Fire*. Many of Webb's fellow writers at the Asia Conference took issue with his argument, but the record of *Fields of Fire* in the marketplace, once it was finally published by Prentice-Hall in 1978, indicates that there are plenty of readers who share his commitment to honoring the soldiers of Vietnam.

With well over a million copies sold, *Fields of Fire* is one of the best-selling Vietnam novels, and its gritty, naturalistic realism has made it a favorite among Vietnam veterans. In each of the four times in the past decade that I have taught a course dealing with Vietnam War literature, *Fields of Fire* has been the text that most fully engaged my students' imaginations. They warmed to the clarity of characterization and structure in Webb's book; some of the more complex narratives (for instance, Tim O'Brien's *Going After Cacciato*, Ward Just's *Stringer*, or James Park Sloan's *War Games*—none of them being, incidentally, of southern origin) left students cold. Whether this student reaction speaks of critical acumen or of something else is uncertain; suffice it to say that Webb's story registers itself forcefully on readers and that it attaches itself to a warrior tradition linked to the South through the background of one of its major characters, Robert E. Lee Hodges, Jr., the figure in the story for whom Webb has the greatest empathy.

The parallels between Hodges's and Webb's backgrounds are significant. Both Hodges and Webb are named for their fathers. Webb's father was a career officer in the United States Air Force; Hodges's father served in the army in World War II and lost his life in the Battle of the Bulge. Although Hodges did not have a living father to shape him into a warrior as was the case with Webb, grandmother Hodges supplied him with a full slate of memories of the past, brining his father back to life in the process of her storytelling. The presence of a grandmother to make the past accessible was a potent element in Webb's own youth; his material grandmother lived with his family until he was eight. In a phone conversation in the spring of 1991,[4] Webb recalled fondly how his grandmother would tell stories of the past every night at bedtime. Thus, with regularity, even in post-World War II prosperous America, Webb heard how his ancestors from Virginia, Tennessee, and North Carolina were involved in the Revolutionary War, fighting with distinction at Kings's Mountain and elsewhere, and he heard the story about the ancestor (Doyle), just off the boat from Ireland, who fought the British in the War of 1812.

Most telling of all, he heard of his people several generations back who had become caught up in the Civil War. His great-great grandmother's brother—from mountain, nonslaveholding people—was in the Davis Rifles; he served under Stonewall Jackson, was wounded at Cedar Mountain, and was killed at Chancellorsville. There was a great-great grandfather who became a forty-three-year-old private in the Virginia cavalry and who started a family tradition after the war by naming his first son Robert E. Lee Webb. There was, on his mother's side, Sam Marsh, who initially joined the Arkansas infantry but later moved to Tennessee and became part of Nathan Bedford Forrest's cavalry. There was Alec Long, also on his mother's side, who died at the Union prisoner-of-war camp at Alton, Illinois. Finally, for a bit of balance that Webb relishes, there was William Asa Hodges (Webb's mother was a Hodges), a Tennessee-born great-grandfather who fought for the Union from Kentucky (two-thirds of Kentucky had gone to the Union after Confederate forces crossed the border from Tennessee in 1862) and eventually saw considerable action (Lookout Mountain, Chattanooga, Kennesaw) in Sherman's long march to the sea in 1864. Stories upon stories upon stories, all with vivid details—the places and people all carefully named, so accurate that, when Webb's research for *Fields of Fire* took him to the National Archives to check the written account of his family, there were no surprises. The oral record that his grandmother had provided him when he was twelve squared with the documentary evidence.

No matter where the Webbs moved, and they moved often according to the various postings of an air force career officer, Webb had roots. He was born into a storytelling tradition, one that came from a place held in reverence, at least partly, for things done on the field of battle long ago. Wherever Webb was, he was of the South, and this heritage eventually worked its way into his first novel—with some changes, naturally, to provide a bit of distance and perspective.

One of the key changes, of course, involved having Hodges lose his father in World War II. This critical detail opened the door to the challenge of recovering the past—literally bringing it to life out of death. The first mechanism in this process for Hodges was the last for Webb: an encounter with documentary evidence, official papers bearing in them certain facts of an earlier time. Early in the story, Hodges discovers a dusty footlocker full of his father's personal belongings from the war, Purple Heart and all. The contents of the footlocker, while not in themselves uniquely southern, serve to set the narrative on a course backward in time. In this regard, both Webb's own life and the fictional case of Hodges prove to have a clear southern orientation.

According to the sketch of Webb's life in Charles Moritz's *Current Biography Yearbook* of 1987, his ancestors "fought in the Revolution and in every subsequent American war" (590). Webb constructs the same historical past for Hodges. Of all the characters in *Fields of Fire*, Hodges most directly reflects the Webb family legacy of service in war. In both the real and fictional cases, the regional orientation is resolutely southern.

The Hodges family lives in a part of Kentucky with allegiance to the Confederacy during the Civil War. There is a monument in the square: "a stolid Confederate soldier peering south toward Tennessee, one of the few in a Kentucky town" (34). Although the Hodges family hails from border country, their bedrock southernness is announced at the beginning of the novel's second chapter, when the protagonist's full name is first mentioned. "Robert E. Lee" almost says it all, but from that clarion opening, Webb builds a twenty-three page chapter dedicated to the warrior of southern heritage.

Webb is clearly concerned with placing the warrior tradition of the Hodges family at the level of mythos, and it draws heavily upon the system of family honor described by Wyatt-Brown in the study mentioned earlier. Because Robert's mother remarried after World War II, there has never been any talk of his natural father, so as not to offend his stepfather, but family traditions exist for Robert nevertheless, in the footlocker artifacts and in his grandmother's stories. By such methods myths are realized, and Robert's action depends absolutely upon the call of the past as it is represented in footlocker and story.

On the "day before he left for Vietnam" (24), Robert visits the footlocker to connect himself with both history and destiny. The footlocker is "guarded by cobwebs," since Robert's visits have not been regular, and in it he finds "the remains of his father," not physical, of course, but emotional. After all, myths play upon us at an emotional, irrational level. There are "two brown army uniforms of World War II vintage," some items from a newspaper about the war in Europe, letters from his father to his mother, a picture scrapbook, and finally the last official documentation of his father's life: "a manila envelope containing the letter which informed his mother that his father had been killed, and three medals, including the Purple Heart" (24).

The detail about the medals is highly significant, at least within the corpus of work produced by Webb to date. Medals are meant to be taken very seriously, constituting the nation's effort to officially recognize acts of valor and service. The front of the book jacket of Webb's most recent novel, *Something to Die For* (1991), shows Webb's own combat decorations, not as a statement of personal aggrandizement, but as part of the text's message about the way medals are properly meant to be understood— although the awarding of medals to participants in the novel's action is shrouded by clouds of irony and even moral corruption. One of Webb's greatest concerns throughout his career as a novelist (and equally throughout his career of public service) involves the danger of misperceiving or misrepresenting the honor that should accompany medals given for acts of valor.

Young Robert E. Lee Hodges, Jr., accepts the meaning of his father's medals and of the other material in the footlocker without question. He is an innocent, although for Webb this condition is not a fault. Robert takes things at face value: "It was enough for him that he had found them, and was able to experience them" (25), but Robert feels an injustice in the fact that he alone values what his father gave in the service of his country, a point shown as he reflects upon the harshness of his father's fate: "How sad to have sacrificed your life for your country, to have faced the bullet on the fields of fire only to have your memory purged as a part of a jealous lover's insecurity" (25). To Robert, then, will fall the task of honoring his father. His action proceeds out of deep family commitment. As Webb quickly shows, the Hodges family has long recognized the importance of living up to the standards of the past. Looking at a picture of his father in uniform, "wearing a defiant solumn bold glare copied from some Rebel ancestor" (25), Robert concludes: "Man's noblest moment is the one spent on the fields of fire. I believe that" (25). In this declaration, Robert's destiny is manifest. He will fight, "because we have always fought," and even though he does "not look a warrior" (25), he will acquit himself decently as one.

However, the story of how Robert E. Lee Hodges, Jr., went to Vietnam would not be so much a reflection of southern culture if it did not also include the presence of Robert's grandmother, for she becomes the voice of the past, providing for Robert the sense of history that tantalized the graveyard witness in Tate's "Ode To the Confederate Dead." Robert regularly visits his grandmother on Sunday. It is a ritual for him that takes the place of religion, but the ritual serves his needs at a deeply spiritual level. During these Sunday visits, he does a variety of chores for her— hoeing her garden, mending a fence, limeing the outhouse—and then comes the meal that she has prepared specially for him. The act of sharing food together has long been crucial to the maintenance of community in the South, and in these meals, Robert and his grandmother create a kind of family communion, which concludes, inevitably, with storytelling that solidifies the past for Robert. Such moments prime the pump of conservatism in nature, and they situate Robert as a person within the realm of mythos:

> Since he was the last it had become perhaps the most important thing in her waning life that he should know of those who went before him. All the campfire stories and the front-porch chronicles, of the wilderness days and the Hodges who had fought and fallen, had dwindled down to him and her. And these tales, these forgotten pieces of history, would be passed to him or die. All the pain and misery and minor successes and major sacrifices would be learned by him or forgotten by the entire world. She was intent, compulsive: she would not let them be for nothing.
>
> So she taught him all the Ghosts, over the years of Sundays, inside the shadows of her kitchen. And this is what he learned, under the patient drone of a suffering voice grown old and dry. (29)

The signal importance of history for people of the South is amply demonstrated by Webb in this passage. In the subsequent details of figures from the Hodges family past, Webb ties his novel to a pattern of historical connectedness that sets the South apart from other regions of the country. As Webb indicates with his portrait of another character,

Snake, who prepares for the combat of Vietnam by surviving on the tough streets of an inner-city ghetto, warriors can come from places other than the South, but it is within southern culture that the tradition of the warrior serves most fully as a driving force. The past in the South is infinitely more than the record of history texts. It is brought to life in the form of real people, remembered people, who participated somehow in weaving the fabric of time. All it takes is someone to keep track of the weaving threads.

The Hodges tapestry (or chronicle) begins with Abednego, a mountaineer of the South during the revolution who is captured by the British. His son, Isham, serves in the militia in the War of 1812, then moves from Virginia westward to Tennessee. One of his sons, Welcome, moves up to Kentucky, raises a large family, and then, as an old man, must face the death of several of his sons in the Civil War, "three of 'em just in Pickett's charge" (30). The report that reaches old Welcome, passed along to Robert by his grandmother, catches all the insanity of the carnage at Gettysburg but highlights the honor of fighting for a cause: "But then the whole row with those Hodges boys was ripped up and three of Welcome's fighting boys dropped down in that field. The ones that made it back said those Hodges never even got to fire their guns, that they'd walked a mile in all that heat and dust and they'd almost made it up to them damn Yankee cannons, but then the cannons beat them to it. They faced the cannons, though! Died on a day of glory!" (31)

What the survivors of that moment could claim was honor, a point reinforced by the interpolated remarks of General Lee himself:

> They all said he was crying, riding on his white horse from group to group, that white beard of his just soaked with tears. Told them he was sorry. Told them they were God's bravest creatures, that they'd earned a glory spot in heaven. Told them it was himself who lost the battle. That's the kind of man our General Lee was, son. That's why you and your daddy both were named for General Lee. He was a man of honor and he cried the day three Hodges died on the glory field. (31)

At the end of the grandmother's recitation about the Civil War dead, Webb enters the narrative in his own voice to summarize: "It was a continuum, a litany. Pride. Courage. Fear. An inherited right to violence. And the pride accumulated, even as the reasons themselves grew more amorphous" (31). Although Webb's summation may seem a little pat, it is undeniably consonant with the overall objective of his development of

Robert E. Lee Hodges, Jr., in the Vietnam era—to show how, at least in the South, present-day persons are linked to patterns larger than the individual self. Myths have that function in the cultural life of a people; by tracing the warrior tradition in the Hodges family, Webb isolates one mythic dimension of the South.

Robert's grandfather "breathed the gas for Pershing" (31), leaving the South for the better part of two years "not for the honor of Old Glory, but for this vestige of lost hope he called the South" (32). The Grandfather returned home, only to live just long enough to survive his son, who, following in his father's footsteps, went off to fight the Germans. Two world wars, two generations of modern Hodges off to Europe: "And, both times, the landscape of the South escaped unmarked, while its cemeteries burgeoned" (32). Those burgeoning cemeteries are both statistically significant as an index of the southern warrior tradition and a reminder of the setting for Tate's "Ode," with its poignant recognition of "knowledge carried to the heart" as it surges out of the past.

Robert E. Lee Hodges, Jr., of course, is amply supplied with knowledge carried to the heart, albeit through the medium of his grandmother, and with this background, he is bound for Vietnam. In fact, the pressure of his past is so great that some sort of wartime experience seems absolutely mandated. As Webb puts it, "If there had been no Vietnam, he would have had to invent one" (34). Webb's vision of this point is even more unnerving now than it was in 1978 when the novel appeared, for in the wake of Desert Storm, which seems to have served the grand purpose—for President Bush at least—of burying the doubts of Vietnam deep in the sands of Kuwait and Iraq, we are given cause to realize how the war of one generation beckons to the next. Here rests the dilemma inherent in the warrior tradition. If one accepts it in principle—and if one inherits it from a culture with a mind for keeping the historical record intact—then the pursuit of war becomes an absolute condition of the culture.

Fields of Fire accepts that principle, and it links Vietnam to a particular form of cultural inheritance in the South. As Hodges takes leave of his grandmother for the last time, he goes off toward Vietnam not with deep commitment to saving "Vietnam from itself" (35) but with a sense of obligation to his ancestors: "And besides, Vietnam was something to be done with, a duty. Not for Vietnam. For honor (and a whisper saying, 'for the South'). And mostly for the bench seat in the town square" (35). The bench at the town square is the location of public story-swapping, the place where Hodges's own war experience will eventually be traded back and forth across time. That bench sustains the values of the culture, and as long as it is still there (the bench may now be outside of town in a shopping mall), the culture will feed the virtue of valor to each succeeding generation. Such a process, including a strong dose of motivation, sent young Hodges out of the town of his birth to meet his destiny elsewhere.

Hodges reaches Vietnam. He fights there with great distinction and is greatly esteemed by his men, but all of his honor and all of his virtues are not sufficient to deliver him alive from the war. Ironically, his death comes as the result of another man's troubled sense of honor. Goodrich (known to his fellow soldiers as "The Senator," because of his Harvard, well-bred background) is distraught that six members of Hodges's unit have avenged themselves in cold blood upon two Vietnamese civilians who were held accountable for the deaths of Baby Cakes and Ogre, two other soldiers in the unit. The Senator files an official report of their misconduct, but before the incident can be investigated, Hodges's unit is engaged by a large enemy force. By not acting aggressively, again a consequence of moral confusion that does not recognize the duplicity of the enemy, Goodrich precipitates a sequence of events that leads to his own wounding. Snake, one of the men accused by Goodrich, gives his life in trying to save the Senator, and then the same thing happens to Hodges, who is killed in the act of trying to direct artillery fire that will secure the unit's safety from attack.

Hodges thus follows his father in becoming a casualty of war, one of the frequent outcomes in the warrior tradition, but he providentially leaves a son, and Webb is explicit in suggesting that the warrior legacy will continue—though the means for its survival involves a megamerger of cultures that could only take place in the late twentieth century. Hodges had married a Japanese woman, Mitsuko, when he was stationed in Okinawa, his Marine Corps assignment before Vietnam. They conceive a child, and although Hodges never sees his son Hitoshi (like father, like son), Mitsuko provides sufficient grounding in the warrior tradition (part Japanese, part southern) to ensure that it will carry forward into the next generation. Hitoshi asks his mother, "What was he like?" (388), and that

opening leads to the fulfillment of the warrior tradition as myth, something that transcends the ordinary temporal boundaries of human existence. All it takes is the telling of the past.

"Your father was—a very brave man" (388), Mitsuko begins. When
Hitoshi asks how his father was brave, he is provided with the code of the
warrior: "He was a brave warrior. He was not afraid to fight in battle for
his country. Once he was shot here, and here, and here—" (388). Despite
those wounds, Hodges had recovered, and he had gone back to battle.
Hitoshi presses his mother further, looking for the key to his lost parent:
"Is it good to be so brave? To fight for your country like that? Was it a
good thing that my father did?" (389). Anyone with a sense of James
Webb's background (member of a family with southern roots, son of a
military man—which reinforced the idea of family tradition—graduate of
the Naval Academy at Annapolis in 1968, Marine Corps officer in Vietnam, and winner of many combat medals, including the Purple Heart)
could predict with absolute certainty Mitsuko's answer to her son: "Yes! It
was a very good thing your father did" (389).

Since Webb is drawing upon the function of mythic material in a
culture, he does not traffic in ambiguity at this crucial moment in his
narrative. He yields to the impulse of commitment, dedicating the future
to the pursuit of honor for the record of the past. Hitoshi says it all:
"Then I too will be a warrior" (389). With that declaration, the saga of the
Hodges family completes one more full revolution. Okinawa is on the
other side of the globe from the American South, but the warrior tradition of the South is meant to reach into the future nevertheless, having
relocated itself in another culture with some of the same tendencies with
regard to honor.

Since publication of *Fields of Fire* in 1978, James Webb has persistently
labored in a variety of ways to sustain the concept of honor. His second
novel, *A Sense of Honor* (1981), turns directly on the matter of ethics in the
world of the warrior—the very issue mentioned so prominently by Westmoreland in his memories of West Point. The story of "Wild Bill" Fogarty
in *A Sense of Honor* is bitterly ironic. Fogarty, who has a southern background, is a first-classman at Annapolis, and he is the ideal warrior person-
ified. However, because of a civilian professor at the Naval Academy who
has strong convictions about individual civil rights, Fogarty eventually
runs into trouble with the official policy of prohibiting acts of hazing.
Fogarty has violated the letter of the policy, and although Webb shows his

actions to be well intentioned and perhaps even necessary to produce the kind of soldiers who will have the courage needed for battle, he is eventually forced to leave the academy. The novel was not nearly as successful either artistically or commercially (just a quarter of a million in sales) as *Fields of Fire*, but it clearly followed in the same vein.

Webb's next outing as a novelist was a book called *A Country Such As This* (1983), and it attempted to assess the standards of the nation. To provide a sweeping scope, Webb traces the history of three naval academy graduates from 1951, the time when they left Annapolis, to 1976—the year of the American bicentennial. Each of the three characters is given his due, but Webb seems to identify most with Judd Smith, who comes out of the mountains of western Virginia. Smith is a rough mountaineer, with a reputation, almost from birth, for creating trouble. By the end of the narrative, Smith is forced to do battle on behalf of the armed forces against the former wife, Dorothy, of Joe Dingenfelder, another of the major characters. A member of Congress, Dorothy is opposed to the escalation of military armament programs. Smith has long since left the military to become a preacher, serving the people of his hometown, Bear Mountain, where the soldier on the Confederate Memorial is still "facing south" (317), but then, sensing that the country has drifted too far away from the commitments of its past, he goes off to Congress (*Mr. Smith Goes to Washington* redux). On the battleground of Washington politics, he faces off against Dorothy. Their combat is fierce, but they finally come to terms with their differences of opinion, which are motivated on each side by a sense of honor and dedication to principle, thus defining the nature of a country such as America.

Webb's career underwent a major shift in the mid-1980s; in 1984 he was made assistant secretary of defense for reserve affairs by President Reagan, and then in 1987, he was nominated by President Reagan to serve as secretary of the navy, taking the place of John F. Lehman, Jr., a civilian without any military experience. Webb accepted the job in order to re-establish the concept of listening carefully to career military officers in the making of military policy. Webb felt that Lehman had too often acted without proper understanding of what military action involves—a problem repeatedly addressed in Webb's fiction. As it turned out, Webb found the task of tangling with politicians to be so unpleasant that he resigned before completing a full year as navy secretary. Once again he turned to the writer's craft, which holds greater possibilities for having an impact on American culture, because, as he had noted earlier upon encountering the dismal thickets of Washington policymaking, "in writing, you can affect people's emotions and attitudes" (Moritz, *Current Biography Year-book* 582).

Something to Die For, which appeared in January of 1991, just as America moved from the posture of Desert Shield to the military action of Desert Storm, confirms all of Webb's long-standing anxiety about the possible abuses of the military by civilian policymakers. For this story, Webb resuscitated the figure of Bill Fogarty, who had been left in official "dishonor" at the end of *A Sense of Honor*. Fogarty is cast in the Hodges mold— son of a military father, with a strong southern warrior heritage, destined to do his duty and die for his country. This time, however, Webb situates the warrior in the middle of a story that has at least as much to do with the forces of government that create the need for war as it does with actual combat.

The South is introduced quickly in the novel's "Prologue," which presents the background of Colonel Bill Fogarty, commander of the 51st Marine Expeditionary Unit. Fogarty's life has been governed by a photograph of his father's being congratulated by General MacArthur for heroic action in Korea in September 1950. Little Bill Fogarty had treasured that photograph, arming himself with courage sufficient to carry him through until his father's return from war. His father did return, but the importance of the soldier image in Fogarty's life only grew through time. Later, even after distinguished service in Vietnam and after considerable achievement in Washington military circles which would guarantee a comfortable civilian job upon retirement, Fogarty has remained committed to the warrior role: "At bottom, he soldiered for the children who sat at home and pondered photographs and prayed that their own fathers might soon return" (10), a notion that he himself recognizes as "medieval in modern America" (10).

The Fogarty family disposition toward soldiering, however, goes back far beyond the father. His mother accepted her only son's decision to enter the infantry with "quiet desperation" (10). Still, in her background, there are the seeds for her son's action.

> But she was of the mountain South. She knew that conflict filled her people's veins, and that she could no more alter the flow of her blood than she could redirect the Tennessee River, which curled past Lookout Moun-

tain near her childhood home, reminding her every day of the Civil War battles that tore at the heart of her ancestors. She knew her son was part of a continuum, that her people had straddled a paradox for thousands of years, wishing most of all to be left alone, but drawn to fighting as naturally as a bird dog thrills at its first flushed covey of quail. (11)

Thus was the stage set for Bill Fogarty, and a photograph of him, taken during the Marine Corps dispatchment to Lebanon in 1983, has been long treasured by his son. At the beginning of the novel, it seems clear that the warrior tradition is certain to last beyond the days of Bill Fogarty.

The South is invoked again in the first chapter, which provides a quick orientation to the political infighting that is part and parcel of making policy moves in Washington. Ron Holcomb, the secretary of defense, is a man of sharp intellect (Harvard undergrad, Yale law), a young Turk on a very fast track through the corridors of political intrigue at the national level, but Holcomb has to use all sorts of stratagems, some above board and some not, to keep his agenda on the move. When he pays a visit to Senator Joe Barksdale, the majority leader, to seek his support in a budding scandal about the loss of technological secrets to the Russians through the duplicity of major Japanese corporations, he runs up against positions for which Harvard and Yale were not the best preparation.

Above the senator's door is "a photograph of Nathan Bedford Forrest, a revered Confederate general who had fought many battles in Mississippi and western Tennessee" (19). Holcomb mentions Forrest to the senator, expecting to score points for some knowledge of the southern general, but he gets a minidissertation on Forrest's character that speaks to issues far beyond his own particular background, which has never brought him close to wearing a uniform. When Holcomb offers a comparison of Forrest to Teddy Roosevelt, Barksdale's scorn erupts:

Teddy Roosevelt made his name in a battle that was hardly more than a skirmish by any standards. Bedford Forrest fought for four years, in all the bloodiest campaigns. He was the only Confederate leader who refused to surrender at Fort Donelson. Led his whole cavalry regiment out, each man riding double with a foot soldier on his horse while the other commanders gave up. Seriously wounded at Shiloh. The bright star at Murfreesboro and Chickamauga. His little brother, who he had raised as a son, was killed at his side there at Brice's Crossroads. He got off his horse and held his brother for a minute, calling for him, then got back on his horse when he saw his brother was dead and won the battle. Wounded four times. Had twenty-nine horses shot out from under him. Killed at least thirty men in hand-to-hand fighting. And what do we remember? An hour on San Juan Hill. (21)

This recitation about Forrest is revealing on two counts. First, Forrest's reputation is primarily secure in the South; he is less likely to be known elsewhere than Generals Robert E. Lee and Stonewall Jackson. Webb certainly studied Forrest in military history classes at the Naval Academy, but that knowledge would not be sufficient for the extensive meditation on Forrest's valor. Webb's southern heritage—particularly the fact that he had an ancestor who served with Forrest—has to be accountable for the way Forrest's military prowess is promoted early in the novel. Second, the steadfastness of Forrest as a military man (Forrest's legendary reputation in the South will be discussed later) serves as a historical parallel (lacking any hint of Forrest's postwar racist activities) to Bill Fogarty. Forrest and Fogarty, of course, are complete contrasts to the civilian orientation to war that Holcomb represents.

The civilians—Holcomb and his president, Everett Lodge (a compulsive poll-watching Washingtonian political creature, who seems more than a little like George Bush)—eventually create the grounds for a brief combat engagement between Fogarty's Marine Expeditionary Unit and Cuban soldiers trying to establish control over the region of Eritrea for Ethiopia. The political maneuvering behind the "war" is far too complex for a brief summary, but to Fogarty, the whole situation makes no sense. He asks his superiors for reasons that he can give his men, so that they will have "Something to die for" (66), but his request is not honored. As events unfold, Fogarty is caught in the role of warrior. He is dispatched to accompany French units maneuvering to meet the Cubans. He witnesses the first engagement of troops. He feels the call to battle. When his own unit is sent ashore, he leads them courageously—at the cost of his life.

The "war" is over in days (in this Webb anticipated almost perfectly the nature and duration of Operation Desert Storm), with the Cubans being hopelessly short of technology and air power, but still the battle claims its victims, with Fogarty at the top of the list. The narrative concludes with a series of ironic awards ceremonies, the harshest being the presentation of the Medal of Honor to Bill Fogarty, posthumously, with his widow accepting the medal. Fogarty's son John is deeply distressed by the loss of his father, naturally enough, but even more so by the note of falseness he detects in the words of President Lodge at the presentation. John does not accept the president's statement, "It wasn't easy making the decision to send our troops into Eritrea" (327), not because John knows the secret behind the whole fracas—that the president never indeed made a decision—but because he feels the words are spoken just to please the "adoring crowd" (327). He quietly accuses the president of killing his father, and Lodge is taken aback by this comment but makes the moment his for the crowd by hugging the boy, an act that allows him to whisper to the boy to stand tall for his mother's sake. John recovers his composure, tells his mother he is OK, but Webb adds: "But he wasn't. And he never would be" (329). In that declaration, Webb has taken his case for the southern warrior to a new point of departure. In essence, the entire tradition stands in jeopardy as a consequence of political maneuvering that borders on moral bankruptcy.

It is an intriguing position for a life-long military warrior to adopt, one that should give the nation cause to examine its mechanisms for finding wisdom in moments when war seems imminent, but in the wake of the Operation Desert Storm victory, any such reexamination is far from likely. If anything, the whole Persian Gulf escapade seems destined to extend the reach of the warrior tradition, at least to another generation of young Americans and probably to regions outside the South as well. The statistics for American combatants during Operation Desert Storm clearly confirm that the South is as vigorously committed to the idea of military action as ever. The army's recruits from the Southeast outnumbered other regions by a 3–2 ratio in 1990, and in most recent years, about 40 percent of new armed forces personnel come from the southern region. Of the 128,027 reservists and National Guard members called for duty during the Desert Shield/Storm period, 52 percent came from the South.[5] It seems clear that the warrior tradition in the South is standing firm, very much at the ready to assert itself whenever the next adversary becomes apparent.[6]

Webb admits that the combative tendencies—the willingness to rush into a fray without regard for possible consequences—remains strong in southern culture. In our March 1991 phone conversation, Webb inquired whether I knew the joke about how many rednecks it takes to change a light bulb: "Four. . . . One to change the bulb, one to write a song about it, and two to go out into the parking lot to fight over it." These days Webb worries that such impulses may at one time lead to catastrophe.

Given the wild flag-waving witnessed in the winter and spring of 1991, when the next war becomes inevitable, there will be plenty of soldiers from the South who will be ready—perhaps eager—to answer the call to duty. It will be their time to honor their families, their communities, and their particular past.

3

In Which Country?

Going away from home—wherever home might be—to fight a war has inherent potential for trauma. War is not meant to be like home life, and as a consequence, the military must prepare soldiers for unfamiliar conditions. Often this process involves training that mimics the expected reality of a war zone. The physical environment of Vietnam alone warranted careful efforts to help soldiers at least anticipate—since they could not fully know Vietnam except by direct experience—what awaited them in the combat zone on the other side of the world. How better to meet this challenge than to take advantage of the South as a locale for the initial coming-to-terms with Vietnam?

As we shall soon see in Bobbie Ann Mason's *In Country* (1985), the South might serve as much more than a conditioning factor for soldiers; it could also serve as a "stand-in" for the entire Vietnam experience, if one had the requisite imagination and the compulsion to make it happen. This point will reappear later in this study with consideration of several other novels, including Dickey's *Deliverance*, but since Mason's text rings some important changes on the function of history which *Fields of Fire* introduced, *In Country* must be examined at this time.

Many of the soldiers who fought in Vietnam were not of southern origin, yet by virtue of military training conducted at southern installations, their orientation toward Vietnam reflected at least a portion of the conditioning that continues to make the South unique. Training in the South for Vietnam made sense, for in that region, soldiers could be given the most practical introduction possible to the feel of heat, humidity, and other discomforts that would be encountered in most of the combat regions of southeast Asia. Recruits entering the main gate of Fort Polk, Louisiana, passed under a sign announcing the degree to which training in that particular environment was their new place of origin: "Welcome to Ft. Polk, Birthplace of Combat Infantrymen for Vietnam." In such fashion did the South assume a crucial, albeit passing, formative role in the background of many soldiers who left the "World" (the Vietnam-bound soldier's reference term for home—the United States) to meet their fate in the jungles, mountains, and deltas of Vietnam.

The Vietnam experience was, following the logic of terminology noted above, "unreal," not of the "World." The experience typically involved a whole set of distancing elements that put the individual soldier into a realm that seemed to have no sensible connection with what had gone before. Soldiers acquired new names almost immediately, spontaneously coined monikers that reflected the impressions that others formed of them. Then came the race against time—a year's worth of days (for marines, an extra month) to be survived. Within that framework, attitudes about life and death often changed radically, with each successive transformation putting the soldier at greater and greater distance from the people he had left at home.

When soldiers returned—whether wounded (physically or emotionally) or in apparent good condition—they typically encountered culture shock. They were exposed to something that those left behind were not, and the combat trip made an immeasurable difference. Many of the narratives that are included in this study deal directly with the problems attending the veteran's return home.

Some soldiers did not return alive. They were the more immediate and obvious casualties of the war experience, lost to the grim facelessness of the body bag and aluminum casket. For soldiers like Hodges in *Fields of Fire*, the future would depend entirely upon memory, and because the

American psyche often does not seem to incorporate much capacity for memory, these soldiers could be lost before long. Against this possibility of loss stand at least two elements of redress.

First, there is a V-shaped, black stone wall not far from the Lincoln Memorial in the nation's capital. The Vietnam Veterans Memorial has proved to be an extremely moving and powerful place for acts of re-membrance to occur. Second, there is the general tendency of the south-ern imagination to remember—the pattern that gave rise to Tate's "Ode." The wall and the cathartic value of remembrance are crucial to Bobbie Ann Mason's *In Country*, a work that simultaneously deals with the case of a soldier killed in the war and with the case of a returning veteran who is almost as lost as the one who is dead.

Mason's Vietnam story emerges from the same southern-oriented Ken-tucky that was home to Robert E. Lee Hodges,[1] and the narrative form of Mason's novel is even more tightly linked to southern customs, because at its core, *In Country* is a paean to remembrance. Knowledge carried to the heart depends upon the sustenance of memory. Mason's novel celebrates the spirit of memory. It demonstrates the absolute necessity of finding the past and coming to terms with it. To avoid this necessity is to put one's self and one's culture at desperate risk.

Understanding the importance of history to a southerner is crucial to grasping the design of Mason's narrative, especially its conclusion. In "Realism, Verisimilitude, and the Depiction of Vietnam Veterans in *In Country*," an essay contained in Philip Jason's recent collection, *Fourteen Landing Zones: Approaches to Vietnam War Literature*, Matthew Stewart, while providing some penetrating insights on Mason's development of Emmett Smith as a veteran suffering psychic wounds, misses the point of the conclusion entirely, assailing Mason's imagery in the last paragraph as being "optimistic to the point of sanguinity" (176). For Mason—for many other southerners—there is indeed great joy in finding a mechanism for opening the past to the present, which is just what happens at the end of *In Country*. Such acts provide the best hope for humanity, and Bobbie Ann Mason's reading of the Vietnam War turns pointedly on the inter-weaving of imagination and memory.

In Country begins on the road. After the novel's headnote reference to a Bruce Springsteen song with a road motif, Part One of the story places three travelers on Interstate 64, heading toward Washington, D.C., des-tined for a visit to the Vietnam Veterans Memorial on the Mall. These

travelers span three generations of southerners. The youngest is Samantha Hughes, eighteen-year-old daughter of a soldier killed in Vietnam
before her birth. Next oldest is Emmett Smith, Samantha's uncle, father-
surrogate, and Vietnam War veteran with severe adjustment problems.
Finally there is Mamaw Hughes, Samantha's paternal grandmother. Mason wisely holds their reason for going to Washington until the end,
filling the center of her narrative with the backgrounds of her characters, a
process that goes deeper and deeper, even as it moves along through a life
of surfaces that sometimes threatens to nullify the concept of depth entirely.

The details of the four chapters in Part One are typical of Mason's craft
as a writer. Stewart notes that she operates with a "style marked by
allusiveness and a minimalistic spareness" (168), firmly within the realistic
tradition. There is no question that Mason is a compulsive student of
American popular culture, and the opening of the book shows the grasp
of that culture on Sam, Emmett, and Mamaw. We are plunged immediately into a world defined by products, media-generated icons, and places
where fantasy reigns: Exxon, Chevron, Sunoco, Country Kitchen,
McDonald's, Stuckey's, a Chevy Chase movie, soap operas, Pepsi, a VW,
Motown sound (Marvin Gaye, Junior Walker, and the All Stars), free
HBO, Bruce Springsteen, "Roadhouse Blues" by the Doors, Howard
Johnson's, Trans Am, Ford Cobra, Buick, Saab, Visa card, gourmet
beefburgers, New Orleans, Miami, San Francisco, Walkman, Holiday
Inn, 7-Eleven, Cokes, Old Crow, "Hill Street Blues," Walter Mondale and
Geraldine Ferraro, Reagan, Joan Rivers substituting for Johnny Carson,
Don Rickles, Las Vegas. Wow! Welcome to modern, state-of-the-art
America. As Sam reflects, "Everything in America is going on here, on
the road" (17), and, yes, she "likes the feeling of strangeness" (17) that
attends this immersion in road culture.

If Sam were completely bound by the confines of images-of-the-mo-
ment, as Mason senses to be the case with Sam's peers in many regions of
the country, especially given the enormously intrusive power of electronic
media, she would be doomed to the kind of windswept "country of the
damned" imaged at the conclusion of Tate's "To the Lacedemonians." If
this were the case, there would be no possibility at all for the story Mason
aspired to build from the ruins of the Vietnam era, but Sam is destined to
be more than just a creature of the cultural immediacy represented in the
long list above. To Mason's great credit, she presents Sam truthfully and

shows the great magnetism of a culture dedicated to escaping the past in order to joy ride in the present, a present that would depart compulsively from all points of ancestral heritage.[2]

Sam knows how good that kind of present feels; during the time she has shared living quarters with her uncle Emmett, she has known considerable freedom, and it appeals to her, a point Mason emphasizes by introducing an alternative vision of Sam's life. Mamaw declares that things would have been different if her son Dwayne (Sam's father) had returned alive from Vietnam—that "he'd have a house down the road with Irene, and you would have grown up there, Sam, and I'd have knowed you a lot better, sugar. And you'd have some brothers and sisters" (13). Sam is horrified by this revelation. Specifically, she "shudders at the idea of growing up on a farm, doing chores, never getting to go to town" (13). In that shudder, Sam justifies all of the anxiety concerning the fate of the South which was expressed by Tate and the other Agrarians. Yet as much as Sam embodies the spirit of rebellion against the ways of the past, her character is balanced by the southern need for history. As the story progresses, this need eventually prevails, opening doors for Sam that would remain firmly closed for many of her generation elsewhere.

Hints of Sam's deliverance into a deeper perspective are included in Part One of the story, cleverly abutting the plethora of contemporary referents. Sam demonstrates an inclination to wonder what is behind the surface of things. She has an active imagination, indispensable for moving in any direction beyond the present moment. For example, at a Sunoco station where the travelers have stopped to fill the VW's gas tank and provide Mamaw with a chance to empty her bladder, Sam watches anxiously as Emmett flicks cigarette ashes near a gasoline pump. Her mind is immediately filled with an image of catastrophe, ironically not far removed from the kinds of things experienced by her father in Vietnam: "A scene of a sky-high explosion, like an ammunitions dump blowing up, rushes through Sam's mind" (5). In the southern imagination, the past intrudes, and Sam eventually follows the course of her imagination to recover a missing segment of her own past.

The opening section of the novel also introduces the history motif as it functions for Sam. In the great tradition of Faulkner, particularly as represented by the intensely sensual presence of the past in *Absalom, Absalom!*, Mason brings the past into Sam's consciousness by means of response to physical sensations so that the past is not so much understood as felt. This point is realized when Sam thinks, while out for a refreshing run, about the Howard Johnson's room that she, Emmett, and Mamaw are sharing: "Sam loves the room, so in a way it seems strange to be running away from it. The room is so clean, with no evidence of belonging to anybody, but it has a secret history of thousands of people, their vibrations and essences soaked in the walls and rug" (12).

Just as young Quentin Compson begins to meet the past in the stiffling hot, dark, and wisteria-scented chamber of Miss Rosa Coldfield, Samantha Hughes starts on her odyssey into the past with her senses in a receptive mode, ready to extract hosts of people, some probably long dead, out of the "vibrations and essences" that they have left behind in rooms they once occupied, no matter how temporarily.

Another of the senses invoked at the outset of *In Country* is that of sound, specifically in the form of popular music. There is some talk between Sam and Emmett on the road about a "lost" recording of the Beatles from 1964, a song that has just been discovered and released. Sam wants to hear that song, to confirm that it exists, and thereby to deepen her connection with a time before her own—but a time that has the stamp of eternity on it as it rides forward in music. As the narrative moves along, Sam's interest in this song is explained, and it proves to be one of the subtle unifying motifs of history in the text.

The southernness of the characters become evident in the novel early in a number of details about manners and customs. Mamaw is crucial in this regard. For instance, when the VW's transmission starts malfunctioning, it becomes necessary for the travelers to stay together in a motel room. Mamaw faces a crisis of propriety, something that can only occur when a person comes from a culture in which social relationships matter and are closely monitored. She immediately voices her concern about the plan to share a room: "I never slept in the same room with a man before that wasn't my husband. . . . What will they think back home? They'll think I've gone wild and started running around. I didn't even bring my good housecoat" (10). Mamaw's world is defined by its respect for propriety. And good food. Mamaw is a harsh critic when it comes to food. When the Howard Johnson's waitress asks the obligatory "Is everything all right?", Mamaw tells her the straight truth: "This chicken's tough. . . . It's deep-fried" (13). Mamaw knows her fried chicken, and it's a sign of the South.

The novel's second part, by far the largest, takes us back to Sam's high school graduation for a new point of departure. The dating of the year is given in code—"the summer of the Michael Jackson *Victory* tour and the Bruce Springsteen *Born in the U.S.A.* tour" (23)—with these music cues both signaling Sam's youth and indicating further development of the idea that musical sounds provide revelatory glimpses into the workings of a culture. Mason knows her Springsteen particularly well, and as his music in the U.S.A. album has a direct link with Vietnam, there are frequent references to him and his texts. Because the military side of the Vietnam War came to a close nearly a decade before the primary action of Mason's story, Sam must work with echoes of the war, and to an ear that wants to hear, Vietnam is still much "in country," deep in the heart of the country that the memory-laden South represents. Mason thus provides a provocative twist to the combat soldiers' terminology for actually arriving in Vietnam, turning the situation around completely, bringing the Vietnam aftermath fully into the open in America.

The speaker at Sam's commencement exercises offers a preachy call for "keeping the country strong, stressing sacrifice," words that call the Vietnam War to Sam's mind, and "it stayed on her mind all summer" (23). Emmett is there as a constant reminder of the war, for Sam links all of his adjustment problems—and a series of physical maladies—to his time in Vietnam. Sam's early experience of Emmett had entailed meeting his friends, hippies who straggled into Hopewell from exotic places on the west coast. As was typical of southern towns, "Hopewell didn't have any hippies, or war protesters" (23), so Emmett's various acquaintances created quite a stir. Emmett has settled down a bit by the mid-eighties, but he still manifests many of the standard "Post Traumatic Stress Disorder" (PTSD) symptoms, a point carefully explored by Stewart in his essay on *In Country*.

Emmett serves, therefore, as a tangible presence for Sam of events lodged years ago in the historical record. He brings the past into Sam's world, but it is still shrouded in darkness. Emmett basically refuses to talk about Vietnam. When Sam presses him for details about the war, he refuses to cooperate, saying, "Your imagination is bad enough as it is. I'm not going to feed it" (54). Irene, Sam's mother, who has recently remarried and begun another family, shares Emmett's concern about Sam's imagination: "You have a horrible imagination, Sam" (57). Later in the story, we see how Sam's imagination is capable of conjuring horrors. Through this study of the imagination, Mason allows that danger might attend the process of fully engaging one's imaginative faculties in life—

but only through such a process can one hope to mend the fracturing of movement through time. Sam's solution is distinctly southern: by dint of her imagination, she will acquire the taste and feel of the Vietnam War, years after its conclusion, almost two decades after it claimed her father's life.

In one of Sam's bantering exchanges with Emmett and Tom, another psychologically wounded Vietnam veteran who is one of Emmett's local breakfast buddies at McDonald's, Emmett suggests that she's getting good information from a "bunch of history books" (48), and when Tom inquires, "What do those books tell you, Sam?" she scoffs, "Nothing. They're just dull history books" (48). Sam reflects to herself about this, and in the process, we realize that for her (and for others presumably), "the books didn't say what it was like to be at war over there. The books didn't even have pictures." Sam is in pursuit of the real Vietnam. History books are of little value. Veterans are loath to say much of anything about the war. She has to look deeper—and wait. For Sam, when the avenues of understanding the war are finally discovered, they turn out to have been near at hand all along. The truth of Vietnam for a southerner lies close to home.

At home with Emmett, Sam watches *M*A*S*H* reruns. They know all of the stories, but they love the feeling of the show anyway. That TV series was, of course, a thinly veiled commentary on the war in Vietnam, despite the Korean setting. Hawkeye's irreverent bantering and basic antagonism to war derived from the nascent ethos of American youth in the late 1960s and early 1970s, a spirit of rebelliousness that began to appear severely dated by the Reagan 1980s, the period that provides the backdrop for Sam's coming to terms with the legacy of Vietnam. With *M*A*S*H*, Sam and Emmett enter a time warp that brings the past into the present, but the television show only enters Sam's world from without, it does not originate in Hopewell. More potent harbingers of the past emerge from within the physical environment known to Sam.

Specifically, Cawood's Pond is part of the local topography. It is essentially a swamp, a place of some danger (plenty of poisonous snakes call the swamp home), with an aura of primitive wilderness that contrasts sharply with life in town. Sam and her boyfriend Lonnie have spent a few nights at Cawood's Pond in his van—and presumably they are not the first teenagers to have broken free from the constraints of town life by seeking the night at the edge of the swamp.

We see Cawood's Pond first at night, after a violent thunderstorm, in the company of Sam, Lonnie, and Emmett. They travel in the van. Sam lies down on the mattress in back, "feeling like a soldier in an armored personnel carrier because she couldn't see where they were going" (34). For this impression, Sam draws upon a key point of information that Emmett once shared about the claustrophobia he had known in an APC. Back in the present, Emmett notices a bulldozer that will be used to reroute the creek and drain the swamp. Thanks to the work of Leo Marx and others, the machine's encroachment upon the wilderness garden has been long recognized as one of the driving mythological forces in American life. In the construction of Mason's narrative, the swamp is crucial. It provides a setting for finding the real Vietnam, and to bulldoze it into oblivion clearly would be an act of violent denial of the past. Later in this study, we shall encounter several narratives that pay the same degree of respect for wilderness in its raw, natural state, usually accompanied by a foreboding sense that the sweep of "progress" will obliterate the experience of wilderness.[3]

Once they have reached Cawood's Pond, Emmett recalls his one fond memory of Vietnam, the sight of an egret, a white bird that he had seen "in the rice paddies, dipping its head down in the water, feeling around for things to eat" (35). Sam thinks perhaps Emmett has been put in a mood of reminiscence by watching *M*A*S*H*, but it soon becomes evident that it is the place—the swamp—that gives Emmett access to the past. On the radio, Bruce Springsteen screams a song from his *Born in the U.S.A.* album, and then while Lonnie and Emmett are outside, Sam hears a new Beatles song through her drowsiness. These musical voices from the past immediately yield to Emmett's flashback to the horrors of Vietnam. He cautions Lonnie to be silent, to cover his cigarette. Lonnie says Emmett has just been spooked by the darkness, that "it wasn't anything" (38). Lonnie is totally a creature of the present, thoroughly preoccupied with where he will get a job and when he will next make love with Sam. Mason shows that, even in the conservative South, there are numerous people who have their sights set almost exclusively on the exigencies of the moment. Sam, on the other hand, is open to the past, and her larger frame of reference allows her to have sympathy for Emmett—and for all he represents.

Soon Sam tries another route of access to the past. She fancies loving Tom Hudson, the other psychologically wounded Vietnam veteran mentioned earlier, but when they go to bed, Tom's impotence prevents their becoming very close. Tom's "wound" calls to mind Jacob Barnes, Hemingway's symbolic victim of World War I in *The Sun Also Rises*. Katherine Kinney reviews this connection carefully in "'Humping the Boonies': Sex, Combat, and the Female in Bobbie Ann Mason's *In Country*," another of the essays in *Fourteen Landing Zones*, and notes that Mason's treatment of the male/female relationship dysfunction is considerably more complicated than what Hemingway offered to his readers in 1926.

Although Kinney's conclusion concerns the cultural roles of men and women as they seem to be redefined by a moment of discovery—specifically the moment when Samantha finds her own name, Sam Hughes, on the Vietnam Veterans Memorial at the end of *In Country*—what Kinney describes could fit just as well the entire business of reconstructing the past as it is practiced by southern writers: "This reconciliation is earned not by denying the differences of age and gender which separate Sam from the Sam Hughes who died in Vietnam, but by Mason's insistent illustration that self and other, male and female are not static, absolute terms but multiple, interactive constructions which can aid as well as hinder imaginative identification" (47). The past as a function of knowledge carried to the heart becomes naturally interactive with the present, a process that helps lift the spirits of both Sam and Emmett by the time we reach the last paragraph of *In Country*.

To get to that conclusion, however, Sam needs something tangible to establish her link to the past. Fortunately, there are enabling documents. First comes a package of letters that her mother had left behind when she moved to her new life with a new husband. These letters are from Sam's father, and they reveal the origin of her name. Her father, writing from the wilderness of Vietnam, had settled upon Samuel as a name for his unborn child—or Samantha, should the child be female. Samuel was his favorite name from the Bible, a book he claimed to be reading nightly. This particular detail incorporates two telling points: first, that Dwayne Hughes comes from a culture that takes its scripture seriously; and second, that the deep past of the Old Testament still has purchase on the imagination of southerners.

Sam's appetite for her father's script—"a childish handwriting, with big circles and loops" (179) in pencil on lined paper—is voracious. She has had a hunger for just this sort of concrete detail to make the past come to life in her imagination. She is surprised, however, to find that her father's mind is more on the fish he would like to catch in Kentucky than on "in country" Vietnam.

While Sam reads, she munches Doriitos—one of the sure signs of teenage America, a culture defined by what it literally consumes. A fragment of Dorito falls onto one of her father's letters, and Sam picks it up "with a moistened finger," an act that brings physical union with the past: "Atoms from the letter mixed with atoms of her saliva, across time" (180). That moment sets the stage for the remainder of the story, and it signifies the dependence of the southern writer upon concrete details to merge layers of history, past and present—the very sort of unity argued for by Tate in his "whole horse" image in "Remarks on the Southern Religion" (*I'll Take My Stand* 155–75). Such an act of union takes place typically through the senses, all part of the legacy that accompanies a strong feeling for place—a feeling dispersed throughout the South.

Sam's next advance into the past is related to the uniqueness of the place in which she lives. Later in the story she is given her father's diary, which had been kept for years by Sam's grandmother Hughes, who judges it to be of little interest to Sam: "I don't reckon it'll tell you anything. He just set down troop movements and weapons and things like that. It's not loving, like the letters he wrote back. Those was personal" (200). Of course, to Sam, the most private thoughts of her father are more valuable than anything else, despite the horrors they betray.

Sam heads off to the mall to read the diary. This is America at its most modern—the bazaar of contemporary commerce in the land of the big PX—a homogenizing pot of interchangeable stores and decors, blended in a fashion to deny the reality of anything outside the sanitized interior of mallspace. Before she can read, she has to deal with the advances of a male admirer who is decked out in a sign of the South—a "Confederate-flag T-shirt that says 'I'M A REBEL AND DAMN PROUD OF IT'" (201). Sam's daunting look puts him off successfully. Then she reads. Her reading uproots her from the pastless mall surrounding her and orients her toward the other Mall where the past rests silently beckoning. As she puzzles out her father's hand, she discovers the ugliness of war—an image of "a dead gook rotting under some leaves, sunk into a little swamp-like place" (203), which calls to mind a similar moment of discovery by Henry Fleming in Crane's *The Red Badge of Courage* and foreshadows Sam's solitary trip to the swamp at Cawood's Pond.

The diary also contains reports of the death of one of Dwayne's close buddies and of Dwayne's first direct encounter with the enemy: "Aug. 14. Big surprise. Face to face with a V. C. and I won. Easier than I thought. But there wasn't time to think. It was so simple. At last" (204). Then a reflection about how the World (home) seems like a dream. And then no more.

It has been enough, however, to open Sam's eyes to the past, with sufficient invocation of the senses to make her father's war tangible: "She had a morbid imagination, but it had always been like a horror movie, not something real. Now everything seemed suddenly so real it enveloped her, like something rotten she had fallen into, like a skunk smell, but she felt she had to live with it for a long time before she could take a bath. In the jungle, they were nasty and couldn't take a bath" (206).

To confirm the reality of this documentary evidence of the past, Sam needs to plunge herself into a parallel experience. She goes home to pack up some food, her sleeping bag, Emmett's space blanket and poncho, and a cooker, then she heads out in search of danger. She ventures to Cawood's Pond—the swamp right there on the fringe of her own community: "Cawood's Pond was so dangerous even the Boy Scouts wouldn't camp out there, but it was the last place in western Kentucky where a person could really face the wild. That was that she wanted to do" (208). Sam must finally meet the past in the wilderness to complete replication of the Vietnam paradigm. For Sam, Cawood's Pond is going to do what the military training command had in mind at Fort Polk, Louisiana, which served as the "birthplace" for Vietnam-bound soldiers. It is "in country" country.

Sam's night at Cawood's Pond affords her an opportunity to review all of the knowledge that has gradually found its way into the center of her being. She reflects on why men kill—why some die and some do not— and she constantly measures her environment against that of the Vietnam that claimed her father. She is "in country" (210), she "was walking point" (211), and when a raccoon surprises her with its beady eyes in the night, "It was a V. C." (213). In Norman Jewison's film of *In Country* (1989), images of what certainly seems to be Vietnam swamp combat are cut into Sam's night at the pond, thus creating a strikingly immediate and total sense of correspondence between otherwise distant locations in place and time.

At 5:15 the next morning, she wakes and senses deliverance. Having passed through her immersion in danger represented by the swamp at night, "She had survived" (215), but there remains a final terror—the threat of an unexpected intruder, one who would do violence to her. She hears footsteps, and her imagination makes the man a rapist. As the footsteps draw closer, she arms herself with the sharp edge of a can of oysters she had eaten the night before, and she gets a further jolt of adrenalin born of danger: "But this was real. A curious pleasure stole over her. This terror was what the soldiers had felt every minute. . . . They were completely alive, every nerve on edge, and sleep, when it came, was like catnapping. No nightmares in the jungle. Just silent terror" (217).

The silence of Sam's moment of terror is dispelled finally by Emmett's whistling of the *M*A*S*H* theme song, "Suicide Is Painless." Emmett is furious with her attempt to find Vietnam at Cawood's Pond, but as anger flows back and forth between Sam and Emmett, they each begin to come to terms with managing the intrusion of the past into their lives. Emmett tells enough of his Vietnam experience to bring heart-wrenching sobs from his body, and he tells Sam that he fears he is permanently diseased by the war: "There's something wrong with me. I'm damaged. It's like something in the center of my heart is gone and I can't get it back" (225). Sam, too, comes to feel badly damaged by her knowledge—distant though it is—of Vietnam. In the days after the Cawood's Pond episode, Sam acts even stranger than Emmett, a manifestation, she guesses, of her own "post-Vietnam stress syndrome" (229).

Somehow she and Emmett must have an experience with the past that makes its presence tolerable, not just intensely tangible. An opportunity for Emmett to recover the center of his heart and for Sam to have one final lasting moment with the reality of her father comes from Emmett's decision that they should travel together to the Vietnam Veterans Memorial in Washington. For the first time in Sam's memory, Emmett takes charge, arranging the details of the trip, even including Mamaw Hughes. Part Three of the narrative is given over to the completion of the journey that was introduced in the novel's opening chapters, and all of the early motifs reappear.

At a shopping mall in Maryland, down the road from the garage where the VW's transmission has been repaired, Sam impulsively buys the Springsteen *Born in the U.S.A.* album, but when she sees a store identical to one that she has visited back in Paducah, she suddenly grasps the concept of franchise homogenization in American culture. Already, in the wake of her Cawood's Pond night, she has felt some distance from the

commercial mainstream of the young in America. Although Sam's road
to maturity is not without occasional switchbacks, she seems generally
prepared for meeting the gravity of the inscriptions on polished black
granite in Washington.

The visit to the wall is charged with emotion, with every detail echoing
earlier moments in the story. Mason takes us through this encounter from
Sam's perspective, although at the very end, Emmett becomes the focal
point. Sam hears a woman remark to a companion, "I didn't think it
would look like this. Things aren't what you think they look like. I didn't
know it was a wall" (240), and when a schoolgirl inquires innocently,
"What are all these names anyway?" (240)—the perfect representation of
a culture without a past—Sam is angry. Then she "realizes that she
doesn't know either. She is just beginning to understand. And she will
never really know what happened to all these men in the war" (240). She
may not have that kind of perfect understanding, but she clearly is at the
threshold of fully accepting the past in a way that will allow it to live
within her.

From the monument directory, they find where Dwayne Hughes's
name is located, on Panel 9E. Emmett tells a park guide who asks if they
need help, "We know where we are" (242), and he spots the name high
overhead. Sam borrows a stepladder so that she and Mamaw can touch
the name. Sam touches the name: "A scratching on a rock. Writing.
Something for future archaeologists to puzzle over, clues to a language"
(244). Mamaw captures the moment in another medium—with an In-
stamatic—but worries about the quality of the picture: "I hope his name
shows up. And your face was all shadow" (244). In terms of what the
whole of the *In Country* narrative posits, the quality of the picture is
immaterial. Dwayne's name has finally shown up, to be seen and accepted
by his daughter, who represents a new generation. The shadowing of
Sam's face symbolizes the way the past exists in relationship to the present, a positive mechanism for realizing depth of perspective for those
who are open to it. Sam is indeed open to it—and then she receives the
final shock of identification when she finds her own name, SAM A
HUGHES, on panel 14E: "She touches her own name. How odd it feels, as
though all the names in America have been used to decorate this wall"
(245). Sam's discovery epitomizes the South's engagement with history, a
process of record keeping and accountability that both assumes the presentness of the past and accepts the long reach of time: everything be-

comes history. Sam has come into maturity by meeting her name inscribed in history.

Then the focus switches to Emmett. He has gone back to the directory, "probably searching for his buddies' names" (244). Just as Sam has had the epiphany with her own name, Mamaw comes upon her suddenly, gushing with a sense of hope inspired by the sight of a white carnation blooming in front of the black wall. Mamaw wonders, "Did we lose Emmett?" (245). In the novel's final paragraph, just three lines of text, Mason pays a final tribute to the value of knowledge carried to the heart from out of the domain of the past. It happens in an explosive image, without words being spoken: "Silently, Sam points to the place where Emmett is studying the names low on a panel. He is sitting there cross-legged in front of the wall, and slowly his face bursts into a smile like flames" (245).

This moment of high drama might well be called "Lost and Found." Through the names on the wall, Emmett has been able to recover the past, losing himself in it momentarily, but the face that "bursts into a smile like flames" is surely a sign of a heart regaining its center. Emmett has found himself again. While Matthew Stewart finds this moment to be "optimistic to the point of sanguinity," largely because it suggests that excruciating post traumatic stress disorder problems will yield easily to catharsis, the moment emerges from a strong tradition in southern letters. Emmett's road to wholeness must pass through the past, a pattern that squares with the work of writers from the South for generations. For Bobbie Ann Mason, then, the answer to Vietnam is indeed "in country"—in the affinity of the South for making the past live.

Unlike James Webb, whose entire career—either as a writer or a government bureaucrat—has centered on issues of national scope (defense and foreign policy, both ideally having purpose and honor), Bobbie Ann Mason has concerned herself in her writing with just regular people and their everyday activities, and yet she, like Webb, often introduces something from the past upon which present action turns. This pattern had emerged a few years before the story of Sam and Emmett began to take shape. It is manifestly evident in "Shiloh," the title story in her first collection (*Shiloh and Other Stories*, 1982). Leroy Moffitt and his wife Norma Jean are having troubles in their marriage. They lost their son Randy to sudden infant death syndrome years ago, and Leroy has recently injured his leg in a highway accident, putting him out of work as a tractor-trailer driver. Despite the things they have shared, and although they have beaten the odds by staying together after the death of their child, their lives have grown apart, but for some time, neither seems to realize what has happened.

Norma Jean's mother, Mabel, inadvertently brings her daughter's and son-in-law's marriage to the breaking point. On her honeymoon, Mabel had gone to the Civil War battlefield of Shiloh (one of the critical turning points of the war, nearly as consequential as Gettysburg for determining the fate of the Confederacy). The memory of Shiloh has been with her for years; Mabel, "accepted into the United Daughters of the Confederacy in 1975, is still preoccupied with going back to Shiloh" (6). Going back to the past, deep into the past—that is the pattern of "Shiloh." When Leroy and Norma Jean eventually take Mabel with them to Shiloh, the past catches up with all of them; the place becomes symbolic of decisive change in the fortunes of those who gather there to meet history.

Unfortunately, Leroy does not have a mind for history. When he says, "So the boys in gray ended up in Corinth. The Union soldiers zapped 'em finally. April 7, 1862" (14), Norma Jean and Mabel both "know he doesn't know any history." Shortly thereafter, Norma Jean tells him that she wants to leave him. He presses for an explanation, but her response is not coherent. The answer comes obliquely, in Leroy's own reflection on Shiloh and everything linked to it:

> General Grant, drunk and furious, shoved the Southerners back to Corinth, where Mabel and Jed Beasley were married years later, when Mabel was still thin and good-looking. The next day, Mabel and Jed visited the battleground and then Norma Jean was born, and she married Leroy and they had a baby, which they lost, and now Leroy and Norma Jean are here at the same battleground. Leroy knows he is leaving out a lot. He is leaving out the insides of history. History was always just names and dates to him. (16)

As "Shiloh" proves, great peril attends "leaving out the insides of history." The same message informs the action of several other Mason short stories, and it looms large indeed over the whole terrain of *In Country*. Mason's southern heritage provides her with a natural means for placing Vietnam within time, by having Sam, her surrogate, be so receptive to working herself steadily closer to the "insides of history."

4

VIETNAM AND THE FLIGHT OF TIME

THE PRIMACY OF HISTORY IN THE SOUTHERN IMAGINATION as it was engaged with the Vietnam War stands out clearly in the work of James Webb and Bobbie Ann Mason. James Webb posits the existence of a deeply embedded pattern of social behavior in southern culture: quick readiness on the part of southern men to respond without hesitation to the call to arms, a code of behavior reinforced through time by the tradition of storytelling. By such ties does the past bind—or oblige—the present to display honor. Bobbie Ann Mason offers in her Vietnam novel a different justification for the past; Samantha Hughes can only come to terms with her full identity by recovering as much as she possibly can (by dint of imagination) from the past, and Emmett Smith can only heal the wounds of his heart by facing the shards of memory that linger from a time otherwise lost. In Sam's case especially, the process becomes a matter of getting through to the "insides of history." If you lack that driving impulse, there is a good chance you are not a southerner. Sam has it.

Before directing the focus of this study to matters other than history, we must test the necessity of history further and examine two more novels—*Machine Dreams* (1984) by Jayne Anne Phillips and *The Floatplane Notebooks* (1988) by Clyde Edgerton; both offer trenchant perspectives on the past and its relation to the Vietnam War. These two novels share a common narrative framework, the introduction of diverse voices to tell a story from diverse points of time, and perhaps even more significantly, each story involves technological developments, with flying machines being the final stage of development. Although the Persian Gulf conflict in the winter of 1991 may be worthy of only a short chapter in the military history of desert warfare tactics—being far too short to embed itself deeply in the national consciousness—Operation Desert Storm nevertheless had as its media centerpiece the employment of fiendishly effective flying machines by America and its allies. As a consequence, it is most appropriate to scrutinize what Phillips and Edgerton saw in the relationship between time and flight as it pertained to the Vietnam experience.

The narratives of both *Machine Dreams* and *The Floatplane Notebooks* approach Vietnam from the long reach of time. Each novel encompasses a large chunk of history; Phillips reaches back to the Great Depression and World War II for the origins of a tale that leads eventually to a climax in Vietnam, and Edgerton angles even further back, to original moments of southern settlement, for definitional details of a culture that finally comes to incorporate combat in Vietnam. While the Agrarian conservatives generally viewed the onslaught of technology with angst, Phillips and Edgerton seem to accept the inevitability of the machines that enable man to fly, but at the same time, they dramatize the continuity of the human condition and reveal the elements of southern life that persist through time, even as time itself flies.

Machine Dreams is a stunningly prophetic text: having seen the past, you know the future. The dedication offered by Phillips signals her sense of linkage between past and present; she writes, "For my family, past and present." Phillips is from West Virginia, which resisted the lure of the Confederacy, but the stamp of the past evident in the dedication and throughout *Machine Dreams* is distinctly southern. The first sentence of the novel moves in the same vein: "It's strange what you don't forget" (1). This perspective comes from a mother's reminiscence provided for her daughter, one generation telling its story to the next, the past seeking a lasting place in memory.

The story commences in Jean Danner Hampson's reconstruction of her early years—the hard times her family faced in the Great Depression when her father lost his lumber business because he had sold too much on credit; the death of her first love, Tom Harwin, from a heart attack; her mother's death from cancer of the uterus; the early years of her marriage to Mitch Hampson; and the birth of her daughter Danner. The story closes with the one paragraph "Machine Dream" chapter, a fantasy sequence that comes from the inner world of Danner, following the loss of Jean's son Billy in a helicopter crash in Vietnam. The pattern of history is set: things and people rise through time, then they fall. Only memory endures, a haunting but enchanting presence.

The table of contents of *Machine Dreams* provides a clear structural pattern for the narrative. After the opening reminiscence and a parallel introductory section for Mitch, Jean's husband, the chapters follow chronologically. On the heels of the "War Letters: Mitch, 1942–45," the chapters leap forward along the track of time, jumping from one character's viewpoint to another's, usually at intervals of two to five years. We touch down in 1946, 1948, 1950, 1956, 1957, 1962, 1963 (twice in 1963, once for "Radio Parade: Danner" and once for "The Air Show: Billy"), 1965, 1969 (twice, for Danner and for Billy), 1970, and 1972. Then off into a vision of the future with Danner's "Machine Dream," which matches perfectly the conditions of Desert Storm.

Beyond all of the events in the story, from beginning to end, there stands a graveyard, ravenously waiting to claim all—often in association with the specter of war, which has no respect for the visions of invincibility and eternity held by the very young. As Jean remembers the class of 1943, she recalls how "all the boys worried the fighting would stop before they could get overseas" (8). Mitch Hampson is one young man of his generation who got to see war, and his reflections on the experience serve to transmute the dream of war's excitement into something less than glorious: "The war swallowed everyone like a death or a birth will, except it went on and on" (52). When Mitch returns to the farmland of his youth some years after his return from the war, he finds just about everything changed—everything but the "wooden church, all falling in on itself, and the cemetery" (53), where Mitch wanders among the stones and reconnects with moments of his past.

A more appalling association between graveyards and time comes out of Mitch's war experience, and in his dream memory of a mass burial on New Guinea, great earth-moving machines represent the advent of the future. Mitch remembers how the New Guineans had treated the bulldozers of the Americans with reverence, "touched the machines hand-over-hand, seeming to measure them as horses are measured, then touched all the gears and pedals, saying Papuan words for the parts" (67). The dominant image of these wilderness-managing machines, however, comes from deep within Mitch's memory core, which is governed by his senses:

> The smell was bad, horrible and terrible and full of death, he couldn't think of a word to say what the smell was, it rose up underneath and around him and he turned to get away. Behind the smell someone kept crying, weeping like a child on and on as the smell broke in the heat, ten in the morning and hot, already hot as hell and the sky a seering bright blue mass over the dried rust red of the bodies. . . . Nothing to do but go ahead, hot metal seat of the dozer against his hips, vibration of motor thrumming, and that kid still crying, some island kid, get a detail over there to keep those kids away, got to get pits dug and doze this mess. . . . What the hell, he was losing his mind, he shoved the gear into forward as the smell assailed him, pushing, pushing back. He felt the give of the earth, just earth, had to think it was all just earth like at Wheeling, working on the Reeder road with Clayton. (64–65)

Earth, just earth, from New Guinea to West Virginia—earth and machines. Graves. It all adds up to a pattern of continuity that one day will encompass Vietnam. The ominous sense of World War II as it emerges from Mitch's memory—pinpointed on the making of a graveyard by a huge machine—casts a spell over the generation that follows Jean and Mitch, culminating finally in the loss of Billy.

When Mitch comes home, he buys a new machine—a Pontiac V-8, a beautiful work of engineering art to polish and caress, a vehicle of choice for a man on the lookout for a woman. During a few moments while Clayton, the uncle who raised Mitch when his father was killed in a coal mine accident, admires the Pontiac, Mitch thinks to himself: "Crazy how men loved cars" (83). As the story moves forward, it seems that man's love for machines is split between cars and airplanes. When just a lad, Billy has dreams of the cement-mixer trucks that belong to his father's business, and later, his imagination is fired by the planes at a local air show in 1963; both he and his sister have their share of sexual initiation in the privacy afforded to the young by automobiles.

Just as the machines move along, generation to generation, so do the graveyards. Phillips brings the two motifs together magnificently in Jean's visit to her mother's grave, something she does in the new family Nash a few hours before a New Year's party to welcome in 1949. She is not good at remembering some major moments in life, having forgotten her first wedding anniversary the summer before: "maybe she just remembered death instead of life. That was bad. But death wouldn't let you forget, would it?" (112). On a cold and snowy, end-of-December late afternoon, her mother's grave beckons. The Nash takes her into the graveyard, where she finally stops beside the family plot, and sitting there in the car, Jean turns her thoughts to the meaning of death and remembrance:

> None of the stones had much meaning to her except the one that was off by itself, she'd just had it put there last summer. Graves: what did they mean? Her mother wasn't even here, if people ever were; she'd hated funerals and left instructions to be cremated. But she'd told them what to put on a stone, when Jean and her brother and sister could bear the expense. And there was a wisdom to it; people have to have a place to make remembrance. Jean looked at the stone. It was smooth granite the color of pewter and relatively small, not even waist high. Yet it had a weight, a power: it marked a place. (113)

Having a place for remembrance matters to Jean, and she prepares herself for the future by gathering the past close. As the fifties yield to the troubled sixties—with troubles in Jean's marriage mirroring the turbulence in American culture caused by the sexual revolution and by the Vietnam War, both of which affect her children directly—machines make it increasingly difficult to keep the past and present connected. Phillips shows that protecting one's own, to say nothing of trying to find one's own way in the culture of confusion, is an increasingly daunting challenge as time courses through the middle of the twentieth century. Early in the story, during Jean's opening reminiscence, one of her hindsights about Danner and Billy serves to summarize the anxiety that attends men and their flying machines as the flight of time takes place: "It turned out I couldn't keep anyone safe. Not you. Not Billy" (26).

A sense of foreboding about where flying machines will take men even tinges Danner's perspective regarding man's first step on the moon. It is the summer of 1969. Jean has asked Danner's father to leave the house, and divorce sadness hangs in the air, but the paper's headline is ecstatic: "TWO STEPS ON MOON, ARMSTRONG PILOTS BEYOND BOULDERS" (272). One small step for man, one giant step for mankind, Armstrong had declared. Man on the moon. What did it mean?

Danner's interest in the moon landing is modest. Her attention had been directed primarily to the background, human-interest angles of the story. After all, "it was just machines" (272). One detail of the account was the recollection by Neil Armstrong's mother, who said he'd had a recurrent childhood dream of hovering over the ground" (272). When Danner shares this insight with the young man she is dating, she gets a response that sets the stage for subsequent events in her life: "I wonder if all the guys flying Hueys in Nam had the same dream" (273).

Brother Billy heads off to college in the fall of 1969, but his heart is not in education. He is lost, uncertain of where he belongs in life. By November, he is ready to call it quits. He knows that he will be subject to the first lottery drawing of the revised selective service system, but given the personal turmoil in his life, he figures that the luck of the drawing makes as much sense as anything for a way to find his future. He dreams of the drawing—innumerable white balls with numbers on them (including one for his birthday) bouncing around "in a machine" (278): "Hundreds of days of white balls tumbling in a black sphere, silent and very slow, moving as though in accordance with physical laws. A galaxy of identical white planets. No sun. Cold, charged planets, simple, symmetrical, named with months and numbers. Nov. 1, no, 305 of 365. Universe stops. Hand reaches in. Suddenly everything in color, and the black sphere turns midnight blue. Crazy dream" (278).

When the drawing occurs in December, Billy's birthday comes up number nineteen—a sure bet for the draft. By early 1970, he is headed off to the army, coolly turning back Danner's pleas for him to run away to Canada. Billy is all confidence, boasting "The fuckers won't do me in. I'll stay off the ground if they send me, get into an air crew. I'll keep my ass in the air" (302). Danner's caustic skepticism is more in line with eventual reality: "Great. Then you'll have farther to fall" (302).

Farther to fall—such is the reward for all of man's apparent progress in mastering the mystery of flight. Billy's view—that being over the ground in Vietnam is far superior to being on it—fuels his enthusiasm for being a chopper door-gunner. He says, "I want to be up, moving over it with my own gun in front of me. If I get hit I want to get hit with plenty of metal around me. This is not crazy logic—we are not talking about the same world, and there is no way to play it safe" (323).

As noted earlier, Vietnam came to be perceived by most soldiers as an entirely different "world" from the one known at home in America. The chief symbol of the war as fought by Americans was a machine: the helicopter. Two recent collections of essays on Vietnam literature and film—Philip Jason's *Fourteen Landing Zones* and Gilman and Smith's *America Rediscovered*—display images of helicopters on their dust covers. In "The Helicopter and the Punji Stick: Central Symbols of the Vietnam War," from *America Rediscovered*, H. Palmer Hall carefully reviews the use of the helicopter by numerous writers to fix the exact nature of American conduct of modern war. As Palmer concludes, "the helicopter was not enough" (160); helicopters saved many wounded soldiers, "but were unable to save the war" (160).

Destructive avengers that they were—and marvellous deliverers of life as well—helicopters failed to deliver victory to the American forces in the Vietnam War. Helicopters crashed, and with them crashed dreams of American technological success. As a consequence, another symbol emerged to represent the placement of Vietnam in American history, and two other recent books on the subject (Philip Beidler's penetrating study, *Re-Writing America: Vietnam Authors in Their Generation*, and D. Michael Shafer's *The Legacy: The Vietnam War in the American Imagination*) bear the image of the Vietnam Veterans Memorial on their dust covers. We have already met the symbolic power of the wall on the Mall in Bobbie Ann Mason's novel. The conclusion of *Machine Dreams* shows how the helicopter as a machine of flight fits into the long view of American culture, a view that comes most naturally to writers from the South.

Billy's letters from Vietnam to Danner describe the use of helicopters. It is spooky business at best: "You're up there in the *chump-chump* of the blades, spotting flashes and firing while the chopper drops low enough to land the grunts. . . . Like Cowboys and Indians, except the Indians are ghosts and they can't lose because nothing really kills them" (328). Then his parents receive a Department of the Army telegram notifying them that "PRIVATE FIRST CLASS WILLIAM MITCHELL HAMPSON, HAS BEEN LISTED AS MISSING IN ACTION EFFECTIVE JUNE 1970 WHILE PARTICIPATING IN AN OPERATION AGAINST A HOSTILE FORCE" (331). The army provides no details about the loss of Billy's helicopter, but one of Billy's fellow soldiers in the 227th Aviation Battalion follows through on his promise to Billy to write to his family. The soldier, SP-4 Robert Taylor, describes the crash of the helicopter under heavy enemy fire, but he suggests that Billy and the other door-gunner may have jumped to safety, although no trace of them has been found.

Unfortunately, there proves to be no further official information concerning Billy's fate. Billy's name, of course, is meant to echo William "Billy" Mitchell, the army officer who was court-martialed in the mid-1920s for insubordination because of his zealous efforts in promoting the superiority of air power; the Billy in *Machine Dreams* is treated no better by the army than was his historical namesake. The story line subsequently moves along to 1972, tracking the efforts of Jean, Mitch, and Danner to deal with the absence of one they all loved. Jean preserves Billy's room as it was in 1969. Mitch mounts an angry campaign to try to develop more news about Billy. Danner bounces along in depression, sleeping with a series of Vietnam veterans and seeing a psychiatrist— remedies that do not alleviate her profound sense of loss.

The narrative finally is resolved in Danner's dream. She has had frequent dreams of her brother Billy, the result of having the mantle of responsibility for him passed along to her by her mother. As the story of the Hampson family unfolds, it becomes clear that Jean and Danner are at the center of their culture, charged with the task of providing a kind of human-scale continuity that parallels the on-going, generation-to-generation male fascination with machines. Danner's dreams show the peril inherent in trying to reach the future through the chief symbol of twentieth-century progress: the machine of flight. In Danner's dreams, "Billy isn't desperate. He's just himself. I'm the one who is afraid, who knows something terrible might happen, has happened, will happen. I'm the one who can't stop it from happening" (371).

Jean could not save Billy. Danner could not save Billy. There was a war, and Billy felt the call to join it. Machines defined the war, and in the fall of Billy's helicopter, the Vietnam War was defined. This process, which proceeds from the past to the present and on into the future through the connective device of man's impulse to take flight in a machine, is crystallized in the conclusive "Machine Dream," a one-paragraph chapter that comes from Danner's perspective. Phillips's style at this point verges on "magic realism,"[1] entirely right for completing the mythic patterns invoked by the novel's epigraphic references to Pegasus. As Danner and Billy are walking in a "deep dark forest," Danner searches for the "magic horse," and Billy "makes airplane sounds" (373). They walk on through the woods, and darkness finally enshrouds them, leaving all to the last sense to depart before death: the sense of sound. Danner hears Billy "imitating with a careful and private energy the engine sounds of a plane that is going down. War-movie sounds. Eeee-yoww, ach-ack-ack. So gentle it sounds like a song, and the song goes on softly as the plane falls, year after year, to earth" (373).

In these final words, Vietnam joins history—history with a long sweep—just what one would expect from a writer from the South. *Machine Dreams* presents Vietnam in a deep context, with a "before" that extends backward in time and an "after" that reaches forward in time. The Vietnam episode in American culture thus is linked by Phillips to eternal patterns. As the Vietnam War figures in *Machine Dreams*, it was not an anomaly. Instead, it connects naturally with an enduring impulse by men to rise over the earth, a quest with dramatic linkage to the South, given the flights of Orville and Wilbur Wright at Kitty Hawk, North Carolina, on 17 December 1903. Although man's machines have become increasingly complex and wondrous, they are still destined one day to fall back to earth. The long reach of time encompasses all, and with this message, Phillips chastens the side of ambition that would have man break free from earthly limits.

Clyde Edgerton's *The Floatplane Notebooks* serves as an apt complement to *Machine Dreams*, although his story leads eventually to a more celebrative view of man's effort to take flight over the earth. Edgerton proceeds with a structure that resembles the one used so effectively by Phillips. There is a time line that reaches from 1956 to 1971, and the major protagonists offer sections of the story from their varying perspectives. Like *Machine Dreams*, *The Floatplane Notebooks* is not centered on combat in Vietnam, not in the way that *Fields of Fire* is devoted to exploring the experiences of soldiers in country. Instead, the focus is placed on the life of a family—the Copelands—over time, which happens to include Vietnam combat in a crucial way.

Edgerton served as an air force pilot in Southeast Asia from 1970 to 1971, so it is not surprising that one member of the Copeland family, Mark, only son of Esther and Thomas (killed in World War II), flies F-4's over Vietnam. It is not upon Mark, however, that Vietnam burns its telling sign but rather upon his cousin Meredith, an E-3 in the Marine Corps, who loses use of both legs when he is wounded in combat. Yet Mark and Meredith are only two of the figures in the Copeland family, and even though the narrative builds in incremental degrees toward Vietnam as an experience of extraordinary import for the Copelands, the story is ultimately about the ways and means of folks who cope with the land and with time. Nowhere is that done better, it would seem from Edgerton's story, than in the South.

The Copelands are people of tradition. They love stories. As noted above, the novel is told from multiple perspectives, but Edgerton employs a variation on this pattern that is not evident in *Machine Dreams*. Although many of the principal characters of the present give us chunks of narrative, letting us know the world from their points of view, some of the interpolated stories are told more than once, and as the tellers change, the stories shift in details and in point of emphasis. In essence, life becomes a storytelling experience, endlessly engaging, endlessly protean in possibility. To tell stories is to live, and to keep telling stories is to make history, and to make history is to join time in two senses: to connect disparate moments and to enter a chronicle of the ages. Through such a process, in Clyde Edgerton's hands, Vietnam becomes locatable in America and in time.

To understand the workings of this process, we should know a bit about the floatplane notebooks that give rise to the title of Edgerton's third novel (after *Raney* and *Walking to Egypt*). They are just what we would guess them to be—notebooks—and they were started with a sense of explicit purpose. In the beginning, a person has a project, something to build. In this particular case, the person is Albert Copeland, father of Thatcher, Meredith, and Noralee. His chosen project, initiated in the mid-1950s, is to build a floatplane that would lift him into the air in flight. He pursues this project over the course of several decades, and his notebooks are gradually filled with the record of his efforts to realize his objective.

Albert's floatplane project gives rise to considerable humor. Consider the following account of a typical notebook entry, as it is described by Thatcher in his youth:

> So when we get home that afternoon Papa writes in his notebook. It says "Record" on the front. He had the date, the temperature, the wind direction, the altitude of the lake, which he said was sea level—hell, I got more sense than that—and then this:
> NARRATIVE ACCOUNT: THE EXPERIMENTAL AIRCRAFT WAS TOWED TO LAKE BLANCA BEHIND OWNERS JEEP TRUCK. ALONG FOR THE OCCASION WAS THE OWNER, SONS MEREDITH COPELAND AND THATCHER COPELAND. DAUGHTER NORALEE COPELAND AND TWO ANIMALS, FOX AND TRADER (DOG NAMES). THE AIRCRAFT FLOATED LEVEL IN THE WATER AND WAS

RUN SUCCESSFUL OUT ON THE WATER AND BACK IN. THIS WAS THE FIRST
TEST RUN. PASSENGERS WERE THE OWNER AND SON MEREDITH. ALL PARTS
WORKED.

 Then it's got Meredith's and Mark's and Noralee's weights and heights.
I'd be there but I'm grown. (17–16)

The methodology of the entire book is discernible from this passage.
Edgerton shows how a culture builds a record of itself, inscribing a version of events that happen through time, and to this process is naturally
attached a kind of sanctifying aura, albeit tempered with a delightful
touch of whimsy. The notebooks, which accompany the family wherever it
travels in order to keep others in the family posted on recent developments and which serve as a point of departure for frequent oral amplifica-
tions of the written document, ultimately become manifestations of the
"Word," with all the mystical and majestic weight given to the idea of the
"Word" by the apostle John in his gospel.

 The words as noted by Albert catch all levels of life, from the mock
heroics of floatplane flying to the mundane accounts of names, heights,
and weights. The children grow to maturity over the course of the narrative, and the notebooks grow through successive stages, keeping track
of Albert's progress and the life and times of his entire family.

 Yet even as the notebooks function to provide a steadying anchor for
the diverse experiences of the Copelands—and in this role they are justly
celebrated—Edgerton proves himself to be a thoroughgoing postmodern
writer in the way that he rejoices in the uncertainty of absolute truth in
the notebook scriblings. For example, the passage from the notebook
cited earlier makes the first attempt at flight sound successful, but readers
are provided earlier with another version that comes from the highly
believable, youthful voice of Noralee. Her account of this moment has
only one of the two engines starting, an imbalance of thrust that causes
the plane to circle out of control, nearly killing Meredith who has jumped
out, then heading back to crash into the shore and throwing Albert into
the front of the plane (fortunately on the side without a whirring pro-
peller). Furthermore, this disparity in the record is signaled even earlier by
Bliss, a woman from outside the family who marries Thatcher. Bliss's
perspective throughout is especially significant because she moves—
through the process of time and the rituals of storytelling in the family—
from the position of outsider to insider. Her newness to the family allows
her to see the Copelands with startling clarity. Even earlier than

Thatcher's version of Albert's notebook entries for the first attempt at powering the floatplane and before Noralee's candid accounting, Bliss has already declared: "Thatcher said one thing happened at the lake, but when Mr. Copeland wrote in down it sounded quite different" (12). In looking at the insides of history, Clyde Edgerton proves to be a perceptive historiographer.

With regard to the general purposes of this study, *The Floatplane Notebooks* accomplishes two goals. First, the narrative manages to find a place for the Vietnam War in the midst of all the cumulative storytelling that occurs between the first and last pages of the book, not making the Vietnam era serve as the end of time (a phenomenon suggested by the movie *Apocalypse Now*) or the beginning of time (the genesis of a new age, as posited by youth culture of the 1960s under the sign of Aquarius), but simply securing the era as a place in time. Second, the narrative reveals self-reflexively the glory inherent in the way stories become modified and amplified through time. History—as a function of stories told about events—is ceaselessly variable, and Edgerton takes joy in this variability. It is the stuff of life. As time moves along, Vietnam, cataclysmic as it was in many ways, will be a story told and retold in endless versions, something that lasts as a part of the culture—lasts as long as the graveyard and wisteria vine that loom so large in *The Floatplane Notebooks*.

When the Copelands travel from North Carolina to Florida every year during the Christmas season to visit Albert's brother Hawk and family, the notebooks are brought along, for updating the Florida Copelands on the creation of the flying wonder and for collecting and recollecting all the family affairs over time. Because this family is from a location noted for having more than its fair share of traditions, the notebooks record, among many diverse matters (some already mentioned), the annual visit to the family graveyard, down a path through the woods behind their house.

It is Bliss who provides the following insight on the crucial nature of the graveyard tradition:

> What an event! Cousins, aunts, uncles, and such got together, complete with picnic lunch, and when their work was finished that graveyard was as clean and neat as a whistle.
> There is a path—wide enough for a car—which goes down into the woods behind their house, and if you walk or drive on it for a little ways you come to another car path which leads to their family graveyard. There beside the graveyard is a little open grassy area, and beside that is a raging

wisteria vine, beyond which is a pond. The graveyard itself is very serene, with shafts of light coming down through tall pines onto the gravestones, which go back into the 1800s. (7)

As an outsider, Bliss is beguiled by the spirit of this family tradition, which serves to orient her to the nature of the Copelands. Her observation of the "shafts of light" suggests that a natural illumination to life comes to those who manage—in the midst of busy lives—to keep track of the past, to know where the dead are buried, and to keep that place well preserved. That is what Allen Tate called for in "Ode to the Confederate Dead," and as a consequence of their attention to the past, the Copelands always have the door open to knowledge that comes from the heart, something that others, without the benefit of these traditions, lack. Bliss feels the difference: "I think about my mother and father's parents and grandparents, buried in large conventional cemeteries—so unromantically—without an entire enclave, an entire force as it were, buried all around them. It seems to me that the tradition of being buried here should be renewed. It's the most peaceful place imaginable: the pond, the wisteria, the majestic pine trees" (44).

Because Bliss appreciates the graveyard tradition of the Copelands, we can be sure that her name works its natural way into the family record, the notebooks. Bliss's and Thatcher's wedding announcement is tucked into one of the notebooks, as well as the birth announcement of their son, Taylor. When Meredith comes home from Vietnam badly wounded, it is Bliss who finds a natural way to release the tension in his body, symbolically easing his passage back into the culture of his heritage. Meredith and Bliss become the perfect antithesis to the spirit of the dead past that so infects the lives of Hemingway's Jake Barnes and Lady Brett Ashley after World War I. In the Copeland family, the past survives Vietnam.

One additional detail about the graveyard needs further consideration. That raging wisteria. It grows prodigiously, and so has to be cut back periodically. There is no stopping it. Moreover, it lives through and beyond each Copeland who has lived on this land, beginning with the first settlers, Walker and Caroline "Puss" Copeland, and it will surely last far beyond the Vietnam-induced suffering of Meredith. The wisteria vine is Edgerton's ultimate means of placing Vietnam—and all other human endeavors, folly or otherwise—in time.

The vine was planted by Caroline Copeland, part of her role in establishing the family in North Carolina. Many things change over time—large matters such as freedom for black people and small matters such as the location of the house on the property—but the vine thrives regardless. The vine's "horrific splendor of purple wisteria blooms" (40) threatens to overwhelm the Copeland family graveyard, but through their yearly ritual of vine-clearing, they manage to maintain equilibrium with the forces of nature. At its heart, Edgerton's story is about the phenomenon of continuity—of keeping the story of humankind going, despite setbacks.

The graveyard and its attendant vine link all things in time. In the spirit of magical realism, the wisteria vine has the function of relating events from times preceding those of the land's present occupants. For instance, following Aunt Scrap's account to Bliss of the first burial in the graveyard, the vine tells of the origin of the graveyard, begun for a field hand, Thomas Pittman, whose heart burst. He was not to be the last to suffer maladies of the heart: "And as he's been joined by others there in the graveyard beyond where the kitchen once stood, I, on blue moons, have seen and heard—still see and hear—them all" (46). The vine tells, too, of dark and dangerous times of national conflict, the sort of thing that might well have brought the American republic to its demise less than a century after its creation. The vine was there when a soldier in blue rode up to the Copeland place, bringing others in blue who plundered the farm and had a good laugh at the unschooled ignorance of Ross Copeland, who had carved "BORN DED" on the stone that marked the grave of his stillborn nephew.

With the vine, it is all there—the loss of a child at birth, the misery of the Civil War catastrophe, the death by virtue of a defective heart. This scope of history is large enough to encompass almost anything of human scale, and when we add the contemporary counterpart to the vine—the floatplane notebooks, which include a Department of Defense telegram reporting the unfortunate result of a hostile action on the other side of the globe—we have the realization of timeless time. Within that construct, Vietnam becomes placed snugly in the bosom of eternity, hard by a host of other sad stories, stories with the power to bring wisdom to maturity if only we might be attentive to them.

At the conclusion of the narrative, Vietnam is still present in the ongoing difficulties experienced by Meredith as he contends with adjustments in living mandated by his war injuries, but the culture is moving forward nevertheless. Although his speech is limited, Meredith has found a way to communicate by using a typewriter. He has even added the last finishing touch to the floatplane by typing out a name for it: *Natural Suspension*. Papa Copeland decides that giving Meredith a ride in the floatplane is called for, and he arranges to have the plane moved to the lake.

At the lake, while the plane is being offloaded from its trailer, the brakes on Meredith's wheelchair appear to fail. This is Thatcher's perception of the moment, but Edgerton leaves room for readers to speculate on the possibility of Meredith's wanting to have his wheelchair roll into the water, where his life would obviously be in peril. It is easy to understand why Meredith would be deeply challenged by having to come to terms with the floatplane, which represents the lively spirit of his years before Vietnam. The pain of confronting the past might impel many people to suicidal thoughts, perhaps even to action. Thatcher sees the near disaster, however, and Meredith is hauled to safety. Then it is time to proceed with the floatplane ride as planned.

The last chapter constitutes less than a page. The type is set in italics, and the style of the passage closely resembles the prose at the end of *Machine Dreams*. Meredith's perspective governs this closing passage, and his description of action proves to justify the name he had generated for his father's floatplane. Somehow, miraculously, the twenty-year project finally takes flight. The natural suspension of the plane moves from water to air, so naturally that it seems without explicit intent, so naturally that the plane's movement above the water and back to it strikes Meredith as being like that of a great bird: "*We were just going for a little ride on the water and that thing started flying—lifted right up, clean and smooth away from the water. We flew out over town, over the house, then looked down at the graveyard, here. Papa flew it back to the lake and made a big, wide turn, dropping down lower and lower, straightened her out and touched down into the wind. Bliss said just perfect, like a swan*" (265).

The floatplane represents the will of the Copelands to let imagination move freely, but always within the steady construct of knowledgeable reference to the past. They always know where they are in relationship to the family graveyard. Two of the Copelands have ventured far away to become involved in the Vietnam War, and one of them has returned home marked for life by the experience of combat in Southeast Asia. Yet at the end of Edgerton's story, the experience of Vietnam is being subsumed in time. This process of natural suspension of events can only happen when there is an appropriate medium to provide lift. A rich historical record, established through a continued relationship with nature (the wisteria vine at the family graveyard) and inscribed by man's hand in the action of imaginative writing about life's projects (Albert Copeland's floatplane notebooks), provides the necessary medium. As long as these conditions are sustained, Clyde Edgerton shows that it will be possible to manage the traumatic upheaval of events such as the Civil War and the Vietnam War.

The Floatplane Notebooks suggests that additional wars are not needed to banish Vietnam into the realm of the forgotten; instead, rather than trying to forget Vietnam completely, American culture should try to pursue two other options: to establish a more regular and natural relationship with its past and to feed its imaginative capabilities. With regard to each option, the world of the Copelands stands as a beacon to magical flight into the future.

REGENERATIVE VIOLENCE;
OR, GRAB YOUR SABER, RAY

AT THE END OF THE CHAPTER on Webb's *Fields of Fire*, brief consideration was given to the propensity that southerners have for violence, a point signaled pointedly in Webb's joke about the redneck group effort to change a light bulb which would devolve into a parking-lot fist fight. It is time now to return to examine this matter more directly and fully. For many years it has been recognized that the South is home to more than its fair share of violence. In a pioneering study, *Violence in Recent Southern Fiction* (1965), Louise Gossett turned to the U.S. Department of Commerce's *Statistical Abstract of the United States* and found that, concerning the incidence of murder, "in 1959, for example, the national rate of 4.8 per 100,000 population was exceeded by all Southern states" (32).

The last thirty years have done little to change that pattern. The section on violence in Wilson and Ferris's *Encyclopedia of Southern Culture* (1989) covers nearly fifty pages, with articles on subjects ranging from activities of the Ku Klux Klan to attitudes about punishing those who commit sin. Studies by Raymond Gastil, Sheldon Hackney, John Shelton Reed, and

numerous others have documented the statistical profile of southern violence and posited diverse explanations for the high incidence of violent
acts. Clearly, the South continues to be a place in which, although manners and decorum strive mightily to keep the ferocious impulses of the *id*
under control, the control mechanisms break down frequently. As a consequence, southern writers who have come of age in the past three decades
have had ample justification to follow in the path of people from the
earlier generation that was considered by Gossett. Through examining a
range of early major figures of modern southern literature—Faulkner,
Wolfe, and Caldwell—who set the "climate of violence," then considering
Warren, Styron, Goyen, Capote, O'Connor, Welty, McCullers, and Grau,
Gossett found that southern writers from the 1930s through the late 1950s
had "made the violent and the grotesque powerful vehicles of their perception of reality" (199). Looking even further back beyond these twentieth-century writers, Kenneth Lynn demonstrated convincingly in *Mark
Twain and Southwestern Humor* that Twain drew upon a rich tradition of
violence—both real and perceived (as embedded in oral storytelling and
written fictive texts)—in the old Southwest, the very region from which
the central author of this chapter, Barry Hannah, comes. Twain's Colonel
Sherburn, represents the epitome of the connection between honor and
violence, as well as Twain's own ambivalence about it. Given such a deep
well of influence in the South, the allure of violence in conjunction with
honor has proved to have staying power. In numerous cases, the young
writers of the South—those whose careers began in the aftermath of
various social upheavals in the 1960s—have located reality in close prox-
imity to acts of violence.

This sustained pattern of violence is most completely realized in the
work of Barry Hannah, whose first novel, *Geronimo Rex*, appeared to
critical acclaim in 1972. *Geronimo Rex* contains a number of savageries. The
novel's protagonist, Harry Monroe, discovers a number of dusty volumes
in the library of Hedermansever College, not in itself a situation normally
expected to generate violence, but in Harry's case, deep reading in the
humanities contributes directly to his eventual fixation on the persona of
the Indian chief Geronimo, who comes to stand for the essence of violence: "What I especially liked about Geronimo then was that he had
cheated, lied, stolen, mutinied, usurped, killed, burned, raped, pillaged,
razed, trapped, ripped, mashed, bowshot, stomped, herded, exploded,
cut, stoned, revenged, prevenged, avenged, and was his own man" (231).

Signs of violence are abundant in the world of Harry Monroe. Even the name of the college in which he matriculates conveys a mordant pun— head/man/sever. It becomes Monroe's challenge to pass through college without having his head metaphorically cut off. To maintain his essential integrity as a man, he assumes the spirit of Geronimo as a guide, and some violence ensues in the pursuit of self-affirmation. Guns and knives are employed frequently as this novel deals with a young man's rite of passage into adulthood in the South.

In an early overview of Hannah's fiction, Donald R. Noble noted in "'Tragic and Meaningful to an Insane Degree': Barry Hannah" that "Hannah's violence is a subject sure to get much attention in the future" (40); more recently, Allen Shepherd's study, "'Firing Two Carbines, One in Each Hand': Barry Hannah's *Hey Jack*," focuses directly on Hannah's violence in the context of southern culture. Again and again in a career that includes nine books between 1972 and the present, Barry Hannah has placed violence of various kinds at the center of his fiction.

Although Hannah himself never became involved directly in the Vietnam War, it was almost inevitable that he would confront imaginatively the violence linked to America's doomed foray into combat in Southeast Asia. By drawing upon a number of friendships with Vietnam veterans, including Philip Beidler, whom Hannah met while he was a writer-in-residence at the University of Alabama, and John Quisenberry, a lifelong friend who went to Vietnam as a pilot, Hannah has been able to develop salient connections between his native South and the conduct of war in Vietnam. For example, in Hannah's 1978 short-story collection, *Airships*, the story of Ard Quadberry, "Testimony of Pilot," draws its inspiration from Quisenberry's war experience. Quadberry flies F-4s off the carrier *Bonhomme Richard* and loves the exotic thrills associated with flight of this sort. One day he returns for a quick touchdown of his jet at the Jackson airport to deliver a message for his old girlfriend, Lilian. In the few instants he can spare on his flight west to San Diego and then Vietnam, Quadberry says, "I am a dragon. America the beautiful, like you will never know" (37). A series of close encounters with death over Vietnam leave Quadberry with an injured back. At the end of the story, he opts for an operation that might relieve his back pain, but Quadberry—the would-be dragon whose taste for peril gives him access to an America the beautiful beyond the knowledge of others—dies as a result of the operation at Emory Hospital in Atlanta. Quadberry's old friend Will tells the story, but since the irony of this loss is so profoundly unsettling to Will, he "will never tell another" (44).

Hannah, in contrast, tells other Vietnam stories. Vietnam figures centrally in "Midnight and I'm Not Famous Yet," another of the *Airships* stories, one later interpolated into the story of French Edward in *The Tennis Handsome* (1983). In "Midnight," Bobby Smith is an army captain in Vietnam. He meets another southerner, "Tubby" Wooten, who comes from "a town just north of Vicksburg" (105), which makes him "hometown" for Bobby, and together they venture into combat by parachuting into the path of an advancing North Vietnamese force. Tubby's response to Bobby's inquiry about reasons for being in Vietnam point to Hannah's own feelings about the need for more than a quietly settled life. Tubby says, "I joined. I wasn't getting anything done but being in love with my wife. That wasn't doing America any good" (107).

Bobby and Tubby are both chasing dreams of conquest. While a part of them might be contented with the vision of dominance contained in one of Tubby's photograph's of John Whitelaw, a masterful golfer and "our only celebrity since the Civil War" (107), they get caught up in a larger scale pattern of mastery over others. Of course, they are not the first to fall into such a pattern of behavior, a point solidly reinforced by Richard Slotkin in *Regeneration Through Violence: The Mythology of the American Frontier, 1600–1860*, which traces the evolution of a compelling mindset that spans centuries and that arguably predetermined America's impulse to assert its influence over the forces of darkness in Vietnam.

Slotkin's thesis is straightforward: "The first colonists saw in America an opportunity to regenerate their fortunes, their spirits, and the power of their church and nation; but the means to that regeneration ultimately became the means of violence, and the myth of regeneration through violence became the structuring metaphor of the American experience" (5).[1] Slotkin carefully shows how this metaphor became embedded in American culture through a host of writers in the first century of the nation's history; he concludes that "regeneration of violence" remained dominant right through the era of the Vietnam War.[2]

While the South has its own orientation toward the use of violence, Slotkin's analysis, which sweeps broadly across American culture, seems applicable to southern attitudes about the Vietnam War. The need to establish superiority over some "other" is as strong in the South as anywhere. Barry Hannah's fiction in general makes violence of various kinds seem necessary, and his Vietnam stories in particular showcase incidents of aggressiveness, usually with the sense that legitimacy in living is affirmed as a consequence.

Bobby Smith eventually comes to realize that war and violence are not guaranteed to produce regenerative energy for American culture, at least not in a simple, formulaic pattern. War is not as prettily heroic as the golfing conquests of John Whitelaw: "Here we shot each other up. All we had going was the pursuit of horror. It seemed to me my life had gone straight from teenage giggling to horror. I had never had time to be but two things, a giggler and a killer" (114). Yet even in this revelation, the Vietnam episode becomes paradigmatic for Bobby Smith as a way to understand life in his native South, the history of which launches itself into Vietnam combat in a bizarrely ironic twist.

The general commanding the North Vietnamese forces is named Li Dap. American intelligence on Li Dap's training at the Sorbonne yields the following detail: "He knows Robert Lee and the strategy of Jeb Stuart, whose daring circles around an immense army captured his mind. Li Dap wants to be Jeb Stuart" (110). Li Dap's audacity, inspired by Jeb Stuart[3]—a daring Confederate cavalry commander in Lee's army—results in his quick capture; his tank becomes mired in a pond as he attempts a bold flanking movement. Bobby and Tubby soon have a valuable prisoner, one who comes to them bearing the stamp of a southern legend of military prowess, and in their interrogation of the general, he betrays a further appreciation of the nuances of American history with respect to the great national schism of the nineteenth century. He relates the conduct of his war "to your war in the nineteenth century. The South had slavery. The North must purge it so that it is a healthy region of our country" (113). Irony of ironies! Bobby and Tubby, both southerners, are engaged in war with the intent to reach a plateau of achievement on a grand scale by besting a national opponent. However, their posture is undercut by an enemy figure who suggests that America's cause in Vietnam is flawed by association with the South's position during the Civil War—both forced to defend the stigma of slavery and doomed to lose if any truth resides in history. Naturally enough, this line of analogous reasoning unsettles Hannah's protagonists. Shortly after this exchange, the fortunes of Bobby and Tubby take a sharp turn for the worse.

Tubby has taken some pictures of General Li Dap, a coup that could lead to his advancement, and Bobby himself expects to advance to major on the basis of capturing the general. However, the North Vietnamese Army states a sudden attack, and Tubby is killed immediately. Bobby rescues the pictures, but then uses his phosporus shotgun indiscriminately to kill any enemy within range, including Li Dap. When an investigation ensues, "the story got out to UPI and they were saying things like 'atrocity,' with my name spelled all over the column" (117). Bobby is soon sent home—as a lieutenant.

Back home, Bobby reconciles himself to leaving the war by thinking of how he got most of his men out of Vietnam alive, but Tubby's loss haunts him. He sleeps around, indiscriminantly, eventually bedding his own aunt, an act that assumes regenerative power in its violence against social norms. In Hannah's rendering, deliverance to a good life often involves sexual activity that reflects a shade of violence; breaking a norm and/or social convention affords the individual access to revitalization.[4] By virtue of committing an act that is taboo, Bobby makes his aunt happy: "All those years of keeping her body in trim came to something, the big naughty surprise that the other women look for in religion, God showing up and killing their neighbors, sparing them" (117). Then the story concludes with Bobby and his aunt watching John Whitelaw play Whitney Maxwell in a golf match, a contest packed with explosive potential: "When they hit the ball, the sound traveled like a rifle snap out over the bluffs" (117). Whitelaw loses, but Bobby knows how to handle defeat. He has had practice. Once you have enjoyed the thrill of a good fight, you have no reason to be dependent on the outcome. As Bobby notes, rhapsodically, "Love the loss as well as the gain. Go home and dig it. Nobody was killed. We saw victory and defeat, and they were both wonderful" (118). In this remark we see the long-term benefits that accrued to the South as a consequence of having had to manage the defeat suffered in the Civil War. Vietnam was an example of something already well known in southern history, thus deeply legitimating Bobby's "love the loss as well as the gain" attitude.

Illuminating as Bobby Smith's war experience is with regard to the intersection of violence and southern culture, Hannah's most ambitious effort to deal with the Vietnam War takes place in a short novel called *Ray*, perhaps the best achievement of his career to date. *Ray* (1980) is a short book, only 113 pages and divided into 62 sections, and it is packed with explosive moments. Turbulence swirls around the story's central figure, a doctor named Ray, and at every turn, there are provocative indications of the South—its history and its violence, which Hannah links together.

Midway through the book, we discover that Dr. Ray has two first names: Raymond Forrest. The name Forrest quietly but surely sends us back in history to Bedford Forrest, the southern general who popped up as a telling sign of Webb's southernness in *Something to Die For* and who will figure prominently in several stories to be examined later, most particularly one of Winston Groom's novels. Forrest's role in the organizational activities of the Ku Klux Klan, a carryover of violence from the Civil War into the period following Reconstruction, makes his stature questionable for anyone outside the South, but Hannah, Webb, Groom, and others obviously find his military heroics to be of transcendent value, and Ray carries the spirit of his namesake as he rushes headlong through the wild times of the 1960s and 1970s, having one experience after another wherein his masculinity is tested and affirmed by his conquest of others. These tests occur in ritualized but real combat (war) and in sex. In either circumstance, Ray needs to achieve dominance. Hannah's fictional world is thus a hell both to pacifists and to feminists.

The most exciting reconsiderations of western culture in the past two decades have come from feminist theorists, whose work of necessity often concerns the use of violence as a means of establishing dominance, a concept that sits at the center of female/male interaction. Susan Brownmiller's *Against Our Will: Men, Women, and Rape* (1975) considered the male use of sexual power to establish mastery over others, and her book includes a section documenting rapes committed by American soldiers during the Vietnam War. Then, as before, rape became a means to deride the enemy by reducing their women to objects for brutal abuse, a point established compellingly by Jacqueline Lawson's "'She's a Pretty Woman . . . for a Gook': The Misogyny of the Vietnam War" in *Fourteen Landing Zones*.

Considering Hannah's tumultuous personal life in conjunction with the evidence of his fiction suggests that he is no stranger to psychological demons of a sexual nature, which warrants a look at a critical perspective that draws out the sex-violence linkage in texts. In "The Violence of Rhetoric," an illuminating analysis of dominant patterns in language in *Technologies of Gender: Essays on Theory, Film, and Fiction*, Teresa de Lauretis reviews the contributions of many cultural theorists—including Jacques Derrida, Jacques Lacan, René Girard, Michel Foucault, Claude

Levi-Strauss—to determine the parameters of control that are set by certain habits of language. Her representation of conclusions reached by Jurij Lotman in a typological study of plot origin has particular relevance to Barry Hannah's Vietnam writing:

> In the mythical text, then, the hero must be male regardless of the gender of the character, because the obstacle, whatever its personification (sphinx or dragon, sorceress or villain), is morphologically female—and indeed, simply, the womb, the earth, the space of his movement. As he crosses the boundary and "penetrates" the other space, the mythical subject is constructed as human being and as male; he is the active principle of culture, the establisher of distinction, the creator of differences. Female is what is not susceptible to transformation, to life or death; she (it) is an element of plot-space, a topos, a resistance , matrix and matter. (43–44)

As we shall see, Barry Hannah's heroes are inveterate penetrators, and they go about their penetration compulsively. This behavior goes on apace whether the "other" is a woman or an enemy in a war.

Ray begins innocently enough, with a style and voice reminiscent of the opening of *The Adventures of Huckleberry Finn*, complete with first person narration: "Ray is thirty-three and he was born of decent religious parents, I say" (4). We can almost hear the sweet naive quality of Huck's disarming introduction of himself at the outset of Twain's most influential story. The "I" narrator of *Ray* rambles on about matters of personal import, with occasional remarks addressed either to Ray or about him. There is, for example, the information about the narrator's relationship with someone called Sister, one of the Hooches. The details concerning her—her identity and background, even her relationship with the narrator—are generally innocuous, but they soon involve a matter that figures largely in the Vietnam War and that hovers as a general issue behind all of the relationships in the life of the narrator. It seems that Sister's "grandmother was a Presbyterian missionary killed by the gooks" (4). This grandmother is not destined to play a significant role in the narrative, but the description of her chosen function in life and of her death immediately satisfies the conditions embedded in countless stories examined by Slotkin as he documented the idea of "regeneration through violence." This practice of extending the sacred precepts of American culture into the realm of others was often carried out with missionary zeal, and in many instances, it involved dispatching Americans into the midst of potentially hostile cultures. Such was the background of Sister Hooch's grandmother, and a similar pattern is discernible in America's vision of itself as having a crucial role in the fate of the Vietnamese people.

The narrative undergoes a violent twist just a few pages into the text. It soon becomes evident that the "I" narrator and the subject Ray are one and the same. The narrative turns on the explosive tension between the objective and subjective visions of life. The age (thirty-three) of this split personality invites us to understand that this character has been around for some time, someone who has been recycled in time. Ray's age and the religiousity of his parents provide a clear and obvious link to Christ, the sort of game played by an earlier writer from Mississippi with a character named Maury/Benji.

The name-game and time-recycling gambit played by Faulkner in *The Sound and the Fury* assumes a major role in the structure and message of *Ray*. With the first-person/third-person split (or perhaps it is a weird union) operating throughout, Hannah suggests that the essential condition of our modern world is division—or fracture—or multiplicity of identity. The only thing that stays constant is the maleness of I/Ray. Certainly there are conditions sufficient to set the stage for violence, and this is just the beginning of the story.

Only a few more pages into the novel, we are informed by "I" (Ray), "I did my part in hurting the gooks back for you, Sister. I flew support missions for B-52 bombers in Vietnam" (10). Retributive justice, achieved with violence by striking back at the gooks for the death of Sister's missionary grandmother, is claimed by the narrator not as a personal motive for going to Vietnam but rather as one of the inevitable consequences to having been part of the American forces engaged in combat at that time in that place. By placing his Vietnam action in the realm of retribution, however, Ray becomes the walking embodiment of the southern code of honor, as set forth retrospectively by Wyatt-Brown. Of course, the "I" (Ray) figure was a pilot, one who, as Ray explains, flew "An F-4, called the Phantom. It's a jet airplane" (10). Ray's military experience essentially duplicates that of Quadberry in "Testimony of Pilot," flying F-4s off the carrier *Bonhomme Richard*.

Moreover, another detail in Ray's explanation is noteworthy here. He is talking to Sister Hooch, a woman with whom he has enjoyed lusty sex, though they have never been married and though Ray has been married to other women during his time of sexual assignations with Sister. Sister is presented in the novel through the perspective of Ray, who covets her as a prize sexual being and not much else. She has a hearty appetite for sex and so makes an easy conquest for Ray. Before Sister is killed by another man who is covetous of her ample charms, she goes about setting herself up in the music-recording business, proving that she has talents beyond those adored by Ray. Ray is enthralled with her feet (yes, this savior/destroyer would gladly wash the feet of women—with his tongue, no less) and with the way she loves loving him, so it is natural for him to speak to her as if she has no concept of what an F-4 is.

Yet Hannah may also be speaking to a larger issue. America at large seems to want to forget Vietnam. America generally has little need for the uses of history and so may soon need the kind of gloss afforded by Ray in his clarification of what an F-4 Phantom was in the Vietnam era.

As a southerner, Hannah is biased toward remembering the past. At one point in the novel, he even has Ray declare: "I roam in the past for my best mind" (95). The past intrudes frequently in *Ray*. The past provides a set of paradigms for violence, for Vietnam, for the energy that Ray has found both in war and in sexual impulses, each of which has taken him to the brink of disaster. The past provides the image of the raised saber, an image so central to the whole novel—even appearing in the last sentence of the story, "Sabers, gentlemen, sabers!" (113)—that nothing else serves so well to represent Barry Hannah's imaginative vision of the South's place in the Vietnam War.

The past is obviously invoked in the opening reference to Sister's grandmother, but before the end of the first section of the novel, deep history has assumed an even more pointed function. A large chunk of history is introduced by Hannah in a secondary plot involving the fortunes of Charlie DeSoto. Charlie carries the name of a famous explorer of the South, "Hernando de Soto, the discoverer of the Mississippi River who perished in 1542, probably of greed and arrogance" (12). Like Ray, Charlie has strong impulses for violence.

Charlie feeds these impulses on history. He has been reading about "the original de Soto according to Rangel, his diarist on the expedition from Florida" (13), and Hannah inserts into the text a two-page excerpt from the alleged historical document. The account deals with a hostile encounter between de Soto's forces and Indians who were under the leadership of Tuscaloosa, in the vicinity of Mobile. It concludes with the following description of the confrontation's outcome:

> The Governor put his helmet on his head. He warned the soldiers. Luis
> de Moscoso and Baltasar de Gallegos, and Espindola, the captain of the

guard, and only seven or eight soldiers were present. Gallegos went for Tuscaloosa, but the chief was hidden in a cabin and Gallegos with his knife slashed off the arm of an attacking Indian. Some got to their horses and killed the savages with lances. I was hit thrice by arrows. Women and even boys of four years fought with the Christians. Twenty-two of us died until the other Christians rescued us with firearms.

At the last, we had twenty-two dead and their fortification was empty. We had killed four thousand of them.

Many pearls and a great store of corn were found.

Tuscaloosa and all his family were dead. We turned the great tall Indian over. A soldier named Stellus had fired the buss straight through his chest from five lengths. (14–15)

Anyone even remotely familiar with the conduct of combat action in the Vietnam War is certain to catch the parallels to Vietnam in this record of de Soto's trip through the South and his battles with Indians as he went about the business of establishing Christianity in the new world. There is the hostility of "women and even boys of four years," conditions that made the ethics of war particularly difficult for American soldiers as they attempted to subdue the Vietnamese enemy in their own land. There is also the emphasis on relative body counts, with the implicit sense that the victors would be the force with the fewest casualties, and there is finally the emphasis on the superiority of firepower, which de Soto's force enjoyed in the defeat of Tuscaloosa. In a sense, then—at least in Hannah's imagining, which is not, naturally, the same as a fully comprehensive history of American combat activity throughout the war—Vietnam had been prefigured in the history of the South.

Hannah adds an additional twist. This pattern of history is relished by one familiar with it: Charlie DeSoto. Charlie's reaction to the exploits of his "perhaps ancestor" comes very close to representing Ray's position on the issue of war and violence; it also seems to be close to Hannah's own views. Immediately following the passage from Rangel's diary, Hannah provides us with a provocative insight into Charlie's response to the past: "Sometimes Charlie DeSoto read that passage to renew himself with his old perhaps ancestor. He got neither any special horror nor delight from it, but it reminded him of the adventurous perversity in himself that he cherished" (15).

Half a page further on, Charlie reflects, "It is terribly, excruciatingly difficult to be at peace . . . when all our history is war" (16). Therein may lie the peculiar rub for southerners and their yen for history. The past is full of war—commencing with the native Americans but eventually including a large slate of "others," domestic and foreign, who have had to be countered with violence—and anyone attentive to the past is likely to be psychologically disposed to walk in the paths of the fathers.

Hannah's vision of the South in *Ray*, then, begins with a wistful acceptance of violence, including war. In fact, war may afford man (literally the male version of the species) the clearest route to claiming a sense of supremacy, exultation in besting all others. Late in the story, as Ray is foundering one more time in the midst of domestic doldrums, he remembers his time in Vietnam. The memory provides an antidote to his peacetime malaise: "Many things have broken down in our nice house. The only glory I see is the glory I saw as a jet fighter. I went through the clouds and brought up the nose of the Phantom, lifting at twenty-one hundred land miles per hour. It was either them or me, by God. I loved those clean choices. And I loved my jet. I loved all those aerodynamics, the rising and diving" (101–2). Clean choices. Clear competition. Dominance. Glory.[5] War provided Ray with opportunities to avenge and destroy, actions that emerge naturally from the "adventurous perversity" that Charlie DeSoto cherished.

At the end of the narrative, Ray captures the sense of necessity for war in a clarion sentence: "Eventually every man's a sword" (108). The image of man as sword functions on two levels: first, there is the man in his state of sexual arousal, with the sword penis being used aggressively to subdue women. In *Ray*, Hannah balances the two levels of meaning, alternating them and virtually equating them. The release of energy is similar in each, and they are offered by Hannah as affording the possibility for ultimate healing, in an ironic way.

At one point in the story, Ray comes upon "a frat boy in an Izod shirt" (64) who had severely beaten an old drunk with a two-by-four. Ray arrives on the scene, calls an ambulance, then asks the frat boy to produce his two-by-four. Violence ensues as Ray gives the college student his due: "I bashed the fuck out of his ribs with it and his grandmother screamed. We put them both in the ambulance. I healed everybody" (65).

Ray is a physician, but he has been to war, which stands for him as a paradigm of reality, and he subscribes repeatedly to the virtue of violence. In the passage above, the doctor "heals" through an act of violence. The savior/destroyer union in Ray's character intrigues Hannah; it operates with the same sort of tension that is built into the "I" (Ray) split in the narrative point of view. Without question, Hannah subscribes to the necessity of some violence in life.

A sexual parallel to this violent healing appears later. Eileen, Charlie DeSoto's wife, has left her husband because she has discovered a lesbian side of herself. She goes to Ray, because he is a friend of Charlie's and because he is a doctor. Ray's response is typical of his general approach to women: " 'Let me fuck you,' I say. 'It will be good for you. Doctor's orders,' I say. 'Come on,' I say, 'you crazy lesbian bitch—ohh, uhh, uhnn, touch it!' " (103).

While "it" is not explicitly identified, the context of the passage and of the novel as a whole make clear the referent: that magical male saber, risen again to set wrongs right, ready at an impulse for the charge to glory.

This conflation of male action in war and in sex is realized most explosively in the various sections of *Ray* which deal with another era of the past and a set of circumstances that allows Hannah to link the Vietnam War even more closely to the South. Most of the narrative takes place in the post-Vietnam era. Ray is a veteran, and his memories occasionally thrust the story line back to moments of action from his time as a jet pilot in Vietnam. Cues to these times of reminiscence are diverse. For example, in Section XVI of the novel, Ray and his second wife, Westy, think that she is pregnant, and they are thrilled at the prospect of a shared child (they each have children from previous marriages, a point of reality that Hannah knows well from his own experience in serial marriages), but the circumstances change: "Two more days and it turns out that she wasn't pregnant, after all. My brain was in squalor and torment. But now it's like another friend I lost in Nam" (57). The Nam cue brings up an interpolated scene from the war in which we see "Edward, lieutenant commander from St. Paul, Minnesota, a nigger who saved my life twice, falling to pieces. There he goes. I should have delivered him. I should have been awaker" (58). The loss of a baby, the loss of a fellow pilot—it is all the same, a universe of convergence upon intensity and pain.

Yet people must rise through intensity and pain. Southerners have a particular expertise in the trials associated with this process, and on a few occasions in the novel, the narrative leaps back a century in time. In these time warps, Ray is a vigorous participant, not just an interested but distant witness as he was in the case of his knowing Charlie DeSoto. The first instance of a total break from the Vietnam period occurs in Section IV. In the preceding section, Ray has gone off to New York to deliver a professional paper; while he is away from Westy, he makes love with Laurie Chalmers, "a Jewess with large bosoms" (36), an anesthetist. On the way home, he feels the panic of betrayal, but once he is in the company of Westy, he turns on his sexual aggressiveness, she happily yields, and he concludes, "Sweet God, there is nothing like being married to the right woman" (39). Immediately after that reflection, coming hard on the heels of intense though contorted sexual relations, a new section begins, told in the first person plural: "We have come up in a meadow, all five hundred horses. We are in the Maryland hills and three hundred yards in front of us are the Federals, about fifty of them in skirmish line. . . . Jeb Stuart is as weary as the rest of us, but he calls for sabers out" (39).

Abruptly, it is the Civil War, and the southern forces under Stuart are about to charge.[6] Their sabers are out. In this action, however, they do not charge. Instead they fire their artillery, devastating the Federals. The battle is over in an instant: "It was too quick for us, Captain" (41), one of the enemy says to the "I" narrator at that point, a figure who soon is clearly equated with Ray. The southern soldiers drink the coffee and eat the steaks of the force they have just defeated. At length, they attend to the consequences of war: "We threw earth over the dead. Stuart went out in the forest and wept. Then all of us slept. Too many dead. Let us hie to Virginia, let us flee. I fell asleep with the banjo music in my head and I dreamed of two whores sucking me" (41).

That last detail typifies the aberrant, hyperactive sexuality that dominates all of the various historical times known to the experience of "I" (Ray). Not only is sex timeless, it is also a center of regenerative activity that incorporates much strangeness, including violence.

Sex and violence, in war and elsewhere, unnervingly seem to be the primary centers that hold humans together in experience. These forces are timeless, a point reinforced emphatically in Section V, which contains just two sentences: "I live in so many centuries. Everybody is still alive" (41). This declaration indicates the main conclusion that Hannah reaches about time: it is all the same. As it was in the campaign of de Soto, so it was in the missions of Jeb Stuart, and so it was in Ray's B-52 support flights in his F-4 Phantom jet over Vietnam, North and South. For the southern writer, the past is alive, a lasting source of knowledge carried to the heart.

Hannah's narrative in *Ray* extracts a full measure of inspiration from the past. Inspiration comes from Vietnam, but even more so it comes from the distant events of the Civil War, specifically the charges under the leadership of Jeb Stuart. Even though "Many of us start weeping and smiling because we will die and we know" (65), once the sabers are out, all else is inconsequential: "Around you there is nothing because the horses are in perfect line. The sun is coming over the raised sabers" (66). In the action related in Section XX, the southerners are again triumphant: "Everybody was killed. One Union private lived to tell the story. If warriors had known this story, we would have taken the war to the gooks with more dignity" (66). Hannah suggests in this passage that all America lacked in Vietnam was a little history—something to provide fealty to the cause, solidarity with one's compatriots, and dignity.

The South, of course, has history. It also has a reputation for producing fine writers, and Hannah manages to have some sport with the image of southern writers, especially poets. Ray assaults one young man who is possessed by the lyric impulse to deliver a poem called "Certain Feelings." Oddly enough, though, while the poem is a virtuoso parody of Whitmanesque free verse, it incorporates many of the same physical objects and notions that find a home in Hannah's fiction. There is a strong, recurrent emphasis on "firearms," "certain feelings about the girls and the guests," and a "certain helplessness I cannot control" (55), all of which figure largely in Ray's life. Ray eventually becomes infected with the poetic urge, as does Mr. J. Hooch, Sister's father. In all of this, Hannah may be manifesting symptoms of defensiveness. We should recall that the Webb joke about the rednecks changing a light bulb included one who would write a song about the act, and far back in Hannah's past there was a time when he fancied himself a poet. By bringing the southerner's zest for language out in the open in a humorous way, Hannah disarms any opposition that might emerge to challenge the shocks and surprises provided regularly by his own prose style. We can all laugh, for instance, at the tongue-in-cheek claim made by Ray at the end of the book—a claim backed by an outrageous example of raw sentiment without artifice:

> *And you can see how my poetry is improving.*
> *I'm climbing the high oak of learning.*
> *I'm feeling the old force of yearning.*

> *(112)*

The example is followed by an exclamatory assertion of Ray's enthusiasm for entering his fourth decade (Ray's age virtually corresponds to

Hannah's). The poetry shows how unchanged Ray is by time, and the last lines of the novel further guarantee the continuation of past patterns into the future. What has happened in the past, however troubled, may again be expected in times to come. In five, carefully selected words, Hannah reiterates the pattern of regeneration through violence: "Sister! Christians! Sabers, gentlemen, sabers!"

Sister's missionary grandmother was killed by gooks. Centuries earlier, good Indians were put in their place by Hernando de Soto's Christians. Ray happily applied his male saber many times to Sister Hooch, who seemed to thrive on his loving. He flew his Phantom like a saber in the sky to strike back at the gooks, and he knew glory in that experience. Ray rode many times into the heat of battle with Jeb Stuart's cavalry, always with their sabers raised as gentlemen, at least in their own image as carried through time. And what has been, will be.

Before turning to examine another set of novels that consider issues from the South's past as they are recycled through the Vietnam War, it is worth noting one final imaginative shift that Hannah incorporates into his story of Ray. In most cases, literary critics and writers are cast as adversaries, but in Hannah's case, that situation has not always pertained. Toward the end of the novel, which merges "Over Hanoi" jet-jockey talk with scenes of Jeb Stuart's cavalry pressing north to attack Washington, "I" (Ray) drops in a quick prayer for one who is well known to many of us who have spent time examining the literature of the Vietnam War: "Christ be with my friend Phil Beidler. He has a polyp on his vocal cords. I thought he might have C. Called Ned Graves in Jackson, Mississippi. Best one in the world with the knife on the throat. Phil was knocking down two packs of Marlboros a day. Like me, he loves his ciggies. Called Ned up. He was drunk, but wanted to fly over and get the C out of Phil. But good old Phil didn't have it" (92–93).

Vietnam scholars know Beidler from his 1982 study, *American Literature and the Experience of Vietnam*, which began a series of much-needed efforts to place Vietnam literature and its themes against an American backdrop. All writers on this subject have had occasion to mention Beidler's work, and he himself has recently pushed further with his assessment of Vietnam War literature by studying the collected works of several writers whose careers were essentially given long-term direction by their efforts to plumb the Vietnam experience. Beidler's *Re-Writing America: Vietnam Authors in Their Generation* (1991) is another superb contribution to the emerging body of critical discourse on this literature, reflecting in its structure assumptions about the importance of continuity that have long been congruent with the interests of southerners. Beidler's own southern-ness shows up prominently at the end of his first Vietnam study, where, in recalling a black GI's comment on the pain of reminiscence about the war, he concludes: "For him, for all the writers represented here, for all of us who care to read what they have to say, the war is not over. It will only be over when we have made it so through a common effort of signification, when we have learned at what cost it was waged for everyone it touched then and now and beyond. Then it will be over. Then we can say good-bye to it. Not before" (202).

Beidler's study incorporates many nonsoutherners, many of whom are as compulsive as he about discerning sense from the Vietnam War, but his final words have the mark of the South upon them, an unabashed dedica-tion to keeping the past as part of one's signification efforts.

Barry Hannah became a close friend of Phil Beidler during Hannah's 1975–80 stay at the University of Alabama, Tuscaloosa. Beidler is still at Alabama, still one of Hannah's close friends, and his influence is obviously reflected throughout *Ray*. Beidler helped Hannah grasp the representa-tive centrality of the Vietnam War; Beidler's own war experience ex-panded Hannah's creative efforts to make sense of contemporary America. Literary scholars are more likely to be damned by writers than celebrated, but Hannah is clearly inclined to pull major surprises out of his craft, hence his paying tribute to a scholar/critic, even as he delineates in *Ray* the constancy, even indelibility, of certain traits of character in the South. When the South rises again (and again, and again), it will rise as it did in the past—that seems to be the basic point of *Ray*—but a good southern writer knows how to make it all look new.

6

CIVIL WAR REDUX:
Brotherhood or Fratricide?

AT SOME POINT FOR THE SOUTHERN WRITER, the story of the Vietnam War inevitably must turn on an issue of enduring central concern in the culture of the South: race relations. The relationship between black people and white people was one of the galvanizing forces behind the eruption of hostilities between the states of the North and the South in the Civil War. The North prevailed in that conflict, which has fascinated Americans everywhere for well over a century now, but the task of working out race relations in the United States is still incomplete, whether in the North or in the South.

In some ways, the South has made the greater progress, at least since the flourishing of the Civil Rights Movement in the 1960s. It was possible, for instance, for Douglas Lawrence Wilder to be elected governor of Virginia in 1989, the highest elective state office ever held by an African-American in the South. Wilder's rise to prominence, including a brief run for the presidency in the 1992 campaign, would seem to suggest that barriers built on racial identity might be on the verge of collapse, gone the way of the Berlin Wall, but the two Germanies involved one people, whereas America has to resolve the division of two races. The divisiveness of this issue was reconfirmed in the 1990 contest for a U.S. senate seat in North Carolina. Senator Jesse Helms, the white incumbent, was opposed by Harvey Gantt, an African-American who had gained wide, multiracial support as mayor of Charlotte, North Carolina. The campaign was close and the outcome unpredictable until the election itself, but the strategy of the Helms camp was to exploit white fears of racial quotas that would jeopardize the success of whites in many areas of competition. The strategy—and its tactics of playing upon long-standing racial anxieties, which obscured several legitimate differences between the incumbent and his challenger on matters of public policy—served its purpose, and Helms won reelection to the Senate. Further South, an even more threatening contest for the Senate took place, as David Duke, a former Ku Klux Klansman, sought to win the right to represent Louisiana. Duke's campaign, while not victorious, raised the specter of dreadful past circumstances when fear drove whites into aggressive repression of black citizens. At this point, then, despite the rise of Douglas Wilder and the success of many other less well-known African-American politicians, it would be premature to assert that the South has found a lasting solution to the problem posed by racial diversity.

Racial diversity was, of course, a distinct problem that surfaced during the Vietnam War. Proportionately, according to percentage of the population, blacks were overrepresented in the kinds of military units engaged most frequently in ground combat, and in those units, blacks were underrepresented at command levels.[1] In the eyes of many observers, Vietnam became a war fought by blacks for the benefit of those who were more privileged by accident of birth. As the war went on and protests against it grew more widespread, it was inevitable that questions of race would add to the tension of feelings about conduct of the war. The protest movement was generally more subdued in the South than in other regions of the nation, but in May of 1970, at Jackson State College (now Jackson University) in Jackson, Mississippi, the protest against the war was conflated with protest about black rights in the South. The Jackson State protest became violent, resulting in the shooting deaths of two black students by white policemen, and the ripple effect of this bloody incident quickly was felt by the black troops in Vietnam.

Countless novels of the war feature moments in which the differences of color become salient determinants of action. James Webb acknowledged the importance of the color line in *Fields of Fire*. A group of blacks in Hodges's battalion form "The Brotherhood," and their tent, "The Black Shack," was off-limits to whites. Some of the men in Hodges's platoon have contact with these militant separatists, and the fragging (use of a grenade to wound or kill a person, typically another member of the same combat unit) of Sergeant Angus Austin, the top noncommissioned officer under Hodges, seems motivated in part by the white Austin's toughness on his black soldiers. The same kind of racial animosity is represented in several of the popular movies about the Vietnam War. For instance, Oliver Stone's *Platoon* includes several scenes that spotlight racial tension within the American forces, and a number of black soldiers in *Hamburger Hill* speak explicitly to this issue.

Apart from Webb's *Fields of Fire*, however, the stories of the Vietnam War from southern writers do not frequently concentrate on actual combat tension between white and black soldiers. Even when a racial split is clearly evident in the composition of combat units, southern writers generally concentrate on two points: first, showing how this split relates to life back in the South; and second, examining the means by which the shared experience of combat might set the stage for improved relations between races. A fair example of this pattern appears in Loyd Little's *Parthian Shot* (1975), which focuses almost entirely on the in-country exploits of a Special Forces A-Team. With the exception of Lance Cranston, who comes from Brooklyn, the team, located at Nan Phuc on the Bassac River in the Mekong Delta not far from the Cambodian border, is composed of southerners.

Sergeant Phil Warren is the medic, a role based on the Green Beret experience of Little himself, who left North Carolina for service in Vietnam in 1964. Second Lieutenant James Wheatley, the team's commissioned leader, is from Norfolk, Virginia. Master Sergeant Wiley O'Hara was born in Laslo, Mississippi, "a rough, mean, nigger-hating town" (10). Warren, Wheatley, and O'Hara are white southerners, and the team also includes two black southerners. First Sergeant Matthew Hood comes from Little Rock, Arkansas; Hood looks white but tells Warren that he is black, thus asserting the positive side of blackness. Staff Sergeant Leroy Santee, of Augusta, Georgia, is unquestionably black. Santee assumes a major role in Little's story, for he is a budding capitalist, and when the A-Team is bureaucratically misplaced (they are physically still in Vietnam although all the official paperwork shows them returned to Fort Bragg in North Carolina), Santee organizes the local labor force into a manufacturing enterprise, Hoa Hao Unlimited, Ltd., complete with division of labor, stock splits, and a $40,000 Small Business Administration loan from the Atlanta Bank and Trust.

Santee sees something of his own background in the lives of the Hoa Hao people in this part of Vietnam. He suggests to Warren that "many Southerners in the United States have oriental blood in them," the result of Asian migration across the land bridge to America, intermarriage with native Americans, and then interbreeding between the native Americans and early southern settlers. The consequence of this mixture is a set of shared values and physical attributes. In Santee's view, "Southerners have a more relaxed, calm way of life. Close to the soil. A lot of our eyes—look at mine—have a decided slant to them" (93). To Phil Warren, Santee looks like a round-eyed American, but Santee persists with his sense of kinship with the Vietnamese: "This land stirs deep, nearly lost racial memories of a time and a country before this life" (94).

Upon the arrival of Hamilton Dupree, grandson of a man who founded a southern textile mill, Santee believes that he has found the perfect partner. Dupree comes across as a man of true refinement, a fellow "fond of the gentle, slower way of life. The old Southern plantation aristocrat, without the slaves. There are so few men of quality, of true aristocraticness in the world" (126). At one point in their talks about manufacturing, Santee asks Dupree whether he sees in Vietnam something of his own background: "Doesn't all this—the smells, the sounds, the weather, the rice, the eyes—especially the eyes—stir a lost chord in your soul. A distant memory from centuries past?" (138).

In Santee's vision, whites and blacks have a shared heritage in the South. This heritage involves an approach to life—agrarian in origin, but with some room for light manufacturing—that more than a little resembles some of the features of southern life celebrated in the essays of *I'll Take My Stand*; in fact, it verges on the optimistic vision of the South developed by Fred Hobson in his "A South Too Busy to Hate" (*Why the SOUTH Will Survive*, 1981), which centers on the phenomenon of Atlanta in the 1960s, so busy with business that it could not afford racial bias. Still, within the province of Little's text, progress toward improved race relations takes place on a scale far smaller than that in Atlanta and much more closely oriented to the traditional South. Later in this study, we will consider a number of other novels that explore the similarities of life in agricultural Vietnam and life in the South, some of them (for example,

Gustav Hasford's *The Phantom Blooper*) offering insights on race relations as trenchant as those in *Parthian Shot*.

Santee's enterprise enjoys success for some time, something that he knows would be difficult to duplicate back home. He addresses this point head on: "It's the first time in my life I ever felt I was doing something more than carrying things. . . . And there ain't no way that will happen back in Augusta, Georgia, for me" (253). So when the Bassac River drops back to its normal level and it is feasible for the team members to attempt a return to the military fold, Santee chooses to remain with the Hoa Hao, the case of the southerner rediscovering the South in a distant place. In such a way, Santee attempts to break free of the struggle that has engaged him from birth back in the land of his origin. It is Phil Warren who perceives how Santee stands in perpetual relationship to Top O'Hara: "It was as if both men were playing the last act of the Old South. Each man to his own role. Top was the cornpone, grit racist, and Santee was the happy nigger dancing in the cotton fields. And it was as if they both knew it and were somehow deeply trapped in the mysticism of it all. It was weird" (18).

Santee and O'Hara play out their roles in the "last act of the Old South," and at the end of the story, Santee breaks free momentarily by staying on in Vietnam with his manufacturing company. Unfortunately, an accidental bombing attack on Nan Phuc destroys "a small textile factory" and kills two Americans (one of them Santee), but at least Santee has experienced a level of freedom and acceptance that many would hope to be one of the first major "acts" of the New South. Hence he is on the road to more consequential developments in race relations, already beyond the "love-hate" attitude that has kept the South locked in place for generations, yet something noted by Hobson as a slowly dissolving barrier.

The remainder of this chapter will be devoted to consideration of four novels—Clyde Edgerton's *Raney* (1985), Madison Smartt Bell's *Soldier's Joy* (1989), Larry Brown's *Dirty Work* (1989), and Harry Crews's *Body* (1990)—each of which explores southern race relations in the context of what happened in Vietnam. In the first three, combat circumstances seem to have been instrumental in drawing the races closer together than would be the norm back in the South.

Raney was Clyde Edgerton's first novel, and it is devoted in the main to the matter of marriage in the contemporary era. The blood runs very warm on one side of the family that Raney and her husband Charles constitute, coolish on the other. Raney Bell's folks are Free Will Baptists, holding deeply entrenched positions on God's plan for the human race. They are full-fledged conservatives. Raney thus inherits set notions about the virtue of racial segregation, about the separate roles of men and women, about the proper conduct of sexual relations between husband and wife—about practically everything. Charles, of course, is a study in contrast on each point.

Charles's mother, Millie Shepherd, is a convert to Episcopalianism, a move toward formalism and enlightenment from Methodism. In fact, enlightenment is practically the God of the Shepherd family; Charles's father is a college math professor and his mother is a public school teacher in Atlanta. They are what Senator Helms of North Carolina—and this story is set in piedmont North Carolina—would denounce as "humanists." Although the Bell family is willing to let Raney follow her heart's desire and marry Charles, from the first meeting of the two families, the differences stand out much more clearly than the similarities. There are grounds for divorce, plenty of them.

The marriage of Raney and Charles certainly has its share of rough and dangerous passages. As the young lovers enter these passages, they are afforded opportunities to undergo a degree of change. *Raney* is told in the first person, from Raney's perspective, which is delightfully naive, like that of her southern literary ancestor, Huck Finn. The book is laced with trenchant humor evolving from Raney's almost nonstop comments and reflections on the parade of domestic troubles that cause her to fall out of step with her cultural background and/or her husband. At almost every stumble, a principle or precept of Raney's Christian belief comes into question.

Again and again, domestic issues hinge on scriptural authority, a legacy of interpreted text handed along, generation to generation, through a considerable period of time spent in the same place by the Bell family. Raney's world is a community through time, its continuity anchored in part by the Bible, in part by the regularity of family gatherings to tell stories. The old tell, the young listen. As often as not, these parts intersect to form a whole: tales that cut with a Christian edge—make that, Free Will Baptist edge.

The couple's honeymoon is not even over before the Vietnam War begins to become a divisive problem for them. Charles had been to Vietnam as a soldier, although at no point does anyone offer explanatory details about the nature of his service. However, it is certain that he made fast friends in country. One of them, Buddy Shellar, is a wedding guest. He and Charles occasionally slip away from the wedding rehearsal to take a nip of some intoxicant, an act that distresses Raney greatly. Charles is adamant in his defense, suggesting at one point that their common experience—"and we were in the *war* together" (14)—justifies what they are doing with the pint Buddy has brought along to the wedding.

The distress caused by Buddy's presence is minor compared to the impact of another friend from Charles's Vietnam days. On the morning after a disastrous wedding night, so disastrous it leaves the marriage unconsummated, Charles makes a long-distance call to New Orleans and talks at great length with his best friend, Johnny Dobbs. He even gets Raney to sing a couple of songs to Johnny over the phone. Raney thinks that Charles's familiarity with Johnny is peculiar from the outset, but as she surmises more about Johnny's background from the calls Charles makes to him whenever there are rocky moments between the young marrieds, her anxiety grows ten-fold.

Raney overhears many of her husband's phone conversations. Their home has an air vent between their bedroom and the living room downstairs, and it is through this vent that Raney catches details that give her a shock. She is first upset that Charles shares his thoughts more freely with Johnny than with her. Charles seems to look upon Johnny with more respect than he shows her. Then comes a major revelation, as Raney infers a troublesome detail about Johnny from some of the things that Charles is saying over the phone: "He went on about Mama for a while and then said something about everybody saying 'nigger' and that when Johnny came to see us for him not to drive in after dark—which I didn't understand until it dawned on me that maybe Johnny Dobbs was a, you know, black. He didn't sound like it when I talked to him over the phone at Myrtle Beach" (31).

The fact that Johnny Dobbs is black poses a particular problem if he should come to visit Charles and Raney. Charles and Johnny might have been close friends in the army—perhaps "roomed together, or at least ate together" (32)—but such intimacy between the races is not yet acceptable in Listre, North Carolina. Raney promises to herself that if Johnny ever visits, he will stay at the Ramada Inn.

Some time later Raney asks Charles if Johnny is "a minority" (61), and Charles says, "he's black, if that's what you mean" (61). Raney cannot imagine her family all together in her house with Johnny Dobbs as a guest. Hesitantly, she explains her reservations to her husband: "Well, Charles, I know you were in the war together and everything but this ain't exactly the war" (61). From this exchange, which ends when Charles notes that Johnny is too busy with law school for a visit right away, it is clear that Vietnam represents one of the watershed events in Charles's departure from the norms of his native culture. In the war, Charles had the freedom to become close to those of another race. Perhaps it was a necessity, not just a choice, but regardless of the specific cause, his perspective has been changed, even though his culture has not moved ahead nearly as rapidly.

Charles comes into conflict frequently with Raney and the conservatism of her family/religion. Rather self-consciously, he takes the role of devil's advocate, eager to jump on remarks made by Raney's kin, challenging the assumptions that lie behind their values and attitudes. In the second section of the novel, provocatively called "A Civil War," the matter of racial prejudice becomes hotly debated in a family gathering. Charles takes on the entire family, asserting firmly, "I don't think skin color makes any difference" (127), a point that meets with uniform disapproval from Raney's aunts, uncles, cousins, and parents. Raney herself thinks that God's plan was for the races to be separate; anything else would be "unnatural" (128). Yet to her credit, Raney wants to be as open as possible to her husband, whatever his notions. After listening to Charles describe the racial argument to Johnny on the phone, she gets "to thinking about Charles being outnumbered and that maybe Johnny Dobbs really was one of his best friends—that something traumatic in the army has caused them to be good friends" (130).

"Something traumatic" has indeed taken place. Charles has been liberated by his army war experience. He is at odds with the prevailing cultural attitudes of Listre, but Edgerton allows Charles a large measure of success in his efforts to draw the white and black races closer together in the South. After a brief period of marital separation, Charles and Raney reconcile, determined to listen more to each other in the effort to work out their differences, and not long after, they conceive a child. The coming of a new generation brings up a whole new set of considerations. Charles proposes having Johnny Dobbs as the child's godfather, and there is talk about baptism in infancy.

The novel closes as it begins—with a news clipping from the *Hansen County Pilot*. The "news" deals with the baptism of Thurman "Ted" William Shepherd, which takes place in the baby's fourth month, at St. John's Episcopal Church, and yes, "Mr. Johnny Dobbs, from New Orleans" (227) is baby Ted's godfather. Looming up from the shadows of Charles's past, from his time in Vietnam, Johnny Dobbs comes to represent a major shift in the direction of improved race relations, but the last detail from the news clipping shows that there are battles still to be fought in the aftermath of Vietnam in the South. Dobbs is "staying at the Ramada Inn" (227). Some compromise has been necessary to keep the marriage of past and present together in order to make way for a future that incorporates a new set of attitudes about the races in America.

The inclusion of Johnny Dobbs in the major sacramental act of the next generation in the South carries considerable symbolic weight. Edgerton's story finishes with a gentle but nevertheless firm sign of optimism. Maybe it was bound to happen, the way things were going for Raney and Charles. After all, they did have a powerful interest in common: the love of music—southern traditional music, to be precise. Charles has taught himself to play the banjo, an attribute he shares with Edgerton, and Raney sings. As they developed their mutual interest and contended with the adversity of disagreement on many other cultural issues, Raney and Charles became steadily better at listening to each other. They had to learn the art of listening, even pay good money to a "psychiatric," Dr. Mary Bridges, to improve their listening skills. All along, of course, they should have known about listening from their experience in music. By listening to the music each other makes, they grow together. Edgerton puts considerable emphasis on music as a medium for bridging differences.

In the last chapter of the story, with the baby still growing inside Raney, she reflects on a new song that Charles has learned. It is called "Soldier's Joy," one of her all-time banjo favorites: "I don't know why he hadn't learned it before. I play it on the record player all the time—it's on the Circle Album. It's the best instrumental recording I've ever heard. Frailing and three-finger picking together. It works on your insides. I listen to it five times straight sometimes" (241).

"Soldier's Joy" emerges from far back in the American past, its lyrics originating in the Revolutionary War. Here, late in *Raney*, "Soldier's

Joy" works on a number of levels of meaning. Charles, a former soldier, is slowly but surely making his way toward joy in life. His marriage is working, and his music is working. Maybe even his ideas for changing his culture are working, and one of the most basic changes that he desires has a clear link to his time as a soldier in Vietnam. Johnny Dobbs is going to join the Shepherd family. That goal, which implies a sense of brotherhood without regard for color, has been carefully shepherded through many trials in the course of Edgerton's story of a modern marriage in the South. It is ironical to be sure, but at least in this instance, the Vietnam War proves to be the means by which to deliver the South to a promising new point of departure in race relations. Hence "Soldier's Joy."

In 1989, just four years after the publication of *Raney*, a novel with the title *Soldier's Joy* was published, the fifth novel to be written by Madison Smartt Bell. Born in 1957 in Nashville, Tennessee, Bell is one of the South's most precocious talents. A summa cum laude, Phi Beta Kappa graduate of Princeton (1979), Bell took an M.A. in creative writing from Hollins College in 1981. Since then, he has lived in diverse places, including New York City and Italy, spent a year (1987–88) at the Iowa Writers' Workshop, and along the way, has produced a slew of fictions, which, until 1989 and the appearance of *Soldier's Joy*, had dealt with locations other than the South, mainly the raw underside of city life in New York. With *Soldier's Joy*, however, Bell returned to his roots, to his home state of Tennessee.

Soldier's Joy is the story of Tom Laidlaw, a Vietnam War veteran, who returns to the hills of central Tennessee to try to reestablish himself on the land of his deceased father. The song is the same one that correlates with happiness for Charles Shepherd, but Bell seems purposefully bent on rebutting, or at least severely qualifying, the optimism of Edgerton's ending in *Raney*.

Bell's story incorporates many of the key elements in *Raney*. Like Charles Shepherd, Tom Laidlaw is engaged in teaching himself to play the banjo. Like Charles, Tom develops a romantic relationship with a fellow musician—in his case, a fiddler named Adrienne Wells. Like Charles, Tom learns to play "Soldier's Joy," and the song proves to be a turning point in his life. Like Charles, Tom has a deep, almost spiritual kinship with a black man, Rodney Redmon, with whom he had shared powerful experiences in Vietnam. This relationship, as in the case of Charles and Johnny Dobbs, proves threatening to the culture to which

Tom has returned, but where Edgerton allowed Charles and Johnny to take a community-sanctioned step forward together, Bell angles for an ending that borders on apocalypse.

That *Soldier's Joy* would reach a conclusion filled with violence and bloodshed spilled for reasons of racial hatred is not surprising, given the edginess with which Tom Laidlaw moves as he takes steps to learn anew the lay of his homeland. He walks with some hesitation because of an injury from the war, a point that surfaces immediately and that hovers more ominously over the whole story than was the case with Charles's Vietnam background in *Raney*. Tom must learn to walk without some of the toes on one of his feet. The injury affects his balance. To compensate, he develops his own internal gyroscope, a pattern that becomes increasingly symbolic of his whole situation as the story unfolds.

Throughout, Bell seems to be writing part of his own story, for *Soldier's Joy* is much concerned with the task of returning to one's native place after a time away. There have been many Vietnam narratives about the plight of the returning veteran, and this issue is not distinctively southern by any means, yet Bell's version certainly reflects his own profound sense of the South. For example, Tom needs to know the land intimately. Because of sleeplessness and habits developed in Vietnam, he goes out often at night when his senses are all engaged. He knows the sounds, the feel, the smell of his land—all in keeping with the land rootedness of the Agrarians. He goes as if by instinct to the family graveyard, passing through it to pay a visit to old Wat Redmon's house. Tom in his youth had learned perhaps more from Wat than from his own father, a pattern of white/black relationship that is echoed beautifully by G. C. Hendricks, a North Carolinian, in *The Second War* (1990), with the lasting indebtedness of Truck Hardy, the white protagonist, to Uncle Goody, an old black man of Truck's community. In sum, Bell's southern novel is a primer of southernness: the almost instinctive identification with the land, the call of the graveyard, the craving to make music, the white child learning from the black man— these motifs all are distinctively linked to Bell's native country.

Tom Laidlaw's night forays help bring him fully in touch with the essential South, but they also mimic his Vietnam experiences. During his time in country, he was a LURP (member of a Long Range Recon Patrol). LURPs were a special kind of soldier, the closest that American troops came to identification with the land on which they came to fight. They went out into the country in small teams, trained to move silently, carry little, and live off the land. They went looking for the enemy, and because they went on their missions in the fashion of the Indians whom their cowboy cohorts in other units were meant to kill, the LURPs knew Vietnam far better than most Americans. In "Unlearning to Remember Vietnam," Donald Ringnalda captures the key sense of the LURPs: "Someone once said that in Vietnam a grunt learned to live in the bush; a LURP learned to be a bush, so thoroughly did he cut himself off and meld with his surroundings" (71). When Tom Laidlaw prowls his native land under the cover of darkness—one time finding a stray dog that becomes his companion, one time observing a raucous family scene at old Wat's place, one time surprising a deer poacher just about to climb to his treetop hunting stand—he reenacts his Vietnam experiences. He finds himself at home again, though, as he declares to Rodney Redmon in explaining how he was ready to cut the throat of the guy jacking deer, "I don't think I knew right where I was at exactly" (309). Vietnam, the South, in some ways, one and the same.

Tom's homeland is simultaneously a place of permanence and a place of change. For permanence, there is the hard pleasure of tilling the land, planting and harvesting crops. There is the banjo and traditional bluegrass music like "Soldier's Joy," a song Tom learns just before meeting Adrienne Wells. There is the rhythm of weather through the seasons in the hills of Tennessee. With all of this, Tom eventually reconnects, but there is also a deeply entrenched racial animosity, perhaps the hardest legacy to dismiss, and when Tom renews his ties with Rodney Redmon, Wat's son, trouble looms.

Redmon has served time in jail after his Vietnam stint. He took a job in the real estate development business with Goodbuddy Clemmons. Goodbuddy is a hustler, always on the lookout for a way to make a quick buck, whether in the quartermaster corps in the army or back home. He is a form of the "new" South, cast in the same mold used by William Faulkner for the character of Jason Compson in *The Sound and the Fury*. Oozing greed, Goodbuddy has visited Tom at his cabin to propose the idea of putting a housing subdivision on the Laidlaw family homestead. Redmon had enjoyed the good life for a few months with the real estate business, but when Goodbuddy's shady financing practices were discovered, Redmon was made to take the fall for fraud.

After his jail term, Redmon gets a job unloading trucks at a warehouse. He lives by himself, simply, but he is troubled in his sleep by dreams of the dead in Vietnam. His dreams of violence follow him to his waking hours, and soon he is attacked by a fellow employee at the warehouse, Timmy Rowan, who cannot stand the idea of working with a black man. Then at the Clawhammer Bar and Grill, Rodney meets up with Tom Laidlaw. Tom gives him a big hug in public. Some other long-established residents of the region, the Giles family, are witnesses to this display of warm affection between white and black, and soon the young Giles men are plotting a night strike against Tom. They plan to burn his place, teach a lesson to the "nigger-lover" (266), but old man Giles, who gradually has befriended Tom, provides a warning, and Tom is ready for the attack. Tom's dog is killed, but he drives his enemies off with a hail of shotgun shells packed with rock salt. When Redmon learns of the attack, his response pinpoints the connection between Vietnam and the South which intrigues Bell: "You been fighting the war over again" (287).

Later, as pressure builds toward a larger confrontation over the issue of race relations, it becomes evident that "the war" is as much the Civil War (or war between the states) as the Vietnam War. History in the South lives, and in "Soldier's Joy (1972)," the last section of Bell's novel of the same title, the inscription of history in the South is traced to its fundamental point: the reckoning of feelings between the white and black races.

Redmon takes some of his meals at a restaurant run by Raschid, a Muslim (who had originally come from the Cripple Creek area, knew Tom and Redmon, and went off to New York City and a series of armed robberies before finding a place in the fold of Mohammad). On the television in this restaurant, Redmon has seen the evangelistic preaching of Brother Jacob, whose text is love between all races and creeds. Brother Jacob calls for the "Children of God" to bind themselves together with a kiss of peace: "We must learn to lay that trap for one another. Not to trap each other into ruin and murder, no, not that. No more, no matter if it's been our habit. But into Christian charity and loving-kindness—I say to you all, children of God, we must *trap* each other into the spirit of brotherly love" (330). Impressed from a distance, Redmon wants to see Brother Jacob in person when he comes to the area to hold a revival.

Not long after Redmon warms to Brother Jacob's message, Tom and Redmon have a heated argument following the death of Wat. Redmon has asserted that his father always preferred Tom to himself and that Tom's family had displaced Wat from land that he had settled on first. Tom meets this hostility with understanding, and he offers to split his land with

Redmon, giving away the best part in the spirit of justice and respect for Wat. To all appearances, Tom is willing to put Brother Jacob's text into action.

Soon, Tom's fate is further cast with Redmon's because of the revival appearance of Brother Jacob. Laidlaw has received notes in the mail warning that harm will come to Brother Jacob. Redmon suspects Goodbuddy Clemson of writing the notes, and when Goodbuddy is confronted on this issue, he tells Tom and Redmon of a plan to shoot the evangelist on stage. The Giles boys and a mysterious Vietnam Special Forces veteran named Fowler are all involved, operating under cover of the Ku Klux Klan. The "goodbuddy" cracker South clearly fears that the multicultural harmony of Brother Jacob's faith will be more appealing in the long run than their own vision of a forever divided Dixie.

Laidlaw and Redmon are confronted with a moral dilemma: how best to protect Brother Jacob and his message of love from falling prey to racially motivated hatred? The quagmire of Vietnam holds them still, for they had acted in unison once before to commit an act of necessary violence. Laidlaw, Redmon, and another man named Ratman had been part of a team led by a soldier named Sevier. On the return trip from a mission, Sevier's leg was broken. He could not continue on their escape route, so he asked his teammates to kill him. They all fired simultaneously, but Ratman drew the short straw to determine who would tell Sevier's widow how he died. In the most wretched of moral circumstances, they had acted together with their weapons.

When Brother Jacob's life is threatened, they decide to act again, again with weapons, and they go to find Ratman to make their team as complete once more. Ratman's harrowing trip to Sevier's widow has left him a complete social outcast, and he confines himself to "Fort Negley," a hidden and heavily fortified section of a community landfill area. After being told of the need to save Brother Jacob, Ratman pinpoints the situation in the course of local history: "This is old stuff here. . . . This goes back to the War Between the States" (427).

Since Laidlaw and Adrienne are to be part of the musical program to accompany Brother Jacob's presentation, they have the opportunity to conceal weapons in their instrument cases. Before the show is to begin, Redmon and Laidlaw meet briefly with Brother Jacob, who mystically perceives that God is stalking Laidlaw, trying to bring him into the fold. "It's just his time" (440), Brother Jacob says to Redmon of Laidlaw.

With the arrival of Goodbuddy Clemson, the Giles boys, and Fowler, there is no way to avoid a bloody ending for *Soldier's Joy*. Raschid is killed. Goodbuddy is killed. Laidlaw kills Earl Giles. Fowler kills Ratman. Then Laidlaw is shot, just as he thinks that his escape is clear. Fowler, the wily Vietnam-trained adversary, slips out of ambush in the woods—just "where we want them" (445), but Redmon comes back to pick up Laidlaw and carry him to the van where Adrienne is waiting. In the final scene of the story, Laidlaw's head is cradled in Redmon's lap. Redmon says, "I won't let you go either way" (465), not intending for Laidlaw to get out of his promised commitment to share the family land.

While Laidlaw's chances of survival are not guaranteed, he is absolutely committed at the end to joining his own fortunes with those of another race, even though it has meant replicating in his own land, the South, all the moral turbulence of violence in Vietnam. Bell obviously subscribes to the nature of progress as outlined in Edgerton's *Raney*, but he differs radically from Edgerton in the perception of cost in blood for future transactions toward a race-free brotherhood in the South.

Larry Brown's first novel, *Dirty Work*, appeared the same year as *Soldier's Joy*, and it brilliantly continues the meditation on race relations and Vietnam begun by Clyde Edgerton and sustained by Madison Smartt Bell. Brown is a Mississippian. He served in the Marine Corps from 1970 to 1972, then joined his hometown fire department in Oxford, rising to the position of captain before retiring in 1990 to write full time. Brown's story is set in a V.A. hospital in the South, years after the Vietnam War has ended, but Brown's marine experience allows him to incorporate flashbacks to Vietnam and the combat wounds suffered by the two protagonists of *Dirty Work*: Braiden Chaney, a black man, and Walter James, a white man. The immediacy of Vietnam is indeed a moving force in Brown's novel.

At its center, *Dirty Work* is a poignant consideration of what brotherhood means. While the ending is not violent in the style of *Soldier's Joy*, it nevertheless demonstrates how searing—as well as tender—are the bonds that tie brother to brother. On one level, Brown's narrative testifies to the fraternity of Vietnam veterans; this fraternity is exclusive, and it carries with it a set of obligations. These veterans must take care of one another, for others in their culture seem not to know them at all. On another level, *Dirty Work* addresses the imperative of reaching across lines of color to realize the ideals of brotherhood, a point entwined throughout with a sense of spiritual mission that is timeless in nature.

Even the structure of *Dirty Work* highlights the idea of equality. Two points of view are balanced, back and forth, as the thoughts of Braiden and then those of Walter emerge, surge, recede, and then finally come to a kind of union. Along the way, nearly all of the southern attributes already noted come to the fore—the compelling desire for history, the call of honor, the proclivity toward violence, the rootedness of experience in the land.

The story commences from Braiden's perspective. He has spent the last twenty-two years in hospital care, having lost all of his extremities in Vietnam. Not able to move about physically, he compensates with mental traveling. As would be expected in a story of the South, Braiden's thoughts often seek the trail of history, and he goes back in time in his mind. When Walter is brought to an adjacent hospital bed, Braiden is on a trip to the Africa of "three hundred years ago" (1) with a vision of how it would have been "If history had been different" (1). He would have been a king. He would have had a son. But even given the superficial difference of experience between Braiden's reality and his imagined alternative to it, the hunting rituals of initiation into African manhood are not so far removed from the actual experiences of his own past, the time of soldiering in Vietnam. At the end of the first chapter, Braiden's thoughts have moved on through Vietnam to rest on the present moment, on his new companion, and on his essential state of being after twenty-two years of hospital confinement: "Old boys that brought him said Brought you some company, Braiden. I said Misery loves it" (10). Braiden's life is misery, for diverse reasons lodged deep and fast in history; his story is a quest for escape from misery.

The second chapter belongs to Walter. He regains consciousness, realizing that he is in a strange environment but not knowing how he came to be there. To be cautious, he keeps his eyes shut and uses his ears to discern as much as possible about his surroundings. He hears a television; the program seems to represent the general foolishness of American culture: "some asshole in a sitcom saying one-liners and canned laughter playing to it" (8). Television intrudes frequently in *Dirty Work*, almost as if it were the center of the modern universe. Although they have no control over the television or what it represents, at least Walter and Braiden share the knowledge that is a wasteland of extraordinary proportions.

When we return to Braiden's point of view in the third chapter, we discover that Braiden finds the subdued, bedbound presence of Walter to be more entertaining than the television that "they leave on all day and night, talking about they detergent and douche bags and I don't know what all else" (11–12). Braiden sees the hospital as a "junk pile," the place where they put you "when nobody else don't want you, when your family don't want you, when your mama gone and it ain't nobody else" (12). But now there is somebody. Another nobody for the junk pile. Walter. Walter's face is a puzzle to Braiden, as is the whole world: "Why it's got to be the way it is. I don't think the Lord meant for it to be like this originally. I think things just got out of hand" (12). The physical conditions of both Braiden and Walter symbolize how far out of hand things have gotten in human affairs. Walter's face is severely deformed from his war wounds, and Braiden lacks arms and legs. The challenge for them is to find a way to recover some sort of original love that was lost along the way from the beginnings of time.

With the moment that Walter opens his eyes, Brown's choice of words signals the kinship that eventually will become part of destiny for Walter and Braiden. The fourth chapter switches back to Walter's point of view, one that immediately focuses on the closest human being in his world at that moment: "He was a bro and he was looking at me. Studying me when I opened my eyes. Like he'd been watching me for a long time just to see how long it would take" (13).

These lines capture the essence of the entire story—the story of Vietnam veterans and of blacks and whites in the long march of history. The slang term "bro" speaks volumes. It is part of a code, emerging from black culture, which needed a tight word to catch the essence of solidarity in black brotherhood, but the word was quickly appropriated in the lexicon of soldiers in Vietnam to denote anyone who had joined their fraternity of combat experience.

Braiden is immediately a "bro" in Walter's eyes, but as the story develops, the idea of brotherhood becomes deeper and deeper until at last it transcends its original demarcation of color. Even as he contemplates the ruin of Braiden's body and they start to exchange backgrounds (each of them has chopped his share of cotton), Walter senses that they eventually will be drawn closer than they are at the outset in their separate but adjacent hospital beds: "I knew one thing would lead to another. It always does" (16). Although the time frame of the story involves only a little more than a night, the resolution of one thing leading to another is held off until the final paragraph, an act of charity terribly powerful and moving, an act of abiding brotherhood.

·

Ever so gradually, the backgrounds of Braiden Chaney and Walter James emerge from the night in the hospital. They have a lot in common. They are both southerners. As noted earlier, they have both chopped cotton. They come from the country. They both went to Vietnam, Braiden through the draft, Walter as a Marine Corps volunteer. Both were wounded in ways that forever haunt their days and nights, but their responses vary. Braiden desperately needs to find escape from reality, whereas Walter's problem is to keep himself within reality, a different task since the sniper's bullet lodged in his brain periodically sends him into unconsciousness.

Braiden's world is more given to fantasy then Walter's. At one point, he recalls with relish a Jimmy Stewart Civil War movie he had watched with his mama the night before he departed for Vietnam. Stewart has a serious arm wound, and a doctor is induced to save the arm only after Stewart promises to reward him with the gift of his prize horse. The arm is saved. The horse is lost for a time. President Lincoln gets Stewart back to his mama, and years later, they find the horse, which they treat with tender care for the rest of its life. It is the perfect story for Braiden: "It was a real heartwarming story. It was a happily ever after" (25). Braiden's life, of course, is not like that, and he requires all the help he can get to endure the tedium of daily routine in the hospital.

Humor is one of the creative antidotes that assist Braiden in dealing with misery, and his humor bubbles with irreverence for the mindless extravagances of American life. His Vietnam experience has given him a radical perspective on the "big PX in the sky," which was one of the favorite phrases used by combat soldiers to describe the essence of their homeland, and as a consequence, he has a delightful tendency to turn cultural commonplaces upside down. For example, he has fun transposing a television soap opera dalliance into the black idiom. He also imagines living five or six thousand years in the future, a time when "they won't even have no damn guns by then probably" (20), but since guns, turmoil, and violence inhabit most of the visions that pass through Braiden's consciousness, more than humor must be invoked to sustain him in adversity.

Fortunately, Braiden has a religious spirit. In fact, he is on intimate terms with Jesus, who comes to sit on his bed. Jesus sits and smokes and talks, answering Braiden's queries about how long his life must last. Jesus tacitly agrees with Braiden's notion that perhaps Walter might be his "savior" by agreeing to terminate Braiden's life. If Braiden were killed, even following a request for such an act of mercy, he could pass into heaven to be with his mama.

Before this escape can be realized, however, Braiden has ample time to exercise his fantasy, with himself as an African potentate. He returns to this realm as often as possible, for it offers all that reality has denied him: "I got lions to kill, and tribes to fight off. Got maidens. Many of them. Many beautiful ones I can touch with my hands" (63).

Braiden had answered the call to serve his country. He had left his mama and their shack in the county near Clarksdale. He had been shot "all to pieces" (161) at eighteen in an ambush in Vietnam and had missed his chance to have a family, to have children: "Supper on the table when you come in from work. Watch them younguns grow up" (15). He has suffered countless indignities through twenty-two years of government care in veterans' hospitals, but he has imagination, and for a few precious moments, he can put the past under his creative command and realize a happy place for himself.

In contrast, Walter slowly comes to realize how his head wound has again ruined any chance for happiness, just as he was as close to happiness as he could hope to come. He had been making love to Beth, a woman with her own severe deformities, her legs having been chewed savagely by a dog when she was little. Their love seemed natural and supremely fortunate. It was not meant to be sustained, however, for Walter suffered a seizure while on top of Beth in his truck, which was parked by a stream that rose quickly in a torrential downpour, eventually drowning Beth. The memory of this terrible moment, which had occurred not long before Walter's meeting with Braiden, comes out of the darkness slowly. It is preceded by a mass of history from deeper within Walter's past.

Walter's father also had been a war veteran, fighting in Europe in World War II, an experience that had "ruined my daddy as much as anything else" (166). Alcohol had been an answer to his father's problems, but just as alcohol often serves to induce Walter's seizures, it held dangerous consequences for the father as well. One time he had killed a man for something to do with honor and Walter's mother. He had spent five years in prison for that act, which had been precipitated by alcohol.

Randall James's second trip to the penitentiary, though, had nothing to do with booze, but everything to do with family honor and with a sense of justice that admits no difference for race. Walter had explained this incident to Beth before they made love, and it serves to foreshadow

Walter's action at the close of the narrative. Randall James had been picking cotton alongside a black man named Champion. They worked for Norris, a white man, who weighed their bags of cotton and paid them accordingly. At length, Champion became convinced that Norris's scales were not accurate, that he cheated them at every weighing.

Champion tells Randall James of his concern and confronts Norris. Norris listens with scorn to the black man's complaint, then dismisses him. At this point, Walter's father joins Champion's cause, and the argument soon turns violent. Randall shoots Norris, calls the police, and waits to be taken off to his punishment. Walter has himself acted with violence in the name of family honor, defending both father and mother, and the incident with Champion indicates that the James family feels a strong sense of brotherhood with blacks. All people are the same to them.

The ending of *Dirty Work* depends completely upon the power of kinship as it transcends social norms. Repeatedly, Braiden has let Walter know that he does not want to live any longer. Early in their brief acquaintance, Walter has asked, "Do you wish you were dead?" (51), an inquiry Braiden answers unequivocally: "Not a minute don't go by" (51). Just what Walter feared. As they get to know each other better, Walter comes to recognize that Braiden depends on Walter's openness to mercy. There is no other way. Braiden's fantasies cannot help, for at some fundamental point, reality must be faced: "It just pisses me off the way everything is. It don't have to be like this. What would this country be like, man, if they never had brought none of us over here? But that's history. You can't change it. Just like this. Just like you" (179). History set up the misery that has come to plague Braiden, but at the same time, it has created the interdependency that can effect Braiden's release from misery.

Walter's father has died, ravaged by war, drinking, and the pain of seeing his oldest son's life so badly damaged by the Vietnam War. His mother no longer wants to live. Beth, the one woman who might have been able to make him feel whole has died as a consequence of his war-created condition, successfully trying as the water surged over her head to hold Walter's head above the surface. Walter has acted for honor, and he has acted for duty. Now he must act for love. He must respond to Braiden's plaintive request, which carries the weight of an imperative: "World don't change for no man. World gone keep going on. Don't make no difference what you do, what I do. World keep turning. God got a plan for everything. Man may suffer in this world. But God got a better world waiting. I been waiting to see it twenty-two years, Walter. You ain't no man if you don't do this for me. I tired, Walter. I tired and I want to go home. Want to see my mama. She waiting, too" (226). Echoing the spirituals of his cultural heritage, Braiden puts his life in the hands of Walter, the one who has been sent to deliver him from misery.

The last chapter of *Dirty Work* swirls with images from earlier moments in the story: a chopper with sixteen men crashing to their deaths in Vietnam, Walter's father getting his Purple Heart, cotton picking in the Mississippi Delta, and Braiden's dreams of "Africa, the vast plains his people had come from, the little houses of sticks and the footprints in the dust" (236). Walter goes to Braiden's sleeping form, standing over him "a long moment" (236). As Walter starts to strangle his brother, Braiden wakes and gives Walter his final message of approval: "He said Jesus loves you" (236). Walter knows better, however, knows that "somewhere Jesus wept," but the act of supreme mercy goes forward, the white man accepting his kinship with the black man, all factored through the shared experience of war in Vietnam.

Body, the latest novel in the distinguished career of Harry Crews, aims toward a rather different conclusion than the one reached by *Dirty Work*. In fact, Crews uses Vietnam as a crucial factor to justify violence that comes out of racial conflict. In some ways, the portrait of Harry Barnes, also called Nail Head in the story, is close to one of the most stereotypical images of the Vietnam veteran, as represented by Travis Brickle in Martin Scorcese's movie *Taxi Driver*—a once decent man transformed by combat horrors into a walking time bomb living on the edge of apocalypse. Nail Head is "a much decorated veteran of the Vietnam War and who did not look right out of his eyes although he had before he had gone to Vietnam" (27). Nail Head is presented as an ordinary fellow who is set on edge by the psychological tension of Vietnam. Without question, his presence in *Body* makes an outbreak of violence at some point virtually unavoidable.

Yet the headnote to *Body* suggests that Nail Head's condition verges on an ideal state of intensity, and it certainly squares with the southern fixation on violence considered in Barry Hannah's Vietnam stories. Crews opens with a note that he has "friends in the world of bodybuilding" and then offers a quote from Karl Wallenda, of the legendary high-wire performing family, before his death fall in 1978: "Walking the wire is living. The rest is just waiting." Wallenda's sentiments could stand equally well for the combat experience in Vietnam, a kind of intensity that put life at a premium and that made postcombat adjustment to peacetime living next to impossible for some soldiers.

Body is about a world-class competitive match of women bodybuilders, a match staged at the Blue Flamingo Hotel in Florida, a locale used by Crews in much of his fiction. The main contestants, those likely to meet in one-on-one comparison of physique for the Ms. Cosmos title, are Shereel Dupont, formerly Dorothy Turnipseed, of south Georgia, and Marvella Washington, a black woman from Detroit. Shereel's family arrives at the Blue Flamingo to cheer on the girl who wanted to be more than just another Turnipseed in Georgia, a state of being that is perfectly fine for Alphonse, Motor, and Turner Turnipseed. She is coached by Russell Morgan, "Russell Muscle," who recognized in her "great bones" (21) the structure to make a great body in championship bodybuilding and who helps keep her weight in line with energetic bouts of sex. Crews has ample fun with the predictable conflicts between the manners of the country Turnipseeds and the struggling aspirations of the Blue Flamingo.

It might be all fun if it were not for Nail Head, who is Shereel's fiancée and who accompanies the Turnipseeds to cheer on their champion body. As soon as he arrives at the Blue Flamingo, Nail Head has a run-in with the room clerk, Julian. Nail Head's fists are ready to fly into action at a moment's notice; he carries a knife and seems eager to find uses for it, one of which entails reconfiguring Julian's nose. Shereel explains to Russell that Nail Head likes to beat up on people; he "finds it relaxing" and it "releases his stress" (34). She knows that he was in a "rat patrol" in Vietnam, obliged to search tunnels like a rat, and thinks that he would be free of tension if he could find "four assholes in a tunnel and strangle them" (35). Unfortunately, the prospects for such a solution are not strong at a Cosmos competition.

All along the way to the story's conclusion, there are echoes of Vietnam. Nail Head comments on the nicknames used by the competitors, a pattern of naming that he had known in Vietnam and that is demonstrated in his own moniker. Russell bets that size no longer wins, a conclusion that applies equally well to the post-Vietnamese era when Americans had to face the reality of defeat at the hands of a much less powerful nation. As the confrontation with Marvella, whose sisters have accompanied her and together form a united black front, comes hourly closer, Nail Head's tension peaks. He recalls moments of racial animosity in Vietnam and is scarcely mollified when Billy Bat—a male bodybuilder—

tells him that modern bodybuilding transcends sex and race differences. Shereel tries desperately to keep Nail Head under some semblance of control, and in response to her entreaties for good behavior, he asserts testily, "I'm by God in control. . . . Always. It's the fucking world that's out of control" (117).

On the day of the judging, though, Nail Head has a Vietnam crazy look. The finals come down to Shereel, the white southern woman, and Marvella, the black northern woman. Crews represents the struggle in stark racial terms. Nail Head's uneasiness is similar to what he felt as he stepped on the plane to Vietnam—with the world never to be the same again. Fearing that Nail Head will try to coerce the head judge to vote in her favor, Shereel asks him to leave the judges alone, and he agrees.

When Shereel loses the contest and as a result commits suicide, Nail Head is free to act. He remembers similar circumstances in Vietnam, goes off to find the head judge in a bar, and straightforwardly destroys the man with a fragmentation grenade. Vietnam thus comes home to the South with a terrible ferocity in *Body*, and the ensuing violence is called forth on grounds of race. Harry Crews, like Madison Smartt Bell, refuses to gloss over the intractability of racial animosity in the South, and unlike Clyde Edgerton and Larry Brown, he does not find hope for a better future to come miraculously out of any Vietnam War experience of blood brotherhood. In race relations in the South, Vietnam proves to be a factor with two sides, neither being sufficient to determine the course of history in any one distinct path, either forward toward a lasting solution of race-free brotherhood or backward toward endless fratricide. The intersection of the Vietnam War and the southern imagination leaves the issue of race relations polarized, with final results held long in abeyance.[2]

Back to Alabama, Heart of Dixie

THE PROCESS OF FITTING THE EXPERIENCE of Vietnam into the southern imagination has many aspects. Southerners have an affinity for history, and thus Vietnam has been joined frequently to the long span of history cultivated in the South. Southerners have particular tendencies toward violence, and thus Vietnam has been measured in such terms. Southerners have wrestled for many generations with the challenge of race relations, and thus Vietnam became a recent factor in that struggle. Southerners have strong impulses toward identification with the land, and southern writers have found their culture's relationship with the verities of the soil to be refracted truly through the prism of Vietnam.

In the case of some writers from the South, however, the process of fully coming to terms with southern life by way of Vietnam has taken time.[1] In the careers of both Winston Groom and Gustav Hasford, each of whom has roots in Alabama (the "heart of Dixie"), more than one novel about the Vietnam experience was required to complete this process. Because Groom is more widely known to have an Alabama connection and since his first novel, *Better Times Than These* (1978), a story of Vietnam combat, appeared a year before Gustav Hasford's novel, *The Short-Timers*, it makes sense to begin with Groom's Vietnam cycle as a way to understand how the passage of time has proved to make Vietnam increasingly southern.

Better Times Than These is a serviceable first novel. Its structure and its distribution of characters owe perhaps more to the influence of the World War II novels of James Jones than anything else, which followed Mailer's career-making novel about war, *The Naked and the Dead*, especially in the distribution of idiosyncrasies among the various characters, but Groom allows no hint of the stylistic pyrotechnics employed by Mailer in his time-machine and chorus sections. The form of *Better Times Than These* adheres to the requirements of naturalistic realism. We meet the Vietnam-bound characters as they begin to gather for the trip overseas. They are part of Bravo Company, Fourth Battalion, Seventh Cavalry—a unit with a history, as Colonel Jason Patch, the commander, informs his subordinates. Once they are in country, Colonel Patch conducts a briefing on the campaign that Bravo Company will undertake in the Ia Drang valley, northwest of Cam Rahn Bay, in the fall and winter of 1966–67. It is still early in the war. Patch says that they will do what the Seventh Cavalry was always meant to do: go fight Indians. This time the Indians are Vietnamese, but that fact makes little difference. An Indian is an Indian, victim of choice for the soldiers of the Seventh Cavalry. Patch's unit will not repeat the mistake of George Armstrong Custer in his leadership of the Seventh Cavalry; this time there will be no underestimating the enemy. Such is the shaping vision of the Seventh Cavalry, but Patch's subordinates are skeptical. The kill ratios look fantastic (enemy casualties vastly outnumbered friendly casualties), yet the enemy seems to want to fight in the most dreadful places.

Bit by bit Groom provides details of the backgrounds of his major characters. They come from across the country. Lieutenant C. Francis (Frank) Holden III comes to the war from a distinguished family via tennis stardom at Harvard; his decision to pursue duty in Vietnam comes from a family tradition of service, but it is distinctly out of sync with the Harvard set in the mid-sixties. Holden finds that he is right for the war, but he dies nevertheless. Irony shadows the fate of other characters as well. Command of Bravo Company is assumed by Lieutenant Billy Kahn, and in Kahn's background, Groom begins to work out the relationship of

Vietnam to the South. Kahn is a Jew from Savannah, an experience that entailed a keen sense of what it takes to be accepted by a culture that is as tightly drawn together as the South. In Kahn's recollection, "Being a Jew from the South was both a blessing and a curse" (53). Although the Kahns were recognized in their Jewishness, they were nevertheless expected to conform to the conventions of Savannah's social life. They were even expected to decorate their home for Christmas, and one year they were informed that their decorative responsibility would be the Five Gold Rings of The Twelve Days of Christmas. This is more than a "religious thing," they were told: "It is a neighborhood thing" (53).

Thus Billy Kahn knows quite a bit about the business of submitting to the demands of a tightly knit community, and he knows about paying his dues if he wishes to be accepted. He had played football in high school for acceptance. He has joined the army to continue his quest for cultural acceptance, but he is not sure that fulfilling this set of cultural expectations will result in anything more than his possible death. After all, the country club golf course next to the Kahn family home was closed to Jews; they had to go across town to a public course. Perhaps the North Vietnamese Army soldiers in the Ia Drang valley will prove to be as intractable as the WASP southerners back home.

Midway through the story, Kahn is faced with the prospect of having to discipline one of his men, a giant black man named Carruthers, who had cut a Vietnamese girl with a knife. Kahn learns from Carruther's file that he too is from Savannah, having lived there "with his mother and two sisters and a brother—no father was mentioned—on a little street near where Kahn's father's junk company was" (24). As Kahn reflects on this happenstance connection with Carruthers, he has an epiphany: ". . . but suddenly it dawned on Kahn that in Savannah—where everybody knew everybody—nobody knew Negroes but other Negroes, except perhaps by their first names, and looking at this file before him, ten thousand miles from home, he realized for the first time in his life that the distances between the races where he had grown up were as incomprehensible as the distances between galaxies" (241–42).

With the story of Billy Kahn, who can appreciate the sense of separateness known to Carruthers, Groom opens up for scrutiny the closed nature of white-dominated life in the South. Nevertheless, despite all of the divisions recognized in the South, there is an element of cohesion that transcends separation. When Carruthers is leaving Kahn after receiving his company punishment, he asks, "Ain't you from Savannah?" (243). Kahn is "dumbfounded" at Carruther's recognition of a bond that stretches across lines of color or religion, but through this exchange Groom seems to hint that the South incorporates all of its people, regardless of their surface differences.

The South is represented more favorably by Groom in the portrait of Private Homer Crump, a Mississippi farm boy. Crump is not given to introspection; he is a person of simple tastes. He likes to eat, having thrived on "great mother-cooking" (69) wonderfully displayed in countless suppers at home, "with pot roasts and mashed potatoes, home-grown peas and beans, hams, yams, corned beef and cabbage, pork chops with applesauce and beets, and corn bread and fried chicken—she as big as a house, he as thin as a rail" (69). Crump has not had the benefit of wide experience in the world; the most exotic thing he has encountered was the "freak tent at the little carnival shows that brought to Tupelo, Mississippi, such interesting exhibits as the hermaphrodite and the woman with three tits" (21). However, when Crump has a rifle in his hands, he is in his element, a natural hunter. Moreover, his courage in the heat of battle is unshakeable. Homer Crump stands squarely for the same virtue of honor on the fields of fire that Webb built into the character of Robert E. Lee Hodges, Jr.

Unfortunately, Billy Kahn becomes caught in the moral quagmire of Vietnam. Several men under his command commit an atrocity—rape and murder of two Vietnamese young women. When Kahn becomes aware of the act, his response is equivocal, and his passive role in covering up the incident results in a court-martial. Soon he is out of the army. The story closes with Kahn's trip to New York for a memorial service for Frank Holden. Although Kahn has been caught by the morass of Vietnam, he wants to honor another who served with distinction. *Better Times Than These* ends on a note that befits the place of honor in the South.

Groom's first novel tackled combat in Vietnam directly. Since Groom had served as a lieutenant in Vietnam during 1966–67, he was well versed in the particulars of battle, and he offers the fictional rendering in straightforward fashion. About a year before Groom's Vietnam tour, there had been intense fighting in the Ia Drang valley, so brutal that it soon became legendary, the stuff of much talk and many stories. Also, at that same time, there was an incident of rape/murder of two Vietnamese women by soldiers from the Eleventh Infantry Brigade, Americal Division, an atrocity that serves as the basis for what happens in Kahn's unit, thus grounding Groom's narrative firmly in fact.[2] *Better Times Than These* is first and foremost a story of combat in Vietnam. The South is introduced through the characters of Billy Kahn and Homer Crump, but in 1978 Winston Groom was obviously more concerned with representing the reality of war action in Vietnam than in placing the war in the context of southern culture and history.

However, as time passed, Vietnam became part of the South for Winston Groom, even as he aligned himself increasingly in his writing interests with southern matters. By the time Groom published his fifth book, *Forrest Gump*, in 1986, he had found a way to embed the Vietnam experience within the culture of his native region (although Groom was born in Washington, D.C., his family has roots in the Deep South; he went to the University of Alabama; and he continues to spend a good portion of each year in Alabama). *Forrest Gump* is quintessentially southern. Its form and style derive directly from *The Adventures of Huckleberry Finn*. The protagonist opens the story with a declaration, in his own voice, that showcases his natural talents as a loquacious storyteller: "Let me say this: being a idiot is no box of chocolates. People laugh, lose patience, treat you shabby. Now they say folks sposed to be kind to the afflicted, but let me tell you—it ain't always that way. Even so, I got no complaints, cause I reckon I done live a pretty interestin life, so to speak" (1).

"Pretty interestin" is indeed an understatement. Forrest Gump manages to be a ubiquitous presence through all of the major events of the Vietnam era—in Vietnam combat, in student protests against the war, in space on a NASA mission. He meets with Presidents Johnson and Nixon in the White House, he meets Chairman Mao, he gets himself to Harvard and to Hollywood (where he is supposed to be a new John Wayne), and he plays a wild bit of football for Coach Bear Bryant at Alabama. Occasionally there are commemorative moments, times at which Forrest Gump is called upon to say something profound; invariably his words of wisdom are the same: "I got to pee" (13, 19, 27, 55, 214). As his high school football coach declares, "Gump . . . you sure got a way with words" (14). *Forrest Gump* is a picaresque narrative, complete with a likable gump of a hero and some wonderfully inventive comic scenes.

One result of this fictional mixture is to place Vietnam in the midst of history. As previously noted, southerners are good at this. In the succession of incident upon incident, Vietnam becomes just a part of Forrest's "no hum-drum life" (228). It is an important part, surely, with the effects of Vietnam shadowing many years of the hero's existence, but perhaps no other region of the country could produce a representative figure so well prepared by cultural background to manage the devastating consequences of Vietnam combat with such a fine sense of balance. No matter what kind of setbacks Forrest encounters, he intuitively knows how to cope with adversity. His is a southern habit.

Forrest's ties to the South are established firmly at the outset of the story with his explanation of his name, how he came to be called Forrest. Southerners would not need the explanation Groom provides, but he surely wanted to reach an audience outside the South, and besides, the explanation given by Forrest allowed Groom a chance to address a central irony in the southern love for history: sustenance of the past involves encounters with some people, ideas, and events that are not always pleasant. In his own "way with words," Forrest explains the double edge of southern history:

> When I was born, my mama name me Forrest, cause of General Nathan Bedford Forrest who fought in the Civil War. Mama always said we was kin to General Forrest's fambly someways. An he was a great man, she say, cept'n he started up the Ku Klux Klan after the war was over an even my grandmama say they's a bunch of no-goods. Which I would tend to agree with, cause down here, the Grand Exalted Pishposh, or whatever he calls hisself, he operate a gun store in town an once, when I was maybe twelve year ole, I were walkin by there and lookin in the winder as he got a big hangman's noose strung up inside. When he seen me watchin, he done throwed it around his own neck and jerk it up like he was hanged an let his tongue stick out all so's to scare me. I done run off and hid in a parkin lot behin some cars til somebody call the police an they come an take me home to mama. So whatever else ole General Forrest done, startin up that Klan thing was not a good idea—any idiot can tell you that. Nonetheless, that's how I got my name. (2–3)

The southern sense of history is powerful, but it sustains not only the light of the past but also the darkness.[3] In such circumstances, it is useful to have "idiots" like Forrest Gump around to tell the difference between light and darkness.

As a matter of fact, Forrest is exceedingly good at understanding the nature of light. In his brief stint at Alabama, where he is recruited to play football, he gets an "A" in one course, "Intermediate Light," but despite the conclusion of Dr. Mills at the University Medical Center that Forrest is an "Idiot savant" (33), Forrest flunks out of college, the army revokes his deferment, which had been given temporarily "on account of I am a numbnuts" (16), and he is off to basic training, then to Vietnam in the season of Tet, 1968.

Vietnam first appears to Forrest as a kind of Asian Alabama. The ground around Pleiku throws up red dust, and the city is fringed with "sad little shanties that is worst than anythin I seen back in Alabama" (47). The war becomes shockingly real and different than home soon enough. Forrest is taking a shower when incoming rounds hit his base camp. Once the attack is over, he sees what war is all about: "They is hardly recognizable as people—all mangled up like they has been stuffed thru a cotton bailer or somethin. I ain't never seen nobody dead, an it is the most horrible and scary thing ever happen to me, afore or since!" (48). The first dead encountered by Forrest are not known to him, and still the moment is horrible.

Some time later, it gets worse. Serving with Forrest in Vietnam is a black man named Bubba, who becomes Forrest's closest friend because of their similar backgrounds in the South, including time on the same Bear Bryant team. Forrest and Bubba even share a dream of going into the shrimping business once they get back to Alabama. That dream is not meant to be, however, for during an enemy attack, Bubba takes two chest wounds. Forrest manages to get across a rice paddy to comfort his friend, and he is able to ease Bubba's last moments of life by playing "Way Down Upon the Swanee River" over and over again on his harmonica, until Bubba utters his final word: "Home" (59). Years later, and toward the end of Groom's story, Forrest establishes himself in the shrimp business, his means of showing respect for Bubba.[4]

Forrest is given the Congressional Medal of Honor for his heroic exploits in Vietnam, then heads off for a series of increasingly improbable adventures featuring recurrent meetings with Jenny, the love of his life, which always culminate in some kind of defeat. Along this peripatetic way, there are many humorous moments with a southern twist. For instance, when Forrest's space capsule falls into the sea, he is picked up by a group of South Sea cannibals under the leadership of Sam, a Yale graduate. Sam knows of Nathan Bedford Forrest, pegs this Forrest as a Harvard man, and plans to put the astronauts, all white, to work chopping cotton. This prospect causes Sam to explain in rhapsodic terms to Major Fritch, the woman who heads the space team: "Cotton, my dear woman, cotton! King of cash crops! The plant that built an empire in your own country some years ago" (127). No matter where Forrest goes, Vietnam or space or the South Seas, he meets vestiges of the South.

By the end of the story, Forrest is back in the South. Jenny lives in Savannah with her husband and little Forrest, who is actually big Forrest's son, although his early academic prowess belies his true father's individual talents. Forrest settles finally in New Orleans, sending the proceeds from the sale of his shrimp business to his mama, to Bubba's dad, and to Jenny "for little Forrest" (227).

Forrest has companions. There is Sue, an orangutang acquired during the space expedition, who plays a mean game of Ticktacktoe, and there is Dan, a wheelchair-bound Vietnam veteran, known to Forrest from his time in country and found by him as a derelict in Washington, D.C. Forrest's gifts for living and for dreaming are strong enough to carry both Dan and himself. Forrest generates income by being the "best one-man band" (228) in New Orleans, they go down to Twain's river "an set on the bank an go catfishin" (228), and every now and then, Forrest reminisces, just the sort of thing that would be expected of a southerner: "Sometimes at night, when I look up at the stars, an see the whole sky jus laid out there, don't you think I ain't rememberin it all" (228). "It all" is almost endlessly expansive, a sense of history that encompasses everything, including—in a major way—the Vietnam War. Given the beguiling storytelling charm of Forrest Gump, it becomes both natural and necessary to remember Vietnam.

Better Times Than These is Groom's story of America lost in the quagmire of Vietnam. *Forrest Gump*, in striking contrast, is his story of Vietnam ensconced in the midst of a "no hum-drum life" (228), as led by a figure totally southern in composition. Gump's humor and his naturally wise sense of history are estimable gifts; they honor the truth of the Vietnam War even as they show how "to do the right thing" (228) in the face of hard realities. *Forrest Gump* blesses readers with a deft healing touch.

Groom's next novel, *Gone the Sun* (1988), again focuses on his native Alabama, a coastal town called Bienville, a locale earlier used by Groom for *As Summers Die* (1980). As was the case in *Forrest Gump*, Vietnam is indelibly in the background, so much so that it shadows almost every move of the protagonist, James Payton Gunn, who is called Beau by his mother and everyone else in the story. Beau Gunn's background resembles Groom's. He was born in Washington, D.C., in 1943 (the year of Groom's birth), his maturation took place in Alabama, and he went to a southern college. Then he went to Vietnam. After Vietnam, he had trouble adjusting to regular life again but eventually found a way to use his talents as a writer—both in drama and in journalism. In the present time of *Gone the Sun*, Beau Gunn has reached his forties, nearly twenty years after the experience of Vietnam. He has become a playwright of note in New York, seemingly far removed from his southern origins.

For Gunn, Vietnam is still a part of the past that will not go away. He is trying to write a blockbuster play, tentatively called *In Fields Where They Lay*, using Vietnam as a vehicle "to identify the thin, almost imperceptible line between compassion and cruelty" (68). Beau Gunn walks with a cane, the consequence of a shrapnel wound in the hip during his Vietnam tour, but it is soon clear that he also has to cope with considerable psychological stress that has carried over from the war. His play is meant to deal with the demons of his past, but its wrenching second act has been plaguing Gunn, and he needs to get away for a time to see if he can work out the language to his satisfaction. The opportunity to get away comes in the form of an offer by an old acquaintance, "Pappy" Turner, for Gunn to return to Bienville and take over the job of editor for the *Courier-Democrat*. Turner not only provides the means for Gunn to go back home to Alabama, but he also serves as the narrative voice to provide additional perspective on Gunn's life.

In essence, Gunn's life is defined by how the South prepared him for Vietnam. He went to Singer Military Academy, and years later, he recalls one of the key Singer rituals: marching to the Confederate cemetery to pay homage to the dead. At age ten, Beau was "convicted" of lying about an incident at Singer, and he feels it still to be a blot on his character, for when he returns to Bienville in the early 1980s, he meets again many of his Singer classmates, "Pappy" Turner among them, and now, as before, honor is a matter of great consequence.

Beau knows the South and its history. One of his darkest nightmares involves a maneuver in Vietnam based upon the classic double envelopment pattern of the Battle of Cowpens in 1781, but in Beau's dream, he never made "the outer loop of the butterfly's wings" (23) and his men suffered horribly as a result. Beau reflects, "For anyone who goes through a war, the experience becomes a benchmark" (110), but his own war was not as clear in this regard as the wars in his family's past, including the Civil War, as experienced by his great-grandfather. Still, Vietnam impells Beau Gunn by tormenting his sense of justice. He wants, above all, to get straight, unequivocably, with the need to honor truth. When he addresses the staff of the *Courier-Democrat*, Beau forthrightly declares his intentions: "I am told there is political corruption in this city. I hear there is racial unfairness. I understand there is unwise spending of the taxpayers' money. We are in the business of uncovering and reporting these things. We must bring them to the attention of the population" (172). By going home to Alabama, Beau Gunn runs head on into the truth, and he pays for this encounter with his life.

Beau finds that he enjoys renewing his ties to the South, particularly the unchanged nature of the place, which he rediscovers in trips out to a hunting and fishing camp deep in the woods. He also goes back to the "old Gunn place on Blackwater River" (182), which he recalls fondly from his youth. There he forms a plan to fix up Hollow House, a cottage that had been built as an icehouse by slaves and in which his great-grandfather used to sit and "reminisce about the War Between the States, in which he had served as a Confederate cavalry officer" (183). The view from Hollow House inspires Beau, and it is wonderfully quiet, almost perfect for improving the disarray of Beau's modern life.

However, the South in the 1980s is subject to extreme pressures for change. As a port city, Bienville is a haven for drug smugglers, and the local oil business portends extensive and aggressive development. Even Beau's father seems to be caught up in the rapid progress of business in Bienville. Soon Beau is consumed by his desire to get to the bottom of what seems to be a mammouth scandal involving oil and a bum murder rap for Tommy Brodie, one of Beau's old friends from the Singer days. By the time Beau, Eric Pacer (who was Beau's radio telephone operator in Vietnam), and a young woman reporter named Eleanor Campbell get to the bottom of the scandal—a scheme that secretly sends domestic oil to Haiti where it can be resold at a higher price since foreign oil is not subject to any price controls—Vietnam comes home to Alabama in a devastating way. Beau's father is a party to the scandal, without seeing any moral problem in what Universal Oil is doing to make its profits, and Congressman Dan Whittle, still another of the Singer Academy connections, is also involved. It is Whittle who commits the act that finally ties Vietnam to Beau's South.

When Whittle's family honor is threatened by disclosure of his role in the Universal Oil scam, he goes to the newspaper office and shoots Beau. As the .45 caliber army Colt pistol is placed between Beau's eyes, he has a flashback to Vietnam, to the scene of interrogation of an enemy soldier— interrogation that would entail severe torture before ending in execution. This shooting scene was to constitute the second act of Beau's Vietnam play, and it has obviously haunted him for a long time, taking the form of a dream in which Beau helplessly witnesses the shooting of the enemy prisoner by a sergeant under Beau's command. In the heart of Dixie, Beau Gunn looks into Whittle's pistol and realizes that he himself was the one to die in his dream, that the moral morass of Vietnam could be encountered anywhere.

The title for Groom's third Vietnam novel comes from "Taps," which serves as the story's epigraph and concludes with the words, "Rest in peace, soldier brave, God is nigh." "Pappy" Turner provides an epilogue that wraps up the details of Beau Gunn's existence following the shooting. He lives in a vegetative state for two years, then dies. He is given a military funeral, and Turner provides "a real nice obituary in the *Courier-Democrat*" (301). The Buck Hollow cottage is left vacant, unfinished. Beau's play gets good reviews in various productions, despite ongoing critical concern about the second-act shooting. And an old black bear that had lived in the vicinity of Beau's delta swamp hunting camp is killed, "like Beau Gunn himself . . . the last of its line" (302).

The import of Groom's third Vietnam-linked novel carries an ominous note, for he represents the moral ugliness of Vietnam as being on a par with conditions of moral turpitude in the emergence of the modern South. Vietnam confirmed Beau Gunn's awareness that betrayal of innocence could bring lasting misery, but it takes his return to the South to show him how grave and deep the betrayal has been to the sense of honor that once was claimed so proudly by southerners for their region. In *Gone the Sun*, Vietnam becomes one more step in a long road of descent from high ideals to competitiveness based entirely on the ambition to make money, and so going home to Alabama has not been an uplifting experience as represented in the fiction of Winston Groom.

Much the same case is found in the two novels of Gustav Hasford. Hasford has not himself returned to Alabama, but as his writing career has developed, he has shown an increasingly intense concern for his southern heritage. Hasford was born in Haleyville, Alabama, on 28 November 1947, the son of Hassel and Hazel Hasford. His father was a factory worker (good background for his son's Socialist connections in the past two decades), his mother a librarian. Hasford served in the Marine Corps from 1966 to 1968, with time in Vietnam as a military combat correspondent. Since the war years, he has lived on the West Coast, mostly California, and he was graduated from Santa Monica City College in 1972. In 1978, he married Charlene Broock, a librarian as his mother had been. The library motif in Hasford's life will be discussed later.

In 1979, Harper and Row published Hasford's first Vietnam novel, *The Short-Timers*; a Bantam paperback edition came out a year later. *The Short-Timers* is a tightly packed book, loaded with explosive language and filled with violent moments. The protagonist of the story is a marine named Joker. Joker's background is not developed in *The Short-Timers*; in 1979, it seems not to have been important for Hasford to link Joker with any place apart from the pervading ethos of Vietnam, an ethos that totally pervades even Joker's military training at Parris Island, South Carolina.

The Short-Timers is divided into three sections: "The Spirit of the Bayonet," "Body Count," and "Grunts." Vietnam is a ubiquitous presence, even before Joker actually leaves his native land for the overseas assignment that makes him first a reluctant witness to the ugliness of combat, then finally a hapless participant. To find traits of the South in Hasford's first Vietnam book, we have to look closely at minute details, for the general pattern of *The Short-Timers* seems to rebut the claims of history that most of the southern writers in this study have brought to their efforts to fathom the Vietnam War. The title of the novel speaks volumes in this regard. As soon as soldiers arrived in country, they became preoccupied with a year's worth of days. The reach of time and history in the context of Vietnam was 365 days and a wake-up, and calendars were carefully prepared to record the passage of those days. Whatever had happened before Vietnam seemed inconsequential, a point underscored by the epigraph from Michael Herr's *Dispatches*, which Hasford uses to orient readers to what will come in "The Spirit of the Bayonet": "I think that Vietnam was what we had instead of happy childhoods" (1). In *The Short-Timers*, Vietnam the present becomes Vietnam the past, thereby displacing any larger sense of history, personal or communal.

Soldiers headed for Vietnam were bound hard and fast by short time. Hasford's prose style is intensely lyrical as a result, for the lyric catches best the intensity of a given moment in time. In the first section of the story, which takes place at Parris Island, "an eight-week college for the phony-tough and the crazy-brave, constructed in a swamp on an island, symmetrical but sinister like a suburban death camp" (3), Marine Gunnery Sergeant Gerheim instructs Private Joker and his fellow recruits in the lyrics of war by which they will live or die.

Some of the lyrics come from actual marching songs sung by military trainees during the Vietnam era, songs that Tim O'Brien used to fine purpose in his compelling memoir, *If I Die in a Combat Zone, Box Me Up and Ship Me Home* (1973), the title coming from one of those marching cadences designed to keep the feet in step and to prepare the marcher for his possible fate. Gerheim makes his own individual contribution to this lyricism with a zest for potent speech images and axiomatic expressions with which he delivers his message quickly and surely to his flock. Gerheim is indeed a minister figure, albeit one charged with the task of promoting the old testament at the expense of the new. His message goes like this: "Our rifle is only a tool; it is a hard heart that kills" (13). And this: "If the meek ever inherit the earth the strong will take it away from them" (14). And "You can give your heart to Jesus but your ass belongs to the Corps" (19). Under Gerheim's tutelage, Joker and his peers are molded into killers, with all softness, kindness, and gentleness driven out, to be replaced by hard, cold steel.

Gerheim himself is hard to the core, hard to the end, calm even in the face of the death that comes through the action of one of his trainees, Private Leonard Pratt, a pathetic young man whose impulse to kill is thrown into overdrive by the cumulative effect of Gerheim's taunting language. At the end, when Leonard uses his beloved rifle Charlene to send "One 7.62-millimeter high-velocity copper-jacketed bullet" through his drill sergeant nemesis, Joker sees an almost supernatural calmness in Gerheim: "His eyes, his manner are those of a wanderer who has found his home. He is a man in complete control of himself and of the world he lives in" (29). Gerheim's steadiness in the face of death qualifies him as a warrior above reproach, a fitting match for the sort of figure celebrated by James Webb in his development of the southern heritage of Lieutenant Robert E. Lee Hodges, Jr.

It is only by his manner that Gerheim could be linked to the South. Hasford provides no personal history for this key figure in the orientation-for-Vietnam stage of his novel. Nor is there a background provided for Private Joker, although a tiny hint of his origin flickers in the passing mention of his real name, the one given him at birth. This mention occurs at a point in country when his commanding officer reads a promotion citation elevating Joker to sergeant, a promotion that offends Joker to the core. As Captain January reads, suddenly we learn that Joker is James T. Davis. Not an unusual name to be sure. There are Davises everywhere. However, by the time Hasford finished writing *The Phantom Blooper* (1990), which carries the story of Joker beyond the narrative of *The Short-Timers*, it is clear to all that Joker's real name was chosen to invoke a luminous figure of the South, Jefferson Davis, who became provisional president of the Confederacy on 15 February 1861, in Montgomery, Alabama, Hasford's home state.

The ending of *The Short-Timers* is nihilistic. Vietnam has come to be unspeakably mean, ugly beyond Joker's capacity to distance himself from it through ironic wit. Even before the horrifying act that closes the narrative, Joker has come to realize that the Vietnam experience has closed a chapter in American life. As a consequence of Vietnam, things will never be the same for America. Certain changes have been absolutely mandated by the impact of war on the combatants: "Those of us who survive to be short-timers will fly the Freedom Bird back to hometown America. But home won't be there anymore and we won't be there either. Upon each of our brains the war has lodged itself, a black crab feeding" (176).

This dark prophecy proves to be true. The Lusthog squad—including Joker, Joker's basic-training friend Cowboy,[5] Animal Mother, a New Guy, and assorted others—moves out on a patrol into the jungle, and Joker is soon faced with an excruciating challenge to his ironic detachment. He must kill his best friend Cowboy in order to release himself and the others of his squad from the control of an enemy sniper who intends to destroy successively each one of the marines as they come out of hiding in an effort to rescue others already wounded by the sniper's bullets. Joker shoots Cowboy, finally acting instead of just joking, reporting what he sees, and keeping his distance.[6] The stage is then set, by his action, for the "black crab" to feed on his brain for the rest of his life.

This haunting continues in *The Phantom Blooper*, Hasford's 1990 novel that takes Joker through the remainder of his Vietnam tour and then back home. *The Phantom Blooper* opens in Vietnam, sometime after the action of *The Short-Timers*. Joker has remained in a combat unit, having lost his position as combat correspondent (the kind of work Hasford did with the First Marine Division in Vietnam). The concept of the "Phantom Blooper" was mentioned once in passing (58) in *The Short-Timers*, but it immediately becomes the subject of much discussion and reflection in Hasford's second Vietnam narrative. In essence, the Phantom Blooper denotes any American soldier who has crossed over to the enemy camp, for whatever reason. These shadowy figures—and there are many scattered throughout the diverse zones of combat—are particularly scary, for they embody the weakness of the American position in Vietnam, suggesting that the United States role in the war is not sufficiently privileged to hold all Americans in unwavering allegiance. Moreover, it seems that the Phantom Blooper is propelled by his conversion to a new plateau of combat ferocity and expertise, able to surpass the skills of the most talented night fighters of Vietnamese origin, or as Hasford explains the concept through the mind of Joker, "He is the dark spirit of our collective bad consciences made real and dangerous. He once was one of us, a Marine. He knows how we think. He knows how we operate. He knows how Marines fight and what Marines fear" (6). The Phantom Blooper thus is an explosive presence in Vietnam, armed with an insider's knowledge of American vulnerabilities.

At the outset of the story, Joker is moving right along on his short-timer's calendar, every day concentrating even more on what is needed to pass through Vietnam alive. He still jokes, of course, about the craziness of Vietnam, and sometimes, particularly when the marijuana is most inspirational, he does his famous John Wayne impressions. One of these impressions opens the door to the southernness of Joker's background. Joker is hanging out with the "First Platoon black street bloods" (21), and once he has enjoyed his fair share of dope, he launches into a humorous discourse, using John Wayne's voice, about "the true story of the War for Southern Independence" (21). Joker places himself on the southern side in that war, which he suggests was really about the freedom to smoke pot: "Jefferson Davis got elected President of the Confederate States of America on a platform of a chicken in every pot and pot in every chicken" (22). Thus does the Vietnam-era Davis invoke the presence of the Confederacy's Davis, a linkage that becomes increasingly profound as the narrative progresses, but even at this early stage, it is clear that James Davis's identity bears the stamp of the South—the South that once broke away from the union of American states over matters of economic, social, and philosophical differences.

James Davis is destined to break away from mainstream America, whether as represented by the Marine Corps force in Vietnam or by the "defense of freedom" slogans used by American politicians to justify the war, but before this break takes place, Hasford inserts an even more radical voice to critique America's Vietnam agenda. The "bloods" have their own John Wayne, and when the humor of Davis's white Wayne is spent, Black John Wayne picks up the theme of rebellion against northern capitalism, "a backwoods preacher delivering a fiery sermon: 'Black Confederacy *secedes* from your Viet Nam death trip'" (24). Black John Wayne continues his sermon, by dismissing Davis as "silly Alabama white trash" (25), asserting that the "devil is a green man, the money man" (25). A Socialist critique of capitalism is Black John Wayne's theme, and Hasford's own politics ride side-by-side with this black man's harsh denunciation of American life.

Soon Joker becomes "lost" to the other side. While hunting the Phantom Blooper outside the perimeter of his unit, Joker is wounded and carried off by none other than the object of his pursuit. In a section called "Travels with Charlie," which cleverly unites a familiar nickname of the Viet Cong with Steinbeck's exploration of America and at the same time inverts Steinbeck's own support of the American role in Vietnam, Hasford reveals how Joker became the "other," became one with the forces aligned to fight the American way of life. As this process proceeds, it becomes clear that life for the "other" closely resembles life in the traditional South.

In his captive state, Joker is renamed "Bao Chi," which is Vietnamese for newspaper reporter, the job he had assumed when first arriving in country. Bao Chi is kept in "the village of Hoa Binh, a Viet Cong village somewhere west of Khe Sanh, near the Laotian border" (59). The Woodcutter, a powerful elder of the village political structure, keeps the American from going to prison in the Hanoi Hilton in order to observe at close hand why Americans fight. Bao Chi is assigned routine tasks that are part of village life, and he comes to know well many of the villagers. As he is studied by the villagers, he studies them.

He quickly understands that his own Alabama background makes him sympathetic to their way of life, though there are some differences. In his Alabama youth, he chopped cotton "to earn a little extra money to throw away on suckers' games at the country fair" (75), and now he is given the task of harvesting rice, which brings pain to the back at the same spot that hurts when you chop cotton, but the rice is harvested strictly for sustenance, and Bao Chi reflects on "Uncle Ho's slogan, 'Rice fields are battlefields'" (75). He knows, "Nobody ever said that back in Alabama, but somebody should have said it, because we had the same war, grow to eat, eat to live" (75). With these words, Bao Chi starts to warm to a vision of life that was once vigorously promoted by his fellow southerners, and his thoughts soon constitute a renaissance of the Agrarian themes from the late 1920s and early 1930s. Through Joker's reborn southern perspective, Hasford describes a way of life that would have been warmly embraced by the *I'll Take My Stand* group:

> The people of Hoa Binh, peasants up to their knees in paddy muck, work in the yellow furnace of the sun all day, dawn to dusk, and they talk, and laugh. Sometimes they sing. Men, women, and children work in harmony with Xa, the land, because the pull of the land is strong. Back in the World, farmers are becoming almost as rare as cowboys and Americans no longer respect the land or people who work the land. In Hoa Binh the ancient bond of centuries, soil, and farmers is still strong. (76)

Through care of their land, the Hoa Bing villagers create a community with a sense of history that Hasford knows was once associated with his native South.

As Bao Chi's appreciation of the Hoa Binh way of life deepens, he gains an understanding of where America went wrong—and why America was doomed to lose the war with the Viet Cong:

> As a Combat Correspondent I was part of the vast gray machine that does not dispense clean information. The American weakness is that we try to rule the world with public relations, then end up believing our own con jobs. We are adrift in a mythical ship which no longer touches land.
>
> Americans can't fight the Viet Cong because the Viet Cong are too real, too close to the earth, and through American eyes what is real can only be a shadow without substance. (91)

Before long, Bao Chi is ready to assume the identity of the Phantom Blooper. He undertakes a long mission with his Viet Cong peers, venturing as far as Khe Sanh city where they strike back at some of Joker's old Marine Corps associates who have been involved in corruption of one kind and another.

Back in Hoa Binh, Bao Chi thinks increasingly of "the Alabama in my mind" (159), a place that has gradually emerged from the obscurity of his marine years and that attracts him greatly as he realizes that he can never be fully accepted by the Viet Cong. Most of his waking dreams involve flashbacks to moments of youth in Alabama. He sees "forests and streams . . . freshly plowed cotton fields full of yankee cannonballs and Cherokee bones" (159). He remembers how he once "found a perfect Indian arrowhead of blue flint lying inches away from a Confederate musket ball" (159), but on his family farm, "I found only enemy bullets. We plowed up so much Federal ordnance that Old Ma used Yankee Minie balls for sinkers when she went fishing for catfish" (159).

Vietnam serves to carry Joker far back to something very important in his past. Before his time in country is complete, he even is compelled to act as his ancestors once did in the Civil War. American forces have determined the presence of an American in Hoa Binh, and they mount a furious attack to bring this wayward compatriot back home. Seeing his close comrades dying at the hands of the combined ARVN/American forces, Boa Chi fires a blooper grenade at the command helicopter. This action repeats a part of the past: "It is the first time in over a hundred years that a member of my family has fired upon federal troops" (169).

However, since the "federal" forces once again carry off the flag of victory (at least in the battle of Hoa Binh), the protagonist of Hasford's story is soon returned to being "Davis, James T., Private E-1, serial number 2306777" (172). Before receiving his Section Eight honorable discharge—"a medical discharge they give to crazy people" (194)—Davis has an opportunity to set his military psychiatrist straight. He did not join the enemy because of allegiance to communism; instead, he says, "I've gone back to the land. When Americans lost touch with the land, we lost touch with reality" (190). With this reiteration of the Agrarian Manifesto, Davis would be a likely candidate to find happiness upon his return to Alabama, but Hasford builds one last twist into his story.

The Alabama of Davis's memory no longer exists. His father has died, apparently from distress caused by the loss of his son to the enemy. When Davis finally gets back to "Alabama, Heart of Dixie" (215), he learns that his father's love of the land has been replaced by the slovenly greed of his mother's new husband, a man who mouths cheap patriotic slogans but who is in every action a corruption of those virtues esteemed by Allen Tate and the Agrarians. To the returning Joker, "an unreconstructed Viet Nam veteran" (215), "The South is a big Indian reservation populated by ex-Confederates who are bred like cattle to die in Yankee wars" (215).

Riding on a Greyhound bus to return home, Davis sees a "black strip of asphalt laid down over the graves of a defeated race of people who lived in a stillborn nation, rolling through a haunted region, over buried battles.

It's Viet Nam, Alabama" (216). James Davis, in innocence, joined the Marine Corps, leaving the South of his youth, and eventually he was sent to Vietnam. At length, he came to realize that the Viet Cong were engaged in a battle once fought by his own southern ancestors. Davis travels far to learn about the nature of the South, but once he is back on his native soil, he understands the pattern of history: "The South was the American Empire's first subjugated nation. We are a defeated people. Our conquerors have cured us of our quaint customs, quilting parties, barn raisings and hog killings, and have bombed us with revisionist history books and Sears catalogs and have made us over into a homogenized replica of the North" (216). This pattern of subjugation appears tyranical, and surely Davis finds sweeping evidence of its power as he tries to connect himself tangibly with the South after the experience of Vietnam.

He unites himself most successfully with the South in his visits to places that carry the knowledge of the heart, places that have history that can be joined to the present life of a lost Vietnam veteran who is trying to find himself. The first sign of the deep past to reach out to Davis is the "Confederate stone soldier . . . of the finest Italian marble," who "pulls guard duty in the center of town, . . . standing tall, leaning on a marble musket, staring intently at the horizon to detect the advance of Yankee armies" (217). In Davis's quest to link himself with the South that he discovered he loved while in Vietnam, he also responds to the family home and the land on which it stands. The house itself is "140 years old," and it was "built by my ancestors with their own hands on the site of a log cabin built by James Davis in 1820" (224). The family's "160 acres were awarded as a bounty land grant for service as a private under General Andrew Jackson," since "in 1814 James Davis fought at the battle of Horseshoe Bend and helped to slaughter Creek Indians so that Alabama could be stolen from them finally and forever" (224). Davis's past is not free from corruption, a point signaled by the fact that he comes upon his family home after walking through country that for him had seemed right out of Vietnam, complete with booby-trapped trees, wired soil, and a blackberry patch that "tears into my trousers legs like concertina wire" (224). Just as injustice once was apparent in the settlement of the South, so it is known again by one of the South's modern sons.

Davis soon has a violent confrontation with the ultramodern, ultraugly South as embodied in Obrey Beasley, his stepfather, and he realizes that his efforts to find the correct spot to fit back into the South must continue. Before he leaves town, however, he makes one more necessary stop, the one mandated by Tate in "Ode to the Confederate Dead." James Davis takes a walk, over the fields to the Rock Creek Cemetery, to visit the past Davises. The graves are all there, some fifty in the Davis family, "going back to 1816" (238). Davis knows the ritual: "Once a year, on Decoration Day, the families of the dead come together and clean off the graves of their ancestors, and remember all of the generations that came before, just as they do on TET in Viet Nam" (238).

Davis is going to his father's grave, but before he reaches it, a deeper past intrudes, in the form of an "impressive granite marker put up by the Daughters of the Confederacy back in the 1930s, when Solomon Davis was buried in his Confederate uniform, seventy years after the end of the War for Southern Independence" (239). Sure enough, "Grandpa Davis was a scout for Bedford Forrest and was wounded at the battle of Shiloh" (239). Standing alone in the Rock Creek Cemetery, James Davis comes to realize that his life comes from the dead beneath his feet, that he learned life from his father, that he had gone to Vietnam to honor the pride that his father, Pleasant Curtis Davis, had in him. The sense of continuity across time is profound here, indelibly southern, in the tradition of knowledge carried to the heart as inscribed by Allen Tate. When writers like Gustav Hasford, long a resident of the West Coast but with roots deep in Alabama, find it necessary to let the imagination run free, and the imagination thus liberated wends homeward and backward, it is certain that time before the present will survive. Hasford places this deep and abiding sense of the past firmly in the conscience of his protagonist Davis:

> The only visible relics of our conquered nation are crumbling brick walls and weed-grown fieldstone foundations and fluted white Doric columns being swallowed by swamp water. Crumbling earthworks, trenchlines and gun emplacements, are silent now in the shades of forests of virgin timber, all garrisoned until the end of time by ragged, barefoot Confederate grunts, sweet old ghosts wailing to be understood.
>
> But the Confederate Dream lives on. The Confederate Dream, a desperate and heroic attempt to preserve from federal tyrants the liberty bequeathed to us by Thomas Jefferson and Benjamin Franklin. Stubborn sinews of the Confederate Dream live on, deep in our genes, a dream recorded silently and permanently by the metal in this soil. (217)

It took a tour of duty in Vietnam and two novels about that experience, but eventually Gustav Hasford rediscovered the South, and by the end of *The Phantom Blooper*, he shows how fully committed he is to the culture of his native place. The next logical step, following this pattern that began deep inside the all-comprehensive horror of Vietnam, would be precisely the one that Hasford had been planning for years.

Hasford's next novel had been in his mind for a number of years, a story he calls *The Undefeated*, "a novel about the life of a private in the Army of Virginia, a Confederate *Red Badge of Courage.*"[7] Unfortunately, Hasford's plans for his Civil War story, one to be told from the southern point of view, caused him to cross over to the wrong side of the law and, in the process, to dishonor some of the qualities that have long been considered virtues in the South. Because the Civil War, unlike the Vietnam War, was beyond Hasford's personal experience, he had to depend upon historical records to provide him with the wealth of detail needed to make a credible fiction. He needed books, lots of them, the kind of unique books that are long out of print, books that libraries hold in common trust for all. He needed those books close at hand, where he cold browse through them, commune with them, steep himself in the feel of the past that they could provide. It all sounds rather inspirational—and innocent enough—but Gustav Hasford, son of a librarian and husband of a librarian, committed a mortal sin for librarians: he took books out of libraries all over the United States and even some abroad, with no intention of returning them until his need for them was over. He stole books, not for profit but for his personal, creative and imaginative use.

When Hasford's pattern of theft was discovered, subsequent to action taken by the director of the California Politechnic State University Library, David Walch, who sought the return of "87 books and two volumes of *Civil War Times Illustrated*,"[8] a collection of 9,919 volumes was discovered in an Alamo self-storage locker in San Luis Obispo, California. The books were packaged carefully, in boxes labeled according to subject, but the authorities were not impressed with Hasford's research methods or with his meticulous storage procedures. Eventually he was brought to trial on charges of theft and interstate transportation of stolen goods, a "class one" misdemeanor in the criminal code. He was found guilty as charged, and although his three-year prison sentence was suspended, he is still subject to the conditions of probation. Presumably, the limits on travel and access to library collections have put a temporary damper on the Civil War story that Hasford so long has dreamed of writing. How ironical that Hasford's long road to the South, one that passed through the perils of combat in Vietnam, would eventually led him to transgress federal law, the very sort of pattern that put southerners into the crucible of the Civil War, a matter destined to be the heart of Hasford's next work of fiction.

8

THE SOUTHERN POET'S VIETNAM

FICTION AND FILM HAVE BEEN THE DOMINANT GENRES in guiding the
Vietnam War experience through American culture. Drama and poetry of
Vietnam are equally impressive in their own right, but both genres, for a
variety of reasons, have been kept in the background. As a consequence,
great attention has been paid to the novels of the war—and to the writers
who have written these stories—but very little is known about the poetry
that comes from the same imaginative wellspring. No one knows this
better than W. D. Ehrhart, who attempted to bring Vietnam poets into
the limelight with a fine collection called *Carrying the Darkness—American Indochina: The Poetry of the Vietnam War*. Avon Books brought out
Carrying the Darkness in 1985, but the collection did not make enough
money to be competitive in Avon's target market, so in a few years, the
rights to the collection were returned to Ehrhart, who faced anew the
dismay of having to promote material that he cherished and felt should be
available to the American public. Fortunately, Texas Tech University Press
was willing to take on the prospect of keeping *Carrying the Darkness* in

print without much regard for annual sales, so it is still possible to find, in one place, a representative grouping of poets who have taken on the challenge of placing Vietnam in the lyrical mode.

Ehrhart's volume includes seventy-five poets, some with just one poem in the collection, some with ten or more. When I talked with Ehrhart about the prospect of examining a set of Vietnam poets with southern backgrounds, we both realized that the southern background is not readily recognizable. In fact, it was difficult to come up with even a few poets who are acknowledged to be of southern heritage. Nevertheless, three poets eventually emerged from the search, three who seem to represent diverse southern issues as focused through the prism of the Vietnam War: David Huddle, who grew to maturity in Virginia; Yusef Komunyakaa, an African-American born in Bogalusa, Louisiana; and Walter McDonald, whose Texas heritage seems in some ways more western than southern but who reflects traits that have been featured throughout this study as southern. Both Huddle and McDonald have applied their talents to the short story as well as to poetry, and each has had books in print since the mid-1970s. Komunyakaa's first chapbook, *Dedications and Other Darkhorses*, appeared in 1977. In the 1980s, Wesleyan University Press brought out three more books by Komunyakaa—*Copacetic* (1984), *I Apologize for the Eyes in My Head* (1986), and *Dien Cai Dau* (1988), the last dealing exhaustively with Vietnam. Huddle, Komunyakaa, and McDonald are all well-established poets, and each has both a southern connection and a significant commitment to the subject matter of Vietnam. Southern poets echo in their lyrics many of the concerns of the South which were noted in the narratives examined earlier in this study. These concerns are voiced often with flashes of Hannahesque extravagance, the sort of thing that was obviously implied in Hannah's mention of poets in *Ray*: the pronounced sense of place and debt to the past, the ability to incorporate Vietnam into a larger context, the stress of race relations, the challenge of soldiering with honor, the vitalizing force of nature, and the brooding awareness that violent impulses lie just beneath the surface of life, ready to seek instant gratification. As they reflect upon Vietnam, southern poets mirror their point of origin.

David Huddle has been away from his native Virginia for years. Like other writers addressed in this chapter, Huddle makes his living by teaching literature and writing at the University of Vermont in Burlington, Vermont, and at the Bread Loaf School of English in Middlebury, Vermont. Huddle's stories frequently involve aspects of Vermont life, so it seems that he has settled fairly well into his home away from the South, but in his poetry, he returns frequently to Virginia—to the people and places of his youth. When his imagination is called upon to probe his Vietnam experience (as a U.S. Army military intelligence specialist, with Vietnam service in 1966–67), Huddle's native South provides the context.

Huddle was born in Virginia in 1942, and attended the University of Virginia in Charlottesville. Shortly thereafter, as the American presence in Vietnam underwent its rapid transformation from providing only advisors for Vietnamese Army units to providing large-scale combat operations with U.S. soldiers involved in all phases of the war effort, Huddle went off to basic training at Fort Jackson, South Carolina, and after a tour of duty in Germany, he went to Vietnam.

In the last three decades, Huddle has published six books. In his three collections of short stories—*A Dream with No Stump Roots in It* (1975), *Only the Little Bone* (1986), and *The High Spirits* (1988)—only two stories from the first volume deal with Vietnam material directly, but the South is often reflected, mostly college life at Charlottesville in the early 1960s. Vietnam is much more significant in Huddle's poetry, although even there, it is assigned its place against a cultural background that extends far back beyond the time of American combat in Southeast Asia. Based upon the way Vietnam is introduced in Huddle's two poetry collections—*Paper Boy* (1979), and *Stopping by Home* (1988)—it seems clear that he feels compelled to remember Vietnam, remember it without having it dominate his subsequent existence. It is also obvious that the best sense he can make of those years of his life comes in conjunction with the world of Virginia that shaped him before his military experience. Huddle measures Vietnam by southern-bred standards.

The Vietnam poems of *Stopping by Home* (the title reminiscent of one of the best-known New England poems of all time, Frost's "Stopping by Woods on a Snowy Evening," a sign that even in the realm of poetry, Huddle has found some kinship with the country of the North) are grouped together in the first section, which is called "Tour of Duty." In "Nerves," one of the early poems, Huddle notes the distance in reality between his military training, conducted at one of the key southern bases for introducing trainees to what they might expect in combat and the actual experience of Vietnam: "Training I received did not apply / because

Cu Chi District was not Fort Jackson" (3). The best that the South could provide in training did not match the truth of the situation as encountered in country.

This theme of distance is advanced further, with delicate precision, in a poem called "Work." At the outset of the poem, Huddle identifies himself in terms of his demographic background: "I am a white, Episcopal-raised, almost / college-educated, North American male" (5). He is a military intelligence specialist, at the moment recording the results of interrogation of a Vietnamese "detainee," a man who describes himself to Sergeant Tri, the interpreter for Huddle, as a "farmer." This is "dull," all of it having happened many times before, but then Tri intensifies the questioning of the "detainee," suggesting tacitly that violence of some sort might break the "farmer" of his lying. At this point in the sonnet, midway through the sestet, Huddle's Virginia background provides a sharp contrast to the present moment: "Where I grew up my father / waits at the door while my mother finishes / packing his lunch" (5). The manners and customs of Huddle's Virginia background would keep a man waiting quietly for his wife to pack a lunch. This kind of background is way out of line for the decision that Huddle must supply in Vietnam: "I must tell Tri what next." In "Work," no antecedent is acknowledged in Huddle's Virginia to provide a set course of action.

"The Air Rifle," a later poem in *Stopping by Home*, hints of more than a little violence as part of the standard fare in Huddle's southern background. This sonnet inventories the arsenal of weapons that was part of the family. From his father, Huddle has inherited a "double-barreled twelve-gauge" (20), and presumably he could claim any of the other family guns, including "the pistol (Mother's favorite) / we thought was a Yankee's, its notched hammer / becoming its rear sight when it was cocked" and several rifles. Once, as a boy, Huddle "aimed a toy at my brother's ear, breathed / once, and triggered merely noise with my shot." As shots go, it was quiet, but it shows how Huddle's boyhood was not entirely without predisposition to violence. The two poems that follow, "Croquet" and "Icicle," add to the sense that Virginia afforded preparation for the basic elements of war.

In "Croquet," Huddle's "Newbern grandmother" and other esteemed ladies of the family play the game of the poem's title. The ladies compete fiercely, even Aunt Stella, with "bones / skewed by childhood polio" (21), who rams her way through the wickets to the end post first, and then Aunt Stella, "in dining room tones / says, 'Keep your manners but play for keeps.'" Manners and gentility were evident in Virginia, but also a sense of playing for keeps.

Occasionally violence breaks free from the hold of manners, as in the incident chronicled by the poem "Icicle." This poem turns on the idea of remorse, one brother's wish that a childhood act might have been different. At one point in the past, the poem's persona has hit his brother in the mouth with an icicle, "for no good reason / except that the icicle had broken off / so easily and that it felt like a club / in my hand, and so I swung it" (21). As the sonnet dwells on this incident of fraternal experience, the "I" at the center wishes for another such moment, a replacement moment actually, in which the icicle might be presented to the brother as a gift, a change of action that "might / help both our lives." The blow of the icicle, one brother against another, defines on one level no more than a blood relationship through time, but on another level, it stands for Huddle's Vietnam preparation, which was not so governed by the decorum of old Virginia as to make him unfit for the challenges of combat. In general, the grouping of poems in *Stopping by Home* reveals Huddle as a man bent on measuring all of his experience with exquisite care, none of it being greater in magnitude or import than any other part, thus securing for the Vietnam War a lasting place in relationship to Huddle's South.

Huddle worked with the same care and to the same end in his first poetry collection, *Paper Boy*. The title image suggests a willingness to look far backward, to formative experiences. In the middle of this collection, at the mid-point of Huddle's life when *Paper Boy* was published, Vietnam appears. The poem that treats Vietnam—"Going, 1960–1970"—is built of fourteen numbered sections, averaging eight short lines each. "Going" can be taken as a paradigm for Huddle's perspective on Vietnam; it happened, but there was a time before, and there have been matters of grave consequence since. Thus the poem wends from a Cadillac ride home from Charlottesville, to Fort Jackson, to Europe, and back to visit Grandad in Virginia before finally (in section 7) delivering Huddle by helicopter to "an old, cracked / French-built tennis court / near the capital city of / Binh Chanh Province" (50). Then there are several evasive sections that show Huddle getting away from Vietnam—in reality or in dreams. Then he is back home, picking up the threads of his life, trying to get his dying grandfather some whiskey, getting married, and seeing his father dance with his bride ("I felt / like kissing him because I'd / been through enough of a / war to know courage when I saw it"), and finally confronting the pain of death when his grandfather dies. As was the case with Clyde Edgerton in *The Floatplane Notebooks*, David Huddle seems prepared in "Going" to preserve the Vietnam era as a part of the larger story of life, which never proceeds long without some kind of pain and suffering, from one generation to the next. The lyric moments of Huddle's poetry freeze time, and yet the corpus of his work admits to the long reach of history. Vietnam has claim to a portion of Huddle's imagination, but the Vietnam era clearly has not displaced the forces of continuity and memory that are part of his southern heritage.

For Yusef Komunyakaa, Vietnam played a seminal role in his development as a poet, although he did not attempt to turn his imagination backward to recollect the Vietnam years until nearly two decades after his time in country. Komunyakaa's army tour in Vietnam occurred in 1969–70, with service as a combat correspondent assigned to the Americal Division, the unit that had been responsible for the My Lai massacre. Komunyakaa turned to reading poetry as a way of finding relief from the violence he had occasion to observe in his reporting role. The title for his collection of Vietnam poems indicates how Komunyakaa understands the essence of Vietnam. *Dien Cai Dau* (dinky dow) means "crazy" in Vietnamese, and this phrase was applied often by the Vietnamese to describe the American soldiers in their country. The collection acknowledges the inherent craziness in the Vietnam War episode for Americans, and at the same time, numerous poems in the collection betray Komunyakaa's concern that the conditions of Vietnam combat had parallels in American culture, particularly in the South. With Komunyakaa, being an African-American, which carries its own legacy of defeat, is interwoven with both the reality of Vietnam and the history of the South.

The South is manifestly present in the merger of emotions registered by Komunyakaa in "Tu Do Street," a Vietnamese locale sought by American soldiers for various kinds of surcease from the anxieties of combat. There would be music. Drugs. Women. As the place congeals in Komunyakaa's imagination twenty years after, it represents much more than an environment of escape into pleasure. The signs are there of America:

Music divides the evening.
I close my eyes & can see
men drawing lives in the dust.
America pushes through the membrane
of mist & smoke, & I'm only a small boy
again in Bogalusa. *White Only*
signs & Hank Snow. But tonight
I walk into a place where bar girls
fade like tropical birds. When
I order a beer, the mama-san
behind the counter acts as if she
can't understand, while her eyes
skirt each white face, as Hank Williams
calls from the psychedelic jukebox.
We have played Judas where
only machine-gun fire brings us
together. Down the street
black GIs hold to their turf also.
An off-limits sign pulls me
deeper into alleys, as I look
for a softness behind these voices
wounded by their beauty & war.
Back in the bush at Dak To
& Khe Sanh, we fought
the brothers of these women
we now run to hold in our arms.
There's more than a nation
inside us, as black & white
soldiers touch the same lovers
minutes apart, tasting
each other's breath,
without knowing these rooms
run into each other like tunnels
leading to the underworld.

(29)

For Komunyakaa, the profound divisions he had known as a boy in
Bogalusa intrude on the multiracial urges of the night, bringing together,
on Tu Do Street, all levels of the participants in the Vietnam drama. The
unions of the night belie the action of "men drawing lines in the dust," a
splintering process that ruled Bogalusa and that has its strong hold on the

American soldiers in Vietnam. In the field of combat, the splintering momentarily abates when "machine-gun fire brings us together," but otherwise, the rules of Komunyakaa's South operate in Vietnam. The poet fully grasps the irony of whorehouse sex, "as black & white / soldiers touch the same lovers / minutes apart, tasting / each other's breath" and senses that this act of union could go beyond the surface of the moment, if only one had the ability to draw back and look more carefully at what was happening. Of course, that is precisely the function of Komunyakaa's poetry. As Vincente F. Gotera noted in his assessment, "Komunyakaa comes to the material with an academic grounding in modernist and contemporary poetics as well as classic surrealism" (289), a background perfectly suited to subjecting Vietnam to the long look necessary to see behind the surfaces. Gotera suggests that Komunyakaa's poetry benefits greatly from the time delay between experience and the poetic act in handling Vietnam, giving a perspective that is not evident in the intense soul-searching in some of the early Vietnam poetry of the late 1960s and early 1970s.

Again and again in Komunyakaa's Vietnam poetry, he confronts the racial gulf that was part of his youth in Bogalusa. The black-white schism courses through the activities of American soldiers in Vietnam. In "Communique," "Bob Hope's on stage, but we want the Gold Diggers, / want a flash of legs / through the hemorrhage of vermilion, giving us / something to kill for" (30). It is show time in Vietnam, with the zany impulses of American culture thrown into entertainment overdrive, something sufficiently energized to satisfy the distraction needs of the troops, who "want our hearts wrung out like rags & ground down / to Georgia dust / while Cobras drag the perimeter, gliding along the sea, / swinging searchlight / through the trees." The moment is loud, driven by the rhythms of rock and roll, the lights are bright, and the legs are white, white, white. For black soldiers, something is missing: "I thought you said / Aretha was gonna be here." Finally, the show makes an effort to strike a balance on the color line, not with Aretha Franklin, but "There's Lola," Lola Falana, singing and thrusting with her pelvis. Lola Falana is another indication of the idea that sexual impulses homogenize, but the poem resists accepting such efforts at transcending the boundaries of race. As one black soldier observes, "Shit, man, she looks awful white to me." Then the show closes, and the performers depart, carrying their fantasex light and sound kaleidoscope airborne with them, leaving the soldiers behind, black and white, "holding our helmets like rain-polished skulls."

The stress of racial conflict is even stronger in "Report from the Skull's Diorama," a poem that appears in the middle of *Dien Cai Dau*, which reflects on the enemy's use of propaganda to drive a wedge between white and black soldiers:

> Dr. King's photograph
> comes at me from *White Nights*
> like Hoover's imagination at work,
>
> dissolving into a scenario
> at Firebase San Juan Hill:
> our chopper glides in closer,
> down to the platoon of black GIs
> back from night patrol
> with five dead. Down
> into a gold whirl of leaves
> dust-deviling the fire base.
> A field of black trees
> stakes down the morning sun.
>
> With the chopper blades
> knife-fighting the air,
> yellow leaflets quiver
> back to the ground, clinging to us.
> These men have lost their tongues,
>
> but the red-bordered
> leaflets tell us
> *VC didn't kill*
> *Dr. Martin Luther King.*
> The silence etched into their skin
>
> is also mine. Psychological
> warfare colors the napalmed hill
> gold-yellow. When our gunship
> flies out backwards, rising
> above the men left below
>
> to blend in with the charred
> landscape, an AK-47
> speaks, with the leaflets
> clinging to the men & stumps,
> waving to me across the years.

(47–48)

Komunyakaa left Louisiana for Vietnam, but he carried with him an awareness of racial injustice that made him open to leaflet propaganda. "Report from the Skull's Diorama" does not misrepresent the ferocity of the enemy, for the night patrol has "five dead" and an "AK-47 speaks" to the departing helicopter with Komunyakaa aboard, but it does open the door to accepting some validity in the idea that "VC didn't kill / Dr. Martin Luther King," a bit of turmoil that sweeps "across the years" to one born in the South.

In "*Dui Boi*, Dust of Life," perhaps the most surreal poem in *Dien Cai Dau*, Komunyakaa brings a spectral son to life, one who comes directly from the anguish of the South, a point driven home by the poem's first stanza:

> You drifted from across the sea
> under a carmine moon,
> framed now in my doorway
> by what I tried to forget.
> Curly-headed & dark-skinned,
> you couldn't escape
> eyes taking you apart.
> Come here, son, let's see
> if they castrated you.

(58)

The soldier in Hue is visited at night by a son, "born with dust / on your eyelids." This son, "With only your mother's name," has "inherited the inchworm's / foot of earth," but he comes across the sea and settles on his father, as *dui boi*, dust. The poem is nightmarish in its sense of desolation and loss, but it gains an added degree of horror from the line that links this soldier in Vietnam with the South: "Come here, son, let's see / if they castrated you." In Komunyakaa's rendering, Vietnam combat is no place to escape the misery known to blacks in the South through the years of suppression and hatred; in fact, combat in Vietnam accentuated the pervasiveness of certain things—like the dust of life (and death), like the misery of racial prejudice—showing how hard they are to dispell: "I blow the dust off my hands / but it flies back in my face." Thus does the pall of racial animosity hang over the black soldier in Vietnam to fight—and very likely to die—for America.

However, by the last poem in *Dien Cai Dau*, "Facing It," Komunyakaa reflects upon Vietnam with greater equanimity. The occasion for this poem is a visit to the Vietnam Veterans Memorial in Washington, a moment that parallels the concluding scene of Mason's *In Country*, although the lead image is now black, not white:

> My black face fades,
> hiding inside the black granite.
> I said I wouldn't,
> dammit: No tears.
> I'm stone. I'm flesh.
> My clouded reflection eyes me
> like a bird of prey, the profile of night
> slanted against morning. I turn
> this way—the stone lets me go.
> I turn that way—I'm inside
> the Vietnam Veterans Memorial
> again, depending on the light
> to make a difference.
> I go down the 58,022 names,
> half-expecting to find
> my own in letters like smoke.
> I touch the name Andrew Johnson;
> I see the booby trap's white flash.
> Names shimmer on a woman's blouse
> but when she walks away
> the names stay on the wall.
> Brushstrokes flash, a red bird's
> wings cutting across my stare.
> The sky. A plane in the sky.
> A white vet's image floats
> closer to me, then his pale eyes
> look through mine. I'm a window.
> He's lost his right arm
> inside the stone. In the black mirror
> a woman's trying to erase names:
> No, she's brushing a boy's hair.

(63)

From the vantage point of nearly twenty years after his personal witness to Vietnam combat, Yusef Komunyakaa can accept the past. Yes, it still contains divisions as he faces the wall and a series of reflections appear on it. Gotera's analysis of this poem catches its method well, calling it a "facing" of the dualities that govern everyday life: "there and here, America and Vietnam, living and dead, night and day, old and young, white and black (i.e., Caucasian and Negro)," all done in a way that "does not declaim, does not decry" (298). Near the end of the poem, there is the beautiful image of the white vet, whose "pale eyes look through mine," suggesting that perhaps Vietnam has cleared the way to truer seeing by the diverse races that make up America. The poem's conclusion—resistance to the idea of erasing names, of forgetting the past—is entirely in line with the other southerners considered earlier in this study, complete with its sense that knowledge carried to the heart by means of memory can be the hope of the future, as caught sweetly in a mother's "brushing a boy's hair."

David Huddle, working with poetry as a counterpoint to his fiction over the course of nearly twenty years, has sinuously embedded the Vietnam experience in the Virginia of his youth. Yusef Komunyakaa, in contrast, took on a host of other settings and issues—New Orleans, for example, in *I Apologize for the Eyes in My Head* (1986)—before concentrating on Vietnam from the vantage point of nearly twenty years hence, and then he found, with recourse to surrealistic techniques and cubist images in the tradition of William Carlos Williams (Gotera 290–93), that his emotional mindscape of Vietnam featured inescapable parallels to his experience of growing up as an African-American in Bogalusa.

In contrast to both Huddle and Komunyakaa, Walter McDonald has been steadily and relentlessly preoccupied with the Vietnam period of his life. Vietnam was the key to his first collection of poems, *Caliban in Blue and Other Poems* (1976), and Vietnam seems to be just as salient in his more recent writing, whether in fiction (*A Band of Brothers: Stories from Vietnam* 1989) or in poetry (*After the Noise of Saigon*, 1988, and *Night Landings: Poems*, 1989). Vietnam is thus a constant for McDonald, shadowing all his days, but always, too, there is Texas—a place where "God's good grace" ("Settling the Plains," *Night Landings* 43) is sung from the hymnbooks, where one can be, if the spirit moves, close to the land and to nature. In a reprise of the theme of violence explored in the Hannah chapter, it seems that violence also has a lasting home in McDonald's Texas/Vietnam.

The violence motif is launched powerfully in the title poem of *Caliban in Blue*, a poem that catches perfectly the exultant thrill of air combat, something known to McDonald through his Vietnam service in 1969–70 as an air force pilot, but something just as relevant in 1991 with its winter show of American pilots' orgasmic activity in the air over Iraq. Indeed, in 1991, "Caliban in Blue" does not seem dated in the least:

Off again,
thrusting up at scald
of copper in orient west
I climb into such blue skies.
Skies even here
belong to Setebos:
calls it air power.
Air power is peace power,
his motto catechizes
as we, diving, spout
flame from under,
off in one hell
of a roar.

His arms like radar
point the spot.
For this, I trained to salivate
and tingle, target-diving,
hand enfolding hard throttle
in solitary masculine delight.

Focused on cross hairs,
eyes glazing, hand triggers switches in
pulsing orgasm,
savage release;
pull out
and off we go again
thrusting deep
into the martial lascivious blue
of uncle's sky.

(11)

Several features of "Caliban in Blue" typify McDonald's poetic style. He frequently avails himself of literary analogues, here drawing upon the Caliban/Setebos material of Shakespeare's *The Tempest*, but elsewhere in *Caliban in Blue*, he calls on James Joyce and Joseph Conrad (with references to *The Secret Agent*, Kurtz of *Heart of Darkness*, and *Lord Jim*), anticipating Francis Ford Coppola's use of Conrad in *Apocalypse Now* (1979) by several years. Given McDonald's many years of teaching creative writing at Texas Tech University, it is perhaps not surprising to find an abundance of allusions, yet McDonald also has a strength of narrative line that distinguishes his poems, and "Caliban in Blue" surges forward with the energy of sex/war suffused. This early poem reveals that pilots find a special joy in riding their instruments of death and deliverance. If it can be taken as axiomatic that men are biologically programmed to find sexual release, then the overlaying of air war on this fundamental pattern gives cause for alarm. McDonald seems caught in the conundrum of recognizing in himself the feral intensity of the pilot's wish to drive jets at full throttle toward targets that promise "savage release," but at the same time he is aware that his attitude clearly puts him on the level of the beast Caliban—rather far removed from the gentle word magic of Prospero, who would strive to bring peace to the tempest within. Several other poems, in *Caliban in Blue* and in his other collections, particularly those that focus on the poet's children, bring out McDonald's sensitivity to the need for transforming the war impulse into gentleness.

Yet McDonald's own war experience makes resistance to the call of war difficult, a point that he makes explicit in a story called "Robert E. Lee Never Flew Jets" from *A Band of Brothers*. This story is one of several in the collection that deal with Randy Wayne and his attitudes toward flying and war. In McDonald's representation of Randy Wayne (yes, clearly kin to John), we can hear distinct echoes of what Barry Hannah did with the stories of air combat he obtained from his friend Quisenberry: "Here in his Phantom, he was among the finest, more powerful than any other profession could make him. . . . An F-4 had been his Harvard and Vietnam his Yale. History books proudly record Lee's humane remark to an aide during the battle of Fredericksburg: 'It's a good thing war is so terrible, or men would come to love it too much.' But unlike Randy Wayne, Robert E. Lee never flew jets" (110–11).

Although this passage contains a provocative reference to a personage not of the South—Herman Melville, who found his imaginative life in the trying exploits of whaling rather than in the more settled rituals of college learning—Robert E. Lee, the South's legendary figure of gentlemanlike war, stands as the key benchmark of feelings in this passage about the attitudinal stance of pilots in modern war. Lee's war was such that he could see its horrors, and his stature allowed him to voice his reservation about the whole business, all part of his aura for latter-day southerners. The pilots, however, do not see that horror, and as the war in the Persian Gulf in 1991 proved, we depend on air power now even more than ever. In the last decade of the twentieth century, American air power is virtually unchecked, either by actual adversaries or by the moral scrupulosity behind Lee's observation at Fredericksburg. Thus the balance between war/lust and a more human gentleness—a balance that was so difficult for McDonald to realize—may have been tipped by technology toward war.

Another poem from *Caliban in Blue* hints that it is not the pilots alone who respond viscerally to the call of violence. In "Interview with a Guy Named Fawkes, U.S. Army"—a poem also included in Ehrhart's *Carrying the Darkness*—McDonald both plays with a distant historical analogue (the Gunpowder Plot of 5 November 1605 involving a soldier who had been serving in Flanders, Guy Fawkes, in a Catholic intrigue to advance their cause against repression) and avails himself of the power of direct quotation to catch the power of the "truth" in a "tell it like it is" moment of the late 1960s:

> —you tell them this—
> tell them shove it, they're
> not here, tell them kiss
> my rear when they piss about
> women and kids in shacks
> we fire on. damn.
> they fire on us.
> hell yes, it's war
> they sent us for.
> what do they know back where
> not even in their granddam's days
> did any damn red rockets glare.
> don't tell me how
> chips fall.
> those are The Enemy:
> waste them all.
>
> (*Caliban in Blue* 15)

At every turn of phrase in "Interview," violence threatens to erupt. The army protagonist, Fawkes, is seething with anger, feeling his honor betrayed by his compatriots at home and his life threatened by everyone and everything in Vietnam. Given this combination of frustrations and haunting demons, the answer comes all too easily, boiling to the surface, an answer for all who might be The Enemy: "waste them all." As the section on "Violence" in Wilson and Ferris's *Encyclopedia of Southern Culture* illustrates, southerners have often found themselves at home with the impulse that closes McDonald's "Interview."

Much of the South's music is produced in Nashville, home to the Grand Old Opry and the hard-thumping heart of the country-western lyrical mode. In a recent poem, "The Songs We Fought For," from the *Night Landings* collection, McDonald suggests that the essence of feelings contained in much of this music lies close to the motivating forces behind southern soldiers like McDonald who were drawn to Vietnam. To understand the reasons that sent southern soldiers to Vietnam one must listen to the songs:

> We drank while half the stars came out for us,
> Willie and Waylon, Hank and Loretta,
> ours in the glow of the jukebox.
>
> Over the laughter and smoke of local
> men and women groping for their lives,
> they sob-sang all we hoped to know
>
> of lonesome love. Nothing like
> songs could break a man's heart
> with the draft and a war in Vietnam
>
> drawing him closer daily. We slumped
> under our Stetsons, squinting
> in blue smoke layered like gunfire,
>
> and bought pitchers of beer for women
> we never hoped to marry. Each time I took
> Sweet Darlin's hand and led her
>
> onto the dance floor, I felt the world
> should end like that, slow-dancing
> close as we'd ever be to another in clothes,
>
> lost in a sad, sweet fiddle-rhythm,
> sliding on polished boots
> and humming softly to ourselves.

(63)

"The Songs We Fought For" clearly shows the sense of fatality that grasps the listeners of country-western music. At the center of things, there is a sense that the heart is meant to be broken, that love is meant to be "lonesome," not sustained in a quiet and settled domestic way, and that "the world should end like that," with one's boots on, "lost in a sad, sweet fiddle-rhythm." Given such a guiding disposition, the war in Vietnam only made the breaking of a man's heart more tangible, more proximate in time, but it was all clearly meant to be, as the "humming softly to ourselves" guaranteed.

Born in 1934, a decade or more earlier than most of the writers examined in this study, McDonald has long since passed into middle age. He has beaten the odds of fatalism for more years than he ever expected, a point he greets with surprise in "The Middle Years," from *Night Landings*:

> These are the nights we dreamed of,
> snow drifting over a cabin roof
> in the mountains, enough stacked wood
> and meat to last a week, alone at last
>
> in a rented A-frame, isolated,
> without power, high in the San Juan.
> Our children are safe as they'll ever be
> seeking their fortune in cities,
>
> our desk and calendar clear, our debts
> paid until summer. The smoke of pinon
> seeps back inside under almost invisible
> cracks, the better to smell it. All day
>
> we take turns holding hands and counting
> the years we never believed we'd make it—
> the hours of skinned knees and pleading,
> diapers and teenage rage and fever
>
> in the middle of the night, and parents
> dying, and Saigon, the endless guilt
> of surviving. Nights, we lie touching
> for hours and listen, the silent woods
>
> so close we can hear owls diving.
> These woods are not our woods,
> though we hold a key to dead pine planks
> laid side by side, shiplap like a dream
>
> that lasts, a double bed that fits us
> after all these years, a blunt
> front-feeding stove that gives back
> temporary heat for all the logs we own.

(79–80)

In the main, this poem is a hymn to the quotidian. Two people sit quietly in a cabin in the woods, a simple place with the safety of simplicity (not like the city). The rhythms of life here are natural. Days are for recounting memories, nights are for listening to the sounds of nature. It all seems so restful, like a dream of quiet smoke and fire. There is also the tension of surprise, surprise that so many years and so much experience of everyday matters (the paying of debts, the raising of children, the loss of parents) have been realized and now can be remembered. Tucked in the midst of these other matters, however, is "Saigon, the endless guilt of surviving." Vietnam is one of the lurking surprises of McDonald's life, mystifying him in his deliverance from death and shadowing his happiness with the sense that he still owes more than he has paid. The temporary nature of human life is signaled by the final line, as well as by a subtle undertone throughout the poem that a person's purchase of worldly goods is never meant to endure. Meanwhile, in the wait for mortality, one best prepares by snuggling close to the bosom of nature, a theme celebrated by southern writers for many generations.

"Settling the Plains" perhaps best captures the spirituality that goes hand in hand with closeness to nature:

> For here and for the afterlife
> they worked and sang, kept time
> with hymnbooks in both hands,
> old songs of God's good grace
>
> in a land so dry they planted
> cottonseeds to prove they believed
> in miracles. They buried their dead
> on plains with no native stones,
>
> deep in the earth to save them
> from sandstorms that pounded
> daily from the west. They prayed
> for rain, the sun so dry for months
>
> they couldn't curse. Rain fell
> in floods like manna twice a year.
> Like Moses, they walked across
> dry land and called on God
>
> to bless them all for doubting.
> They believed whatever they put
> in the dirt would live if it was
> God's will and the wind blew.

(43)

In this poem, McDonald recognizes the God-centered fatality that dominated the people who settled his part of the country, trying to push King Cotton to its utmost western limits. Such a faith in contingency by "God's good grace" could prepare a person for just about anything, whether "the sun so dry for months" or some sort of unpleasant business on the other side of the world, a situation not actually invoked in "Settling the Plains" but clearly provided for in the poem's representation of abiding faith. *Night Landings* is made up of a mixture of poems about Vietnam and poems about Texas, the Southwest of cactus and mesquite. Twenty years after his Vietnam service, Walter McDonald is still trying to work out the connections between Vietnam and Texas.

A poem called "Nearing the End of a Century," from *After the Noise of Saigon*, shows how fully McDonald recognizes that drawing knowledge from past experience—centered on Vietnam—is crucial to the American entrance into a new century:

> *Let his be clear that we are men of sun*
> *And men of day and never of pointed night.*
> WALLACE STEVENS
>
> Night of the comet, space without angels,
> only our eyes to find whatever light
> is there. The stars are rose-ember
>
> over coals already gray. Orion
> rises angry in the east.
> Night after night he prowls the same
>
> black forest of stars, tracking
> the spoor of nothing he remembers.
> In zipped twin sleeping bags
>
> before Saigon, we claimed billions of stars
> to wish on, perfectly foreign,
> the absolute absence of meaning.
>
> We counted myths made up by others
> like us, needing to believe in something,
> projecting filaments like spiders
>
> spinning tales to turn stark fear
> to faith. Somehow we survived that war
> and raised our share of children.

Nights, you turn for me to hold you,
although I have no answers.
Our best minds query a comet we'll

never see again for clues. Rockets probe
the one unanswered question, millions
of light years back toward beginning,

before myth. We say whatever is,
we'll accept. But we must know,
we must know something.

(22–23)

"Nearing the End of a Century" is not about the quotidian; it concerns itself with ultimate matters, and Vietnam is directly at the center of things. Myths were needed in abundance to "turn stark fear / to faith," but Vietnam nevertheless turned the innocence of wishing on the stars into a kind of emptiness that still has not been answered. Even surviving Vietnam (as a person, as a people) poses more of a question than an answer. Yet the conclusion of the poem harkens back to the pattern of Tate's "Ode to the Confederate Dead," calling upon the imagination to ceaselessly roam over the past, going back in history—surely passing Vietnam as a key point on the way—moving to the time "before myth," for "we must know, / we must know something." McDonald forsees no quick answers to the profound questions prompted by the Vietnam War episode, but he asserts that the backward look is the only way out, the only way to knowing something.

9

YOU MUST GO HOME AGAIN, BUT WHAT IS HOME?

THOMAS WOLFE'S FINAL NOVEL, *You Can't Go Home Again*, appeared in 1940, the second posthumous assemblage of Wolfe manuscript material under the editorial direction of Edward Aswell. Despite the novel's innate peculiarity in terms of its reaching publication, with a much larger-than-usual role for the midwife, *You Can't Go Home Again* did two things: it completed Wolfe's lifelong struggle to place himself against his past, and it created a handy title to be borrowed (or adapted) whenever writers wanted to address the entire business of homecoming—returning to one's place of origin—an experience made daunting, sometimes terrifying, by the baggage any voyager is likely to bring back home and by the changes that almost inevitably will have infected the place known as home. Kenneth Lynn availed himself of Wolfe's title when he scrutinized the profound consequence of Mark Twain's return to the New South in 1882, part of Twain's effort to get himself writing again on his Huckleberry Finn story. Lynn asserted that Twain found in this engagement with his past enough energy to complete his Huck story, but there was also a great deal in the New South that Twain met with grave concern. In a sense, Twain made Huck stand for the best that could be imagined in such a past, but by the end of the novel, Huck had to move on, heading west. Home was not a place where he could remain. In Wolfe's case, or in the case of his surrogate, George Webber, crucial things had happened after the writer had left home, and those things, cumulatively, put effective return in jeopardy. Truly, Wolfe/George Webber could not go home again.

We have already witnessed a number of variations on the theme of coming home, an inescapable telic matter for the person who goes off to war. Wars—even the one in Vietnam—prove to be finite. The soldier goes away, the soldier comes back home. When the soldier comes home dead, usually the story ends, although exceptions have been made, as in the case of Samantha Hughes's father in Mason's *In Country*. More typical, however, is the narrative that turns on the stress of finding the home that the soldier left behind, stress accentuated by the experience of battle. Clyde Edgerton handles this matter in his two Vietnam stories; Madison Smartt Bell's Vietnam novel centers on the problem of returning home; Larry Brown's *Dirty Work* depends completely upon the desperate condition of a veteran who cannot really come home from his war experience; adjusting to home after war is crucial in Harry Crew's account of Nail Head in *Body*; and, on a more up-beat note, Winston Groom's *Forrest Gump* tracks the endless ironies of all that might attend the return of a hero. The books mentioned above happen to be southern in focus, but of course there is nothing uniquely southern to the story of the soldier trying to go home. Homer told that story; so did Ernest Hemingway in his "Big Two-Hearted River" sequence; and so have many nonsouthern writers of the Vietnam era.

Yet before passing on to the study of a text that takes its protagonist out of a home in the suburbs and into a zone of danger (although only a few miles away) that virtually replicates Vietnam combat (and that may constitute for him an alternative sense of home), we should consider the notion of "home" for the southerner and think of the options that the southerner has for imaging the essence of his or her home. In the summer of 1989, I had the pleasant experience of being a fellow at the NEH Institute on "The Southern Writer and the Southern Community," held at Chapel Hill, North Carolina, under the direction of Louis Rubin and Joseph Flora. The program of the institute, even in its title, suggests that a person writing from the South should expect to have a place in a community, something that, vaguely at least, might be a part of his or her sense of home. The readings we examined that summer finally suggested to 'me that there are at least two distinct orientations to the idea of belonging— of being home—that percolate in southern writing.

Very briefly, the options for home involve domestic relations on the one hand (a family, including the reality or promise of children, within a social structure) and the natural habitat on the other (being part of a place at an almost prehuman level, animalistic, deeply and truly rooted to one's origin in nature). Although the camps are by no means mutually exclusive, it seems that women writers have been more inclined toward the first sense of home, while male writers have gravitated to the latter representation of belonging (of really being where one wants to be and being comfortable in that place). The same split roughly pertains to central protagonists as well, with the women having a stronger and more vital feel for family ties and the men being drawn to identification with the physical sense of nature outside the domestic/community environment.

Winston Groom shows this latter inclination in the story of Beau Gunn, who is most comfortable in the delta swamp, where he is linked closely to the old black bear. Earlier, Faulkner had employed the same theme, particularly in *Go Down, Moses*. One of Faulkner's few functional families (most of them are severely dysfunctional), the McCallums in *Sartoris*, are successful because their home is so close to nature. Standing behind all of this is the paradigm of Huckleberry Finn, the quintessence of bonding with nature and the full rejection of the Widow Douglas/Aunt Sally image of home.

In contrast, Eudora Welty, although clearly fascinated with the ramblings of King MacLain and others in *The Golden Apples*, including Virgie Rainey as a key wandering spirit, and placing them at home in nature rather than within the boundaries of culture and the physical confines of a house, is equally concerned with the challenge of maintaining social contracts. This is represented in the life of the music teacher, Miss Eckhart, who, although having no children of her own, is consumed until the end of her teaching career with the goal of passing on her love for music to the next generation. At the end of "The Wanderers," Virgie seems to be coming to terms with the web of her involvement with the associations of what home means to her, for as she sits in the rain, before her eyes and filling her world are the courthouse, the Confederate soldier, the graveyard, and the passersby in MacLain. Virgie's unique sense of connectedness is finally rounded with the mythic matter of the ages—Perseus and Medusa—even the horse, bear, leopard, dragon, and swan. At the end of *One Writer's Beginnings*, Welty evokes the word "confluence" (112) to speak to the central concerns of her life, and she draws attention to the end of *The Optimist's Daughter* as an example of how lives are ideally meant to merge, even in the course of wide traveling (or despite death, as in the case of Laurel and her dead husband, Phil). Following Welty's lead, Bobbie Ann Mason, while allowing Samantha her crucial time in nature to connect with her father, incorporated as a major part of her narrative the crucial importance of multigenerational orientation to domestic life. Samantha does not travel alone to Washington, D.C.; she travels in the company of her uncle, Emmett, and her grandmother, Mamaw, all of whom are to go back to Kentucky together after having solidified their togetherness at the site of a national monument to those who had died in Vietnam, a place that has functioned as the spiritual home for many estranged veterans and for the grieving families of those soldiers who failed to return. Almost all of Jayne Anne Phillips's *Machine Dreams* is dedicated to the travails of trying to sustain family connectedness in the face of male adventures.

In sum, either there is an abiding sense of connectedness to others to make the essence of home, or there is primal connectedness to nature as a home. In the last writings of George Webber to Foxhall Edwards in *You Can't Go Home Again*, Wolfe incorporates flashes of both kinds of connectedness, although the nature link is predominant. The fact that his last words are written rather than spoken shows that he is partially estranged from others, physically removed from them at least, but has not lost the hope of being with them. The last chapter, "Credo," involves extensive reminiscence of the past, the environment of George's early years which would seem to constitute the home to which he cannot return. George finds himself caught in "a giant web . . . the product of my huge inheritance—the torrential recollectiveness, derived out of my mother's stock, which became a living, million-fibred integument that bound me to the past, not only of my own life, but of the very earth from which I came, so that nothing in the end escaped from its inrooted and all-feeling explorativeness" (667). Here we see memorialized the southerner's sense of being caught in the past, but for George Webber (and hence for Wolfe himself), the details that follow are equally important, for they flesh out the real heart of his past—and home. Webber's consciousness is bombarded with the sense impressions of his youth, and fully two-thirds of the twenty-five or so remembered sensations are directly linked to nature, particularly the feel of each of the seasons. The nature imagery finally resolves into Webber himself, a plant impelled to "go back, stem by stem, root by root, and filament by filament, until it was complete and whole, compacted of the very earth that had produced it, and of which it was itself the last and living part" (668). Thus the book ends in irony, with George imaginatively joining himself to a home in nature, although he is physically far from that home, while America, his native land, seems in his estimation to be lost to its people.

Such a background, particularly Wolfe's anxiety about the means of relating to the place that was home, provides a rationale for examining two recent texts concerning the Vietnam War in order to illustrate divergent options on the veteran's effort to return home. Sydney Blair's *Buffalo* (1991) accentuates the importance of connectedness to others as the key to making it home after Vietnam; Pat Conroy's *The Prince of Tides* (1986) brings the Vietnam veteran home to his place in nature. Sydney Blair's novel *Buffalo* involves the post-Vietnam adjustment difficulties of Raymond McCreary, who lives in an old schoolhouse in the vicinity of Charlottesville, Virginia, where Blair herself lives and works. Upon Ray's return to Virginia at the end of his Vietnam tour, his relationship with a woman named Priscilla dissolves, in large part because she had been protesting the war. The breakup of this relationship impedes Ray's linkage to others in his effort to return home. Now, years later, he has begun a relationship with another woman, Vivian, and their love moves gradually in the direction of marriage and children, but the pull of Vietnam is still strong, particularly because of the recurrent visits of a war buddy, Bullet, a man who is severely affected by his combat experiences and who is prone to seek adventures that involve more than a little danger.

As Ray draws closer and closer to settled domesticity, Bullet's persistent waywardness and rambunctiousness become increasingly problematic. During Vivian's pregnancy, Bullet takes on a new adventure, the ownership of a herd of buffalo, strange creatures of the wild west brought to the rolling hills of western Virginia. One of Bullet's observations about the nature of buffalo seems to indicate Blair's understanding of his compulsive roaming nature, which is shared sporadically by Ray: "Thing about the buffalo is, they keep taking off, escaping and marauding and doing whatever they damn well please trompling everybody's corn and potato crops" (119).

Bullet's buffalo do not stay where they are supposed to stay; they repeatedly roam. This roaming tendency, while perfectly right for a beast in nature, has shattered Bullet's family life, and it is directly at odds with the kind of life that Ray must adopt in order to meet the needs of Vivian and the child that they are expecting. The buffalo simply does not recognize the concept of home that is necessary for family nurturing.

Ray has a difficult time releasing himself from Bullet's influence—and hence, of all that Vietnam stands for in his life. Blair takes particular care to acknowledge the appeal of people like Bullet. He is the type of person about whom stories are created, whether self-created or created by others, narratives that move naturally through incidents far removed from the ordinary. For example, Bullet says that he had once eaten the head of a newborn kitten, and Ray has occasion to reflect on this story, all part of his effort to contend with the way Bullet functions in life. What Ray thinks goes directly to the center of the importance of stories in the South: "Ray knew there was always the remotest possibility that Bullet had actually done this horrifying thing, but still, it was easy for such stories to circulate: people loved having someone on whom they could foist all the atrocities and fantasies they themselves hadn't the nerve or stomach, the depravity, perversity, or imagination, to commit. Bullet probably never touched the kitten, but he certainly kept other people's lives in check" (121).

In this passage Blair addresses her culture's dependence upon stories that transcend the ordinary, and her narrative incorporates those qualities of excess precisely because it deals with Vietnam veterans, people who have had direct access to a measure of atrocity, depravity, or perversity beyond the limits of normal experience. Indeed, their excess may serve to keep "other people's lives in check."

At length, and none too soon, Ray takes a stand for the virtue of keeping his own life in check, resisting the buffalo's urge for roaming and marauding. Bullet has arrived once again, just as Ray and Vivian are celebrating their marriage with a large party. Social connectedness, in preparation for healthy domesticity, is at a peak. Vivian is due to deliver their baby at any minute, and yet Bullet wants his Vietnam friend to put his life in jeopardy one more time, to stray from the norms of his culture, to range beyond the limits. Bullet asks Ray to let him store a large stash of home-grown marijuana (another legacy of the Vietnam era) in the schoolhouse basement. Discovery of the stash, which represents transgression of the law, would ruin the future for Ray and Vivian. When Ray proves reluctant, Bullet forces the issue, moving his plan forward without permission, but even as Vivian is in the throes of childbirth, Ray discovers his friend's plan and acts to destroy the marijuana. In a final moment of violence that reinvokes Vietnam, Ray punches Bullet, who then takes after Ray. Bullet fires his 30.06 caliber rifle at Ray, who feels like the buffalo that Bullet had killed in a "mad-minute"[1] outburst of frustration caused by the uncontrollable roaming of his animals. Ray escapes death, however, and as the marijuana burns in the background, Ray and Bullet finally mange to move out of the tyrannical hold that the past has exerted upon them.

At the end of the narrative, Ray turns to go back to his wife and newborn child. A nightmarish vision of his own mortality enables Ray to find a way to return to a more settled way of life. He finds a way to go home to the South of endurance, as symbolized magnificently in the person of Faulkner's Dilsey, who managed always to be in line with the world of nature but at the same time was dedicated to the preservation of family life, continuity over time. The call of the future, of family responsibility, has at last superceded the buffalo impulse, and Blair's novel presents this turn as being absolutely necessary for any kind of livable future.

Pat Conroy provides an alternative slant on the galvanizing appeal of total freedom to step out from settled domesticity in order to protect the integrity of one's individual life. For Conroy, the license for radical freedom is legitimate only when it is used in the service of protecting such fundamental things as nature. *The Prince of Tides* is the story of the Wingo family; the narrative centers on Tom Wingo, whose life bears a resemblance in a few key details to that of Conroy. Tom's father, Henry, is a shrimper who lives on Melrose Island, at the mouth of the Colleton River on the South Carolina coast. Tom's mother, Lila, is a beautiful woman who taught Tom and her other son, Luke, to "love the lanterns of night fishermen in the starry darkness and the flights of brown pelicans skimming the curling breakers at dawn" (4). As Tom recalls, she "saw the world through a dazzling prism of authentic imagination" (4), totally enthralled with the wonders of the natural world.

Of the writers considered thus far, Conroy comes closest to Wolfe, both in the ambitious (sometimes in need of editing), autobiographical reach of his fiction and in his lushly romantic style, which resonates with sensations born of nature. Conroy's own past is built into *The Prince of Tides*, from the Atlanta suburbs where his family stayed while his father—a military man—was away in the service to the coastal region of Georgia and South Carolina, known to Conroy during his time at the Citadel in Charleston. His love of the past and his place in the South is poured into his style. Conroy's story ranges over the middle third of the twentieth century, along the way detailing Henry's World War II and Korean War experiences and Luke's Vietnam War tour, but the Wingo fortunes are ultimately tied to Melrose Island and the nearby town of Colleton. Conroy uses the Wingos to define the essential South, as Tom shows in assessing the driving forces of his life: "I am a patriot of a singular geography on the planet; I speak of my country religiously; I am proud of its landscape. I walk through the traffic of cities cautiously, always nimble and on the alert, because my heart belongs in the marshlands. The boy in me still carries the memories of those days when I lifted crab pots out of the Colleton River before dawn, when I was shaped by life on the river, part child, part sacristan of tides" (5–6).

Tom is born of the river and tides (his birth took place in a terrifying storm that nearly inundated Melrose Island), and the marshland of his youth means more to him than anything else. Unfortunately, the forces of change are omnipotent, and eventually, Melrose Island is lost to the Wingo family, a hundred years after it was won in a horseshoe game by Tom's "great-great-grandfather, Winston Shadrach Wingo," who "had commanded a battery under Beauregard that fired on Fort Sumter . . . died a pauper in the Confederate Soldier's Home in Charleston and refused to speak to a Yankee, male or female, until the day he died" (3). Despite the long heritage of the Wingos in the purity of nature on the South Carolina coast, they lose this physical bond to the land when the United States government takes over the entire town of Colleton to develop a facility for the production of nuclear armaments. This turn of events depends, ironically, on Lila's long-repressed need for a life of refinement, something that Henry never could master but that she finds in a new husband, Reese Newbury, once her children are grown. The Wingo family story, then, is an enactment of the worst fears of the Agrarians—brutal corruption of the nurturing land in order to sustain national growth on the international scene.

The Prince of Tides is full of violence: the rape of Lila by a giant primitive called Callanwolde, initially encountered by the family while they were staying in Atlanta; the rape of Tom's twin sister, Savannah, and the sodomy of Tom by Callanwolde's associate deviates; Luke's heroic efforts to carry a dead lieutenant back to the ship after a Navy SEALs mission in Vietnam; the massive manhunt for Luke Wingo when he tries singlehandedly to deter the government's project for the land around Colleton, a hunt that ends in Luke's cold-blooded murder as he attempts to surrender; and finally, the repeated attempts by Savannah to commit suicide. Conroy's South is violent to the core.

In each of the episodes of violence and/or challenge to the traditional, nature-oriented life of Melrose Island, Luke is the key Wingo, the one who acts aggressively to follow his instincts for decency in life.[2] When Callanwolde and his cohorts threaten Lila and the children, Luke saves them from death by sending his pet tiger, Caesar, into the house to kill the intruders. When an enchantingly pure white dolphin, called Carolina Snow by the Colleton folks, is captured by mercenary hunters who transport the dolphin to Miami for exhibition in a zoo, Luke organizes and executes the plan by which he, Tom, and Savannah drive to Miami, breach the zoo's security, retrieve Carolina Snow, and put her again in the waters of Colleton River. When Luke is left alone deep in enemy territory with a dead pilot, he answers the supreme call of honor to the dead, later simply telling an admiral who asks why Luke had done so much for someone whose life was ended, "SEALs don't leave their dead" (465). When Colleton falls prey to the needs of national security, Luke objects vociforously. He is convinced that his government is stupid, and he traces the strength of his rights to object partly to his service in Vietnam: "I'm a goddamn American. I fought a war so I could say no. I earned that simple right" (513).

In point of fact, however, Luke's identity is more southern than American. He forms a plan to have Colleton secede from South Carolina, and for justification, he quotes the text of Jefferson's Declaration of Independence and notes, "Our forebears died at Bull Run and Antietam and Chancellorsville" (509)—all of this forming a paradigm of secession to serve the cause of individual rights against tyrannical government. Furthermore, Luke knows full well the importance of his association with a specific place, the place that nurtured him, the place that gave him a reason for going to the other side of the earth to join a war: "My country is my home. It's what I can see from this window. It's only about forty square miles of the planet Earth. But it's what I love and what I fought for" (514). Tom and Savannah are obvious foils to Luke's steadiness and forthrightness of purpose; each of them tends to drift and vacillate, but in diverse ways.

Savannah and Tom know that they lack Luke's stability. As they meet to wrestle with their obligations to save Luke once he has begun his SEAL-like operations to disrupt building of the nuclear facility, they are confronted with their own liabilities. Savannah sees Tom as weaker than Luke: "I've got serious doubts about the choices you've made in your life. I don't see any direction to your life. I see no ambition, no desire to change and take chances. I see you floating along, slightly detached from your wife and children, slightly alienated from your job, not knowing what you want or where you want to go" (532). In the following chapter, when we consider the character and campaign of Lewis Medlock to give Ed Gentry a strong anchor in the bosom of nature in Dickey's *Deliverance*, we will find precisely the same issues with which Savannah, Luke, and Tom contend in *The Prince of Tides*. Here, Luke is memorialized as the prince of tides; there, the mantle of river master is passed from Lewis to Ed.

As Savannah completes her indictment of Tom's detachment and alienation, Tom responds provocatively with a counter observation: "That's what makes me an American, Savannah. . . . There's nothing rare about that" (532). Hence Conroy provides a definition of the American late in the twentieth century: a person lacking direction, drifting along in possession of little but a vague sense of alienation. To this vision of the American, there is a distinguished literary history, of course. Savannah's description of Tom's detachment and alienation could be applied equally well to Huckleberry Finn in his meandering drift down in Mississippi, and Twain was the southerner who defined the American better than anyone before or since.

However, in *The Prince of Tides*, Conroy employs the image of the American adrift in a negative way—as a cautionary note about a pattern that will not suffice. Set against this pattern of error, which could likely lead to doom for the culture, is an alternative, all within the same Wingo family of the South. Luke Wingo. Tom is as much of the South—Melrose Island specifically—as Luke is, but Tom somehow missed the call to action that distinguishes Luke. At every turn, Luke took the initiative. Luke is the one who went to Vietnam, and Luke came home with the training he needs in his effort to thwart the encroachment of brutal forces that have no connection to the land and no reverence for it.

Of course, Tom envies Luke, a sentiment obviously shared by Conroy. Tom gives explicit voice to this: "I've envied him his freedom to step out in the full fury of his beliefs armed with a passion that I'll never know or feel. I'm jealous that Luke can alarm the whole countryside by that cold, unknowable rapture he brings to every article of his simple goddamn faith. The reason I need to stop him, Savannah, is because, in the deepest part of me, I believe in the rectitude of his private war with the world" (533).

Tom and Savannah eventually track down Luke in the Colleton River marshes, and they talk him into surrendering, which he does, only to be killed in the act of surrender. The loss of Luke serves as a poignant indictment of America's weaknesses in the post-Vietnam era. Luke is an old-fashioned conservative, in the southern sense. He is absolutely of a place, and he wants to keep that place as it always has been. He has an "unknowable rapture" in the faith that stands for the preservation of the natural world; he is at war with the "modern" world, the one that incessantly tries to alter nature. As a consequence, Luke carries in his own spirit more than a little of Huckleberry Finn, the aspect of his character that keeps him morally superior to the changing tides of social conformity and "progress." Luke's conservatism, his impulse to resist change, is born of the land. He knows that respect for the land is the truest way to a virtuous life, that respect for the land incorporates respect for the past. Luke is more than willing to die to sustain this respect.

Luke Wingo's efforts perfectly amplify the sentiments of Allen Tate's "Ode to the Confederate Dead." Luke has the conviction necessary to act in defense of his heritage—for him, the ultimate affirmation of going home. Vietnam was a crucial juncture in Luke's development, and he assuredly dies with knowledge carried to the heart. By setting the central action of *The Prince of Tides* in the deep South, Pat Conroy opens the door to my contention that many of the most important forces brought into play in the Vietnam War were indigenous to the culture of the South, so much so, in fact, that James Dickey's *Deliverance* can be read as one of the truest and most revealing novels of that war.

Vietnam in the South: *Deliverance*

Of the writers of the modern South, perhaps no one has more enthusiastically embraced the mission of being a southerner than James Dickey. He has said as much many times in interviews ranging over his long career. The point was brought up in a 1966 interview conducted by Carolyn Kizer and James Boatwright. Boatwright observed that a recent *Life* magazine piece had mentioned that Dickey was not southern, and Dickey rose to that challenge:

> I have one central feeling about the South and myself and that is the best thing that ever happened to me was to have been born a Southerner. First as a man and then as a writer. And yet I would not under any circumstances want to feel that I was limited in any way by being a Southerner, that I was expected, say, by other people to indulge in the kind of regional chauvinism that has sometimes been indulged in by Southern writers. One has a history which is intimately in one way or another bound up with the history of one's own people and one's own ancestors and people who live in the same region one does. The South has a tragic history, as everybody knows, but it has given me as a human being a set of values, some of which are deplorable,

obviously, but also some of which are the best things that I have ever had as
a human being. (17)

Dickey wears his southernness naturally, not as a constricting habit but
as a legitimizing force behind his values. He has an identity shaped by his
place of birth, and throughout his life, that identity has given him cause to
forge ahead as a person and as a writer.

At various times, Dickey has spoken directly to the problems of American culture. On one such occasion, he developed the image of the "energized man," one who could blast through the inertia of his times. As is his
wont, being a man of ingrained humility, Dickey began "The Energized
Man" essay with a disclaimer separating himself from the figure he would
shortly depict, but both Dickey's poetry and his fiction carry the heavy
responsibility of imparting energy; Dickey always wants others to move
vigorously as a consequence of reading his work. Always he would provide an antidote to dullness in existence, a condition that he finds endemic
in American culture:

> One gets the impression of moving among a vast number of well-meaning
> zombies; one moves among them, also, as a kind of well-meaning zombie
> with regrets. The enormous discomfort that settles on Americans as they
> grow older: the enormous discomfort that settles on them in the midst of
> all their Comforts, and we can spell that word with a capital, is that their
> lives—their real lives—seem somehow to have eluded them: to have been
> taken away from under their very noses. (163)

The Americans that Dickey has in mind hold on to vague memories of a
more active life, when they were young and full of purpose, but they
succumb to inertia and "things like . . . well, comfort" (163). The results
of this pattern are not pleasant, at least in Dickey's understanding. He sees
nothing less than appalling emptiness and despair:

> With drift, habit, and the general sense of the purposelessness of life sets
> in a genuine malaise: the malaise that lends a gigantic helping hand to
> filling the alcoholic wards of hospitals, to filling the insane asylums and the
> divorce courts. There has never been, I expect, an unhappier people. And at
> the very center of this unhappiness, I am convinced, is the feeling, not only
> that we are not using our energies properly, as we have been meant to use
> them, but that we are hardly using them at all, in any significant way. (164)

Not using one's energies—in any significant way: therein rests the
central problem for the American in Dickey's time, which is the last half of
the present century.

In "The Energized Man," Dickey announces poetry as the solution to his culture's malaise. Poetry is the means for deepening experience, deepening in the direction of connectedness with the surrounding world. The poet is "the energized man standing against the forces, the vast, sluggish forces of habit, mechanization and mental torpor . . . against the forces of comfort and the deadly sense of drift that threaten more and more each day" (165). Dickey concludes his essay with a call to pay abiding attention to the poet, the energized man, and surely, with a lifetime of labor as a poet behind him, Dickey does not dissemble in his conclusion.

However, much more poetry is written in America than is read. While Americans have indeed fallen prey to the malaise of the comfortably settled life—and while they have been demonstrably unhappy in it—they have found ways periodically to break out of dullness, but almost never, it seems, through the "imagination as glory," another phrase used by Dickey to characterize the defining function of poetry. Instead, at intervals rarely exceeding twenty years, in a pattern that now extends over more than two centuries, Americans find themselves called by necessity to go to war. War demands the application of all of one's energies, in what at least has the illusion of being a "significant way." War pushes people to discover the fundamentals of human existence. War brings people to the threshold of nature itself, far away from the settled malaise of the comfortable life. War brings out the ferocious animal tendencies locked inside the confines of every civilized person in society. War brings people face to face with violence. War brings people to confront themselves and their enemy "others" at primal levels of being. War brings people to know the essences of nature with which Dickey has been enthralled his entire life, the visceral nature that his poetry and fiction celebrate at every turn. As John Hellman argues quite successfully in *American Myth and the Legacy of Vietnam* (1986), the war in Vietnam was perceived subliminally by Americans as another errand into the wilderness, a task that satisfied the deep cultural need for transcendental significance, for some kind of action far beyond the ordinary.[1]

The novel *Deliverance*, a story that smoldered in James Dickey's imagination throughout the most crucial and trying years of the Vietnam War and finally came to completion in 1970, addresses itself so directly to the fundamentals of nature called into play by war that it illuminates the Vietnam experience as much as James Webb's *Fields of Fire*, albeit in a radically different way.

When Dickey started work on *Deliverance*, in 1962, America's Vietnam episode was beginning to move inexorably toward the full-scale combat conditions that rose to a peak in the late 1960s, then fell to the eventual withdrawal of U.S. forces in 1973, and was followed two years later by the collapse of the American-backed regime in South Vietnam. The American involvement in the early 1960s most closely resembles the conditions set forth in *Deliverance*. Those were the days of the Green Berets, who went to Vietnam to serve as advisors to their South Vietnamese counterparts. The Green Berets were conceived as a unique force of specially trained and equipped men—the bravest of the brave, the toughest of the tough—and their orientation to the wilderness was total. They were prepared to live off the land, and although they were not officially supposed to be involved directly in combat situations, their assignments were such that they were prepared to use all the available weapons of war. In self-defense, they were prepared to kill, with knife or rifle. To become a Green Beret, a person had to scale cliffs, swim rivers, hunt animals and kill them, and such a person had to have not only an aptitude for this kind of physical performance but also an attitude that relished it. The Green Berets were conceived as a special force of American manliness, and they were the first force to try their luck against the manifold tests of war in Vietnam, which with its jungle terrain presented an almost perfectly designed wilderness.

Dickey worked on *Deliverance* off and on for eight years. In an interview with Terry Roberts, published in *Night Hurdling* (1983), Dickey explained his sporadic approach to the writing of his first novel:

> I came up with the whole plot of *Deliverance* in five minutes. It was eight or ten years before I brought it out, but that's misleading because it implies that I worked on *Deliverance* for eight or ten years, and nothing but. I did six other books at the same time, and these were more important to me than *Deliverance* was. I had no stake in the game as a novelist. I had never published any prose fiction; I had never even published a short story or written one. But the poetry was moving along well, so *Deliverance* was way down the ladder of priorities. I did work on it every know and then, and suddenly I saw that it was possible to finish the thing. And then somebody came along and offered me a contract for it. At that time I only had 90 pages written of a very rough draft, but Houghton Mifflin bought it anyhow and paid me a modest advance. I went on and finished it, and brought it out in '70, I guess it was. Immediately there was a movie contract, a paperback contract, it was in 30 languages, and much more bewildering complexity ensued. (237)

At the time of the interview in the early 1980s, Dickey told Roberts that he was tired of *Deliverance,* but there is no denying that he had used the novel to speak directly, forcefully, and provocatively to issues that have been part of both his life and his poetry at every turn (Dickey served his country in both World War II and Korea, and he has a considerable body of poetry that reflects his war experience)[2]—and in the process, he reached an audience infinitely larger than he had reached through the medium of poetry.

When James Dickey appeared at the University of North Carolina in the early 1970s to take part in a symposium on the South, he read from several of his works, including a section of *Deliverance*—the part in which Ed Gentry scales the river gorge in order to place himself in a position where he might kill the mountain man who shot Drew and who would, presumably, shoot Ed, Bobby, and Lewis. It was obvious to all who heard Dickey reading that he thrilled to the excitement of the action described in his fiction. That was at a time, of course, when America's involvement in Vietnam had moved far along on its course toward eventual disintegration. The Green Berets had been supplanted in 1965 by large numbers of combat troops, army and marine. Following the great surprise of the North Vietnamese's Tet offensive in 1968, American public opinion had gradually drifted away from its enthusiastic support of the Vietnam War. The power of American manliness had been challenged to the point at which it no longer seemed supreme. Trips to the wilderness could bring results that were not fully anticipated at the outset.

Yet, in 1970, when *Deliverance* appeared in print—and again in 1972 when the movie version appeared (with the script by Dickey, who also appeared in the film as Sheriff Bullard)—the story was enthusiastically received by American audiences, both reading and viewing. It seems clear that Americans were still fascinated with heroic efforts to use one's energies in a "significant way," even as a massive-scale national experiment in such behavior was wending its way toward defeat.

Dickey, the consummate southerner, knew full well how certain virtues pass through defeat and emerge, virtually unscathed. In his interview with Roberts, Dickey had occasion to address himself again to his personal debt to his southern heritage:

> The main thing is a sense of family: the integrity of the family unit. This doesn't mean just the immediate family, but includes the in-laws, the cousins and other people with the same blood. The sense of kinship is one of the

things I like in Southern life. I also like the remnants of the old Southern tradition, as full of hot air as a lot of it is. There's still a lot in it that's good. I still believe in the things that Stonewall Jackson and Lee and those people felt were valuable: courage and dependability and other old-fashioned virtues that go all the way back to the Greeks. I still think they're virtues, and the sense of them has been strong in the South. (239)

Where better to summon all of those old-fashioned virtues—courage and dependability and all the rest that go back to the antiquity so favored by southerners, a pattern invoked at the outset of this study in the consideration of Allen Tate—than in a venture into some sort of wilderness? Such a pattern is discernable in the Vietnam foray, and the same pattern anchors the action of *Deliverance*—right in the South.

In the same year that *Deliverance* appeared, Dickey also brought out *Self-Interviews*, a collection of thoughts that gathered the poet's sense of the world at the mid-point of his life. One of the chapters of that book, "Teaching, Writing, Reincarnations, and Rivers," contains a hint that Dickey had Vietnam in mind, distantly at least, as well as other matters taken up in the course of this study of the South. Dickey recalled Tate's "Ode to the Confederate Dead" and reflected at length on the essay Tate wrote to explain the composition of that poem. He understood the linkage of stopping by a Confederate cemetery and Tate's reading of Zeno and Parmenides:

> When I read that in Tate's essay, it hit me like a blinding light; that's really what the poetic process is. It's that kind of personal connection of very disparate elements under the fusing heat of the poem's necessity, so that they create the illusion of belonging together and illuminate each other by providing an insight by association. . . . There's a linking-up of the worlds of the Classical disciplines and the American Civil War in a way that not only comes to seem plausible but also necessary. This idea was extremely interesting to me, and it still is. (55–56)

Dickey's observation underscores the habit of southerners noted throughout this study to find linkages between the present (Vietnam) and the past. Just a page later, when Dickey set out to show how such a pattern of associations might figure in his own poetic imagination, he lighted upon nothing less than a tantalizing image taken from the Vietnam War: "These personal associations are important; nothing could be more important in poetry. As for Dean Rusk as a pair of scissors or a jungle creeper—now that might be an interesting idea: Vietnam is mostly jungle! 'The American jungle creeper'! The incongruity of him, with his bald head and so on, might yield something genuinely good poetically, because areas of association to which more than one person can respond are opened up by it" (57). Yes, it is only a fleeting remark, but telling nevertheless. Dean Rusk, a fellow southerner, one associated with the Vietnam War during the Johnson years—a jungle creeper, Vietnam, the American jungle creeper. By the time *Deliverance* was published, Dickey surely had the Vietnam War at work in his imagination.

Further on in the same chapter of *Self-Interviews*, Dickey draws even closer to the business of Vietnam. This time he is attempting to explain why certain efforts in poetry are inept. The case in point is a fellow poet of Dickey's generation, Robert Bly, who had taken a strong position in opposition to the war.[3] Dickey hits Bly hard:

> The most high-minded humanitarian sentiments in the world do not suffice to create a good poem. Look at Robert Bly. Robert Bly has no talent at all, but he keeps writing for a pre-tested public, the literary anti-Vietnam public. And when he says something to the effect that Dean Rusk is a bomb waiting to be exploded in a dark hanger, everybody applauds, because this is an anti-Dean Rusk sentiment. Whether or not it's expressed with any kind of poetical, or even human, power is beside the point. The sentiment that one wants to believe is expressed, so everybody applauds. But it's no good as verse; it's absolutely lifeless. The poets who have any kind of commitment to the high calling that they've chosen for themselves will not allow themselves to be stampeded into official propaganda for any cause, no matter how admirable. If you want, propagandize, but *coercion* to propagandize is no good; it will only cause you to write orthodox poetry. Whether it's orthodox poetry in favor of the Victorian world view or in denunciation of the Vietnam War, it is still orthodox, and orthodoxy is the worst enemy of the poet's sensibility and of his freedom to select his own subject by virtue of what moves him as a human being.
>
> One could say that one is a monster *not* to be moved by Vietnam. But monstrousness has always been a part of poetry. It was considered monstrous of Baudelaire to write about the sexual lives of lesbians in Paris. But he wished to do it. He didn't write poems in praise of empires; Victor Hugo did. Baudelaire wrote about the situation between two perverted beings in the depths of Paris, because that was what his emotional makeup caused him to do. One must be free to do this. One must not be coerced. There must be no dictatorship over the sensibility, but a freedom. And it's the *last* freedom! (72)

Without question, Dickey's imagination was fired by Vietnam, and he found a way to free himself sufficiently so that he could plumb the whole business of the war to its depths, concentrating on the driving elements of his culture and celebrating the "energized man" in action. How ironic it is that twenty years after the appearance of *Deliverance* and Dickey's denunciation of Robert Bly, Robert Bly is one of the key figures in a movement to rediscover the maleness of man, a process that typically involves trips into the wilderness to strip away the superficiality of settled comfort in order to set the stage for more primitive and elemental sensations of being. In *Iron John*, Bly has finally returned to the Dickey camp, at least in orientation to the physical life, if not in artistic talent.

Without ever claiming to do so directly, James Dickey took on the American experience of Vietnam in his novel *Deliverance* and incorporates the whole Vietnam episode. There is a "Before" section, which lays out the driving psychological and cultural forces that sent men into the physical and moral wilderness of southeast Asia, but here the setting is the wild mountain gorge of the Cahulawassee River and the people for whom the gorge is home. There are sections that treat the horrifying discovery of violent and primitive human behaviors that attend deep penetration into the wilderness, and there is an "After" section, with Dickey as prophet indicating the lingering effects of the Vietnam years. Even as this reading of *Deliverance* argues for its being an analogue of the Vietnam experience, it also must be recognized that the story is perfectly located in the South—that Vietnam was *of* the heart of the most conservative region of America, proceeding from its history and passing into its history, the land and its people locked in a ferocious embrace the tenacity of which sets up the way to deliverance. *Deliverance* is a story of Vietnam. *Deliverance* is a story of the South.

Deliverance opens with Lewis Medlock showing Ed Gentry a map of the area into which they will shortly venture. Lewis provides what military unit commanders would call an operations order for a mission into territory that could be dangerous. Start here, move there, take note of everything there because that intelligence could be important. As Lewis moves his pencil over the details of the map, it seems to Ed that the hand holding the pencil has "power over the terrain" (3), an illusion of total power that attended the early years of American involvement in Vietnam.

Ed Gentry is thoroughly southern, but his life has fallen into the pattern described unfavorably by Dickey in his essay on "The Energized

Man." There is about Ed "the enormous discomfort" that settles on Americans "in the midst of all their Comforts." Ed is happily married to a woman named Martha, who serves his needs with attentive care. He has established a reasonably successful career as an executive in a small advertising agency in Atlanta, and his home in the suburbs is perfectly adequate in terms of comfort, but Dickey introduces signs aplenty that Ed's existence falls far short of the ideal in terms of "using our energies properly . . . in any significant way."

Lewis Medlock is a total contrast to Ed, and Lewis serves throughout to give voice to Dickey's main concerns about the hazards of the settled life. Lewis has a wife, children, and money, but he lives in order to test himself against the greatest challenges he can find, and most typically, the challenges he seeks lurk in the wilderness, far from the routines of a settled life. He has feverishly applied himself to master a series of skills that take him into nature—archery, flyfishing, spelunking—and he has worked just as hard to develop himself into a wonder of finely toned muscles. Ed has been a willing follower in many of Lewis's self-improvement projects, marveling always at the "complete mystiques" that Lewis develops in his approach to finding consummate challenges to his abilities. Ed is full of admiration for Lewis, for Lewis's capacity for determination: "Lewis was the only man I knew who could do with his life exactly what he wanted to do. . . . He was not only self-determined; he was determined. . . . So I usually went with him whenever he asked me. . . . He was the only man I knew determined to get something out of life who had both the means and the will to do it, and it interested me to see how, as an experiment, this turned out" (5–6).

Thus the stage is set for action in *Deliverance*. Lewis is the point man, the one set to lead the way into the wilderness. Ed, more a follower than a leader, is still much taken with the level of excitement that the promised wilderness river ride will provide.

Others will join the adventure, of course—Bobby Trippe and Drew Ballinger. As Ed notes, they are rather different in their motivation: "They were day-to-day happy enough; they were not bored in the way Lewis and I were bored, and Bobby, particularly, seemed to enjoy the life he was in" (8). It is important for the Vietnam War parallel to realize how Dickey differentiates his four characters. They are not all macho men, driven by boredom to seek the intensity of danger by going into the wild. Nevertheless, the impulse to enter the wilderness is powerfully present in the culture of the South, and it is strong enough to draw Bobby and Drew out of their settled element—to make them leave wives and children and jobs, all part of an experiment in connecting with primal forces of human nature. In the canoe trip on the Cahulawasee River, as well as in the jungles of Vietnam, the experiment "turned out" to have some ferociously surprising results. Not all would return home from this adventure, and those who did return would come back to their place in settled society forever altered by their discoveries about the nature of morality outside the "comfort" of home.

The passage into the wilderness begins for Ed before he actually sets forth with the others on the drive to the starting point, a spot on the river beyond the backwoods town of Oree. A series of exchanges between Ed and Martha in their bedroom on the morning of 14 September, his departure date, provides a clear sign of the primitivism—something primal in human nature—that beckons from far beyond the suburbs. When Ed wakes her, Martha queries him about his reasons for going into the woods and asks if he really wants to go. Ed dissembles in his answer, giving the reason vaguely as annoying problems in his studio work, suggesting that the trip with Lewis will solve his problems. Martha then asks if it is her fault. Ed's response, spoken and unspoken, illuminates the forces behind his quest: "'Lord, no,' I said, but it partly was, just as it's any woman's fault who represents normalcy" (27). Ed seeks a world beyond a woman's normalcy, and he is going into the woods to find it. Others of his generation went to Vietnam, but the purpose for many soldiers was just the same as Ed's.

Following this conversation comes an act of sex. There is not much time before Lewis's arrival, but Martha is very accommodating. The position the lovers take in this act of conjugal love is significant. Martha presents her posterior to Ed, and penetration takes place from behind— the standard mating position for animals. Later in the novel, there is another variation on this particular positioning of bodies for sex, a variation that in its male-to-male perversity, derives absolutely from the imagination that is peculiar to the human species of animal.

One more detail, though, is important about Ed's pleasure with his wife. While buried in Martha's heat, Ed sees in his mind's eye another image, one derived from the look of a girl who had modeled the day before in Ed's studio: "The girl from the studio threw back her hair and clasped her breast, and in the center of Martha's heaving and expertly working back, the gold eye shone, not with the practicality of sex, so necessary to its survival, but the promise of it that promised other things, another life, deliverance" (28).

Thus Dickey first sketches out the way to deliverance. Ordinary, fundamental acts—such as sex—are not quite sufficient. The imagination must be actively involved, and this takes the input of experience beyond the ordinary. Fantasies are the key to the universe, here symbolized by the primordial symbol of the all-seeing gold eye, and one must act in pursuit of fantasies—hence the impending venture into wilderness, a pattern that will take one back to one's darkest origins.

Then comes the road trip that carries Lewis, Ed, Bobby, and Drew from the suburbs to the mountain wilderness. As Lewis puts it, "out of the sleep of mild people, into the wild rippling water" (36). On the drive, which suddenly plunges the men into the "red-neck South" (38), Lewis and Ed have an illuminating conversation about survival, the code of wilderness people, and the pursuit of fantasies. Lewis seeks the simplicity of bare survival: "Life is so fucked-up now, and so complicated, that I wouldn't mind if it came down, right quick, to the bare survival of who was ready to survive" (43). He knows that others can make themselves content with less, but for them, he holds little respect. The people of the mountain South live closer to the survival level than folks with Ed's background in the suburbs, and Lewis tries to fill him in on the alien culture to which they are traveling. There is "some hunting and a lot of screwing and a little farming. Some whiskey making. There's lots of music, it's practically coming out of the trees" (45), and the mountain folk "don't think a whole lot about killing people" (45). All of this, of course, sets the stage for specific incidents in the subsequent narrative—incidents that match a great many of the surprises and horrors encountered by American soldiers who found themselves in a culture that they had not taken the time to understand before they were thrown into it. Lewis knows that the alien culture of the mountain people can be dangerous, but he relishes the excitement of passing through it. For him, it is the way to deliverance, realization of an intensity that transcends the limits of ordinary experience.

In response to Lewis's ruminations about the call of the wild, Ed generates a label for the pattern he discerns. He says Lewis has a "fantasy life" (49), a point accepted as accurate by Lewis: "That's all anybody has got. It depends on how strong your fantasy is, and whether you really—

really—in your own mind, fit into your own fantasy, whether you measure up to what you've fantasized" (49).

To support his position, Lewis tells several stories about besting the challenges of the wilderness. On one of his earlier trips into the woods, Lewis had fallen while rope-scaling a steep river bank, breaking his ankle. He had managed, however, to drive himself to climb the rope and hobble out of the woods. The experience has done nothing to deter him; in fact, it has given him motivation to go back in pursuit of "that intensity; well, that's something special" (51). Anyone captivated by television's scenes of war in the early days of Desert Storm in January of 1991 was under the spell of intensity. The Green Berets in the early 1960s were charged by the call of intensity as they went out on their missions in Vietnam, and many of the other soldiers who eventually followed their lead were equally drawn by the mystique of survival in wilderness conditions.

Once Ed and the others reach Oree, they have their first encounter with the mountain people, the "others" whose very difference might constitute danger. Wars inevitably turn on confrontation with enemy "others," people who must be represented as morally subordinate to the standards of one's own culture. So it was in the moral wilderness of combat in Vietnam, and so it proves to be in *Deliverance*. When a person willingly enters the wilderness world, he must be prepared to survive on the terms established by the wilderness. Reversion to the primitive often proves to be not very difficult, as the primitive side of humans is always present, hidden not far below the surface. Of course, some basic instincts are not destructive, as is proved by the enchanting duet that Drew Ballinger plays with the mountain albino boy. Although the boy's eyes are askew, his banjo's musical vision is more than equal to the efforts of Drew on his Martin guitar.

As the wilderness-seekers head on to their entry point and cross a bridge high over the river, Ed sees it as "green, peaceful, slow," not "deep or dangerous, just picturesque" (61). Countless soldiers registered exactly the same sentiments when first seeing Vietnam from the air on their approach to that distinctly foreign land.

With Lewis's speedy driving they are soon at their destination. Exiting the car, Lewis and Ed take their first actual plunge into the woods. Immediately, the ground seems to Ed to be less than hospitable. He looks for snakes and questions his presence in such a potentially hostile environment. "Why on God's earth am I here?" he thinks to himself. Dickey does not wait to provide an answer but shows an image of Ed reflected in the car window, an image directed straight to the heart of Ed's condition in life at that moment:

> I was light green, a tall forest man, an explorer, guerilla, hunter. I liked the idea and the image, I must say. Even if this was just a game, a charade, I had let myself in for it, and I was here in the woods, where such people as I had got myself up as were supposed to be. Something or other was being made good. I touched the knife hilt at my side, and remembered that all men were once boys, and that boys are always looking for ways to become men. Some of the ways are easy, too; all you have to do is be satisfied that it has happened. (69)

How quickly Ed slips into his former self—the boy struggling to be a man, an ancient figure struggling out of the shell of a modern settled man. The rituals for this rite of passage are well documented in southern literature; William Faulkner, for instance, captured them particularly well in the boy's hunt for Old Ben in "The Bear" from *Go Down, Moses.* Perhaps if these forays into the fundamentals of nature involved only creatures less than human, the results might more regularly be salutary and beyond regret, but the war in Vietnam involved confrontation with people "others," and so does Ed's effort to be "explorer, guerilla, hunter." By the second day of the three-day journey, Ed will have been brought face to face with murder, and then he must go the next step—to assume the role of hunter of his fellow man. Lewis's speculations about the intensity of survival against hostile elements, in this case including human beings, becomes realized in bone-chilling fact.

On the quiet shore of the river, Bobby and Ed are surprised by two natives, who quickly act on the base impulse of requiring sexual service from the outsiders. Bobby is raped, forced to take the same position relative to his violator in the woods that Martha had willingly assumed for her husband. Ed would also have suffered another similar indignity from the other mountain man if Lewis had not arrived surreptitiously on the scene. Lewis kills one man with an arrow through the chest, but in the ensuring confusion, the other "enemy" flees into the woods.

At this point, *Deliverance* has arrived at moral ground zero. The four men conduct a lively debate about their proper course of action. Whose rules pertain in the wilderness? A murder has taken place, justifiable within the confines of the specific circumstances, but justice will be administered by the dead man's kin. Under Lewis's prodding—but with

Drew holding out for the moral code of civilization as known back home—the men finally decide to bury the dead mountain man. The land will soon be flooded by the river, which is being dammed, and if there is no dead body, there will be no murder trial. It is a moral code designed by exigency, just the sort of thing that served a great many soldiers in Vietnam, where phrases like "If it moves, it's VC, so waste it" gave rise to occasional acts of indiscriminate killing. By the time *Deliverance* was published, the My Lai atrocity had come before the American public with the devastating shock to the sense of moral superiority with which U.S. forces had been dispatched to do battle with the enemy in Vietnam. The series of murders in the wild in Dickey's novel illustrates the inevitability of the moral conundrums that pursue the person who strays far from the confines of a regular life.

Even as Lewis, Ed, Bobby, and Drew return to the river, they are confronted with more intensity than they had expected. The river itself proves hostile, a worthy adversary to thwart the energies and skills of the voyagers, and the surviving mountain man comes back to kill and haunt them. Drew is killed, Lewis breaks his leg in the rapids, and Bobby is frantic with fear. It falls to Ed to effect deliverance from the heart of the wilderness.

All of Lewis's efforts to make Ed into a survivor are brought into action. Ed must use all of his physical power to scale the cliff of the gorge. Then he must bring down his enemy with a single shot of his bow and arrow. This is war, at its most gruesome and ugly core, the ultimate moment faced by soldiers fighting in the ambiguous wilderness of Vietnam, but Ed rises to these challenges. There comes the moment when Ed is on the threshold of killing the mountain man: "We were closed together, and the feeling of a peculiar kind of intimacy increased, for he was shut within a frame within a frame, all of my making: the peep sight and the alleyway of needles, and I knew then that I had him, if my right hand just relaxed and let the arrow tear itself away, and if my left hand did not move, but just took up the shock of the vibrating bow" (191). When the release of this intensity comes, the shot goes true, still all within a frame of Ed's making. He had taken on the challenge of the wilderness, and now he takes on the responsibility for killing in order to get through the wilderness.

The act of killing leaves its mark on Ed, for he falls from his tree stand, and in the fall, one of his arrows runs through the flesh at his waist. The wound of this adventure becomes his Purple Heart in Vietnam terms. He succeeds in cutting the arrow out, and this moment brings its own epiphany: "There had never been a freedom like it. The pain itself was freedom, and the blood" (195). This ultimate moment of intensity serves as the climax of the story, all the rest being a long denouement involving the safe passage of Ed, Lewis, and Bobby back toward the world they had left behind not long before.

That world is already changing. The river's dammed water is fast forming a lake to serve the recreational needs of the settled suburbanites. Since Drew has been lost, Ed takes on the new responsibility of serving as father-surrogate to his children. Not surprisingly, Drew's widow rejects Ed's offer for Martha to spend a few days with her. She wants Drew, but he is lost forever, one casualty to represent the many lost in Vietnam.

Ed's experience in the wilderness has been such that it cannot be shared with others who were not there with him. When Martha inquires about his wound, he puts her off with an oblique explanation. What happened must remain locked within, his burden to bear for the rest of his life.

Dickey's conclusion to the narrative shows how fully he accepts the necessity of adventures such as Ed's—and at least analogously, by American forces in Vietnam. Two paragraphs in the "After" section explain directly the extent to which wilderness forays from the past will continue to inform actions of southerners far into the future:

> Another odd thing happened. The river and everything I remembered about it became a possession to me, a personal, private obsession, as nothing else in my life ever had. Now it ran nowhere but in my head, but there it ran as though immortally. I could feel it—I can feel it—on different places on my body. It pleases me in some curious way that the river does not exist, and that I have it. In me it still is, and will be until I die, green, rocky, fast, slow, and beautiful beyond reality. I had a friend there who in a way had died for me, and my enemy was there.
>
> The river underlies, in one way or another, everything I do. It is always finding a way to serve me, from my archery to some of my recent ads and to the new collages I have been attempting for my friends. (275–76)

Dickey's South knows how to handle the past, knows how to claim even the most trying and treacherous of experiences, knows that knowledge carried to the heart comes compellingly from facing the wilderness, whether in the woods or in war. Survivors of this kind of intensity carry the past in their hearts, and surely, although there is a report from Martha's younger brother that the next generation, "the one just getting out of high school" (278), is willing to be content with a more sedate kind of approach to nature (as represented by visits to the marinas on the lakes that have been created by the damming of wild rivers), in all probability, the culture of the South will again find itself in need of situations that call for the use of one's energies to the fullest extent and in a "significant way."

It happened in the Civil War, it happened again in the Vietnam War, and the southern imagination is distinctly predisposed for it to happen again, even as it did during the Desert Storm episode. And again, sometime in the future, when the next generation comes along.

At the end of *The Immoderate Past: The Southern Writer and History*, C. Hugh Holman reiterated the premise of his study: "The past has been and still is an inescapable element of the southern mind, not as a myth, not as a retreat, not as a mask, but as a mystery to be understood, as a burden to be borne, as a guilt to be expiated, and as a pattern which can—if anything can—point us to the future" (101). Holman's study, with its title drawn from Tate's "Ode to the Confederate Dead," was published in 1977, just a few years after the collapse of the American-backed government in South Vietnam. At that juncture, Vietnam had not really been engaged in the southern imagination as a mystery in historical time, although I have argued here that James Dickey had already located the essence of Vietnam within the South, as represented by the characters, action, and moral dilemmas in his novel *Deliverance*.

With the publication of James Webb's *Fields of Fire* in 1978, the pattern described by Holman began to be applied to the mystery of Vietnam. Although there have always been mythic overtones, particularly for writers like Webb, the process of embedding Vietnam in southern time has clearly not been driven by the impulse to turn the Vietnam War into myth. Instead, Webb and other southern writers in the past fifteen years have wanted to place the Vietnam War in a continuum of human experience, not because it was a good war or a bad war, but because it happened, and knowledge of lasting value comes to the heart through the medium of time.

Hence this study examines a wide variety of patterns for linking Vietnam to the long chronicle of history in the South. Writers from other parts of America do not typically approach the Vietnam War with the same sense of a deep and abiding past, but a host of southern writers locate the war against a layered background of time. Along the way, numerous other aspects of southern culture resurface in the narratives and poems devoted to the Vietnam War. Identification with values associated with the land, a central theme of *I'll Take My Stand*, which was written by a group of southerners two generations earlier, appears frequently as a mark of southernness, and in many cases, texts of the Vietnam War from the South turn tightly on the issue of race relations, long a matter of special importance to southern writers. Along the same lines, honor (to the family and to the community) is often correlated with the impulse to violence, a linkage that has been of concern to generations of southerners. In brief, southerners found in Vietnam a strange but provocative reflection of their own cultural past.

Southern soldiers went off to the Vietnam War with baggage that was not exactly the issue of the U.S. armed forces. Robert E. Lee Hodges, Jr., of *Fields of Fire*, carried a mammouth legacy in his name alone. In some cases, it took experience in Vietnam to make the special baggage apparent (for example, the scheme of development found in Gustav Hasford's two Vietnam novels), and sometimes it was not until those soldiers returned home that the realization of what had been carried really emerged. Such was the circumstances of Tom Laidlaw of *Soldier's Joy* and Luke Wingo of *The Prince of Tides*, who, in defense of his native land (the coastal tidewaters of South Carolina), claims the right to resist the federal government's encroachment because of his service to defend freedom in Vietnam—an orientation toward rights that connects directly to the secession of eleven southern states to form the Confederacy during the Civil War.

Even Ed Gentry of Dickey's *Deliverance*, who goes only as far as the "jungle" wilderness of north Georgia for the ultimate test of his humanity (both in its physical dimension and in its moral temper), finds himself caught in hazards to his being (both physical and moral) which verge directly on the reality of combat in Vietnam. Ed survives his three-day trial in nature, and the experience will stay with him always, sometimes sustaining him, sometimes haunting him. The necessity of going where he did, and doing what he did, arose because of the place of his birth, and in the end he appears sanguine about his maturation.

In Ed Gentry's condition after his return from the wilds of the river gorge and his exposure to "others" who live there, we can see the general tendency of the South in the years following the Vietnam War. The war has been lodged in experience and in time, where it will remain to carry knowledge to the heart. Neither rejection of any particular experience from the war nor denial of the whole episode is deemed sensible by the southerner. The contemporary southerner is not obliged, either, to celebrate the experience as an ennobling "lost cause." Instead, the writers scrutinized in this study reach for the entirety of experience, including the agony of loss in an arena clearly not governed by tidy dogma or by any reassuring precepts, knowing that it must be borne forward, must be sustained to be received by the next generation. Incrementally the whole grows, with the Vietnam War incorporated into a larger pattern, neither suggesting anything glorious as a result nor portending any particular triumph to come, but growing nevertheless. If anything, the stage is simply set for further events, perhaps as similar to the Vietnam War as the Vietnam War was to akin to the Civil War for southerners of the present generation.

Notes

Chapter 1. THE VIETNAM WAR IN SOUTHERN TIME

1. The connection between history and literature in the South has been established decisively in a number of studies. Perhaps the fullest and best analysis of the connection was provided by C. Hugh Holman in *The Immoderate Past: The Southern Writer and History* (Athens: University of Georgia Press, 1977). Holman argued that the South's concern for history was well established before the watershed event of the Civil War and that history became more significant—not less—as a consequence of that war. More recently, in his perceptive study, *The Edge of the Swamp: A Study in the Literature and Society of the Old South* (Baton Rouge: Louisiana State University Press, 1989), Louis D. Rubin, Jr., amplified Holman's position on the primacy of history in the South even before the Civil War. In his introductory chapter, "The Old South and Historical Causality," Rubin asserts the following: "Historical knowledge is best seen, perhaps, as a continuum in time and space, in which interpretation—the assertion of causality—is arranged in a linear, chronological pattern in order to be understood. So that we are continually engaged in introducing our knowledge of newly discovered events into an already existing scheme, an activity that both alters the pattern itself and also causes what we believe are the meanings of the events to be modified as well" (3). The compulsion to look behind the present is offered by Rubin as a defining tendency of the southerner, one that he uses to explain his own efforts: "But the historical habit, noted earlier, that was more or less mine by community inheritance, was not long in impelling me in the direction of what had come before the moderns—of, that is, the past" (6).

2. Numerous attempts have been made to pinpoint the key identifying characteristics of southernness. Following on the heels of the people responsible for *I'll Take My Stand* was W. J. Cash and his *The Mind of the South* (1941), a provocative, albeit idiosyncratic effort to map the origins of uniqueness in the way the people of the South viewed life. Many subsequent studies have built upon—or questioned—the positions established by Cash, who died not too long after his book appeared. For example, Michael O'Brien, in *The Idea of the American South, 1920–1941* (Baltimore: Johns Hopkins University Press, 1979) contends energetically with Cash's thesis. Other noteworthy efforts along this line include Clyde N. Wilson et al., *Why the South Will Survive*, essays by fifteen southerners, published in 1981 by the University of Georgia Press as a fifty-year update of *I'll Take My Stand*; Richard H. King's *A Southern Renaissance: The Cultural Awakening of the*

American South, 1930–1955 (New York: Oxford University Press, 1980), Richard Gray's *The Literature of Memory: Modern Writers of the American South* (Baltimore: Johns Hopkins University Press, 1976), Fred Hobson's *Tell About the South: The Southern Rage to Explain* (Baton Rouge: Louisiana State University Press, 1983), and Lewis A. Lawson's *Another Generation: Southern Fiction Since World War II* (Jackson: University Press of Mississippi, 1984). Certainly anything by the sociologist John Shelton Reed would be illuminating as an exercise to highlight features that distinguish the South.

3. Carlos Baker, ed., *Ernest Hemingway: Selected Letters, 1917–1961* (New York: Charles Scribner's Sons, 1981), 605. This letter to Cowley, dated 14 November 1945, linked a MacLeish poem, "The Young Dead Soldiers," with Tate's "Ode to the Confederate Dead." Most of Hemingway's correspondence regarding Tate was favorable. They met occasionally, in Paris and elsewhere, and Hemingway felt that Tate's critical judgment was excellent. Hemingway joined Tate and others (including MacLeish) in an effort after World War II to keep Ezra Pound from being treated too harshly for his wartime support of the Fascist governments.

4. An insightful analysis of the linkage between the "Ode" and "To the Lacedemonians" was made by Donald Davidson in "The Meaning of War: A Note on Allen Tate's 'To the Lacedemonians,'" in *Allen Tate and His Work: Critical Evaluations,* ed. Radcliffe Squires (Minneapolis: University of Minnesota Press, 1972), 232–41.

5. Fred Hobson, at the end of "A South Too Busy to Hate," his contribution to Wilson's *Why the South Will Survive*, makes this point about Americans/southerners in similar terms, suggesting that the American "gives little thought to what occupied any particular spot fifty years before, to what happened there. The Southerner may not, either—but, with his tradition, he should" (54). Hobson can be reassured by the writers included in this study that the tradition is honored thoroughly.

6. Serious reflection on the placement of Vietnam War literature within the American cultural heritage was given a powerful boost by Philip D. Beidler's *American Literature and the Experience of Vietnam* (1982). More recently, book-length studies of note include John Hellman's *American Myth and the Legacy of Vietnam* (1986), Thomas Myers's *Walking Point: American Narratives of Vietnam* (1988), and Susan Jeffords's contentious *The Remasculinization of America: Gender and the Vietnam War* (1989). Several collections of essays have also served to bring the Vietnam experience into focus from a wide variety of perspectives: William J. Searle's *Search and Clear: Critical Responses to Selected Literature and Film on the Vietnam War* (1988), Owen Gilman and Lorrie Smith's *America Rediscovered: Critical Essays on Literature and Film of the Vietnam War* (1990), Philip K. Jason's *Fourteen Landing Zones: Approaches to Vietnam War Literature* (1991), and Michael Anderegg's *Inventing Vietnam: The War in Film and Television* (1991).

Chapter 2. VIETNAM AND THE WARRIOR SOUTH

1. In *Cavalier and Yankee: The Old South and American National Character* (1961), William R. Taylor took on this whole issue in a thorough manner, and at

the center of his study touched upon the "mythmaking ethos" (189–93) that was behind nineteenth-century development of the "cult of chivalry" (Chapters IV and V) in the South, all part of what he saw as a "sustaining illusion" (143–341) leading up to the Civil War.

2. These statistics (and considerable other factual information about the presence of the war effort in southern states) were originally developed in research that went into my "Vietnam War" essay (670–71) for the *Encyclopedia of Southern Culture* edited by Wilson and Ferris.

3. It must be noted, of course, that the South was not the only place where Vietnam training and staging took place. The marines used Camp Pendleton (California), and the army used Fort Ord (California), Fort Lewis (Washington), Fort Carson (Colorado), Fort Riley (Kansas), and several other locations to prepare soldiers for Vietnam service.

4. In response to a letter seeking specific details about Webb's family history—who fought where and how this information first came into Webb's possession—Webb called me on 15 March 1991. Although he had been extremely busy with interviews about Desert Storm and with promotional activities for his latest book, he was most generous in supplying details about his family's past. It was evident that the past is vitally alive in his mind, and when I mentioned the idea of "the presentness of the past," he said he liked that view very much. It was what allowed for the possibility of pride—of accountability—knowing that an individual's achievements will be measured against something that has gone before.

5. These statistics were contained in a newspaper article, "Keeping Tradition, South's Enlistees Abound," by Julia M. Klein, in the *Philadelphia Inquirer*, 10 February 1991, 22A. Klein cited Defense Department sources of the Army Recruiting Command at Fort Sheridan, Illinois, and the military services of the National Guard Bureau.

6. It must be acknowledged without equivocation that patriots reside in all regions of the United States. In every past war, good soldiers have come from everywhere; the future is likely to continue in the same vein regarding the distribution of warlike impulses throughout the nation. The point of this chapter is simply to examine the way battle-readiness has been sustained in the South by forces that swirl with mythic energy. The statistics introduced briefly suggest that the phenomenon is real, not merely mythic in nature.

Chapter 3. IN WHICH COUNTRY?

1. Of course, this is home country to Mason herself. In "Women and War: Bobbie Ann Mason's *In Country*," Sandra Bonilla Durham cites an interview that Mason had with Wendy Smith in which Mason revealed how her sense of characters and action preceded the linkage to Vietnam, declaring that Vietnam surfaced "out of my unconscious" (45).

2. Robert H. Brinkmeyer, Jr., in "Finding One's History: Bobbie Ann Mason and Contemporary Southern Literature," similarly draws attention to the affinity of Mason's regard for history with the position of Tate's "Ode," specifically with regard to the story "Shiloh" and *In Country* (31).

3. It should be noted here that John Hellman's contentious study, *American Myth and the Legacy of Vietnam* (1986), focuses directly on the wilderness myth; Hellman argues persuasively that the American fascination with entering the wilderness and subduing it formed a potent basis of the motivation behind the whole Vietnam episode. Only Hellman's conclusion—that the failure of American policy in Vietnam meant the essential loss of the wilderness myth, thus necessitating new mythic points of departure as represented in George Lucas's *Star Wars* trilogy—seems off the mark. The literature of Vietnam from the South certainly points to the idea that fascination with the world of the swamp remains strong.

Chapter 4. VIETNAM AND THE FLIGHT OF TIME

1. The term "magic realism" is most frequently used in discussion of works by Gabriel García Márques, Jorge Luis Borges, and others who take liberties with strict reality in their fiction. In an interview with Raymond Leslie Williams, García Márques observed that he is "quite disrespectful of real time and space," leading to production of a novel that "contains historical elements used poetically" (136). Philip Beidler, in "Re-Writing America: Literature as Cultural Revision in the New Vietnam Fiction," deftly suggests that certain Vietnam texts—notably Tim O'Brien's *Going After Cacciato* and Stephen Wright's *Meditations in Green*—reflect the ingredients of "magical realism" (6). Julius Raper's "Inventing Modern Southern Fiction: A Postmodern View" argues that the South has been home to this type of vision for some time. For instance, Raper mentions certain features of Faulkner's "The Old People" from *Go Down, Moses* as having kinship with the efforts of García Márques, and he links this pattern as well to John Barth, (*Chimera* and others), Walker Percy (*Lancelot*), and David Madden ("The Singer").

Chapter 5. REGENERATIVE VIOLENCE; OR, GRAB YOUR SABER, RAY

1. Highly ambitious and contentious, Slotkin's work has not been without challenge, even as he built upon *Regeneration Through Violence* with a subsequent study: *The Fatal Environment: The Myth of the Frontier in the Age of Industrialization* (1985). Reviewing *The Fatal Environment* for *American Quarterly*, Sam B. Girgus addressed two particular liabilities in Slotkin's general critical approach: "Two flaws of some concern in *Regeneration Through Violence* become major problems in this new work. Successfully resisting the impulse in his new book to elide or compress any idea, interpretation, or sentence, Slotkin immediately develops a pattern of contradiction and confusion. Also, the penchant for presentation in *Regeneration Through Violence* (interpreting the past in terms of *Apocalypse Now*) imposes an overwhelming ideological bias on this new book" (300). Despite the hazards of overgeneralization and inflicting contemporary, post-Vietnam angst upon the deep past, Slotkin's provocative analysis of sweeping cultural tendencies seems well worth taking seriously.

2. In a recent master's thesis, "Romancing the Land: American Land-Based Mythology and the Vietnam War," Caron Schwartz Ellis has carried Slotkin's analysis further forward with a cogent interpretation of "regeneration through

violence" in some of the best-known Vietnam War films released over the past fifteen years.

3. James Elwell Brown "Jeb" Stuart, a native Virginian and graduate of West Point in 1854, committed his estimable military talents to the Confederacy. He led a charge in the First Battle of Bull Run which helped secure southern victory in that engagement. Thereafter he began to refine cavalry reconnaissance techniques, frequently going behind enemy lines to obtain information about troop placement and movement. Unfortunately for Stuart, he became part of the effort to find scapegoats for General Lee following the southern defeat at Gettysburg, where Stuart did not provide Lee with timely information about Union troop locations. Stuart was killed protecting the city of Richmond from the attack of General Philip Sheridan in May 1864. Stuart's reputation suffered as a consequence of Gettysburg; he is not mentioned, for example, in the essays of *I'll Take My Stand*, where both Donald Davidson and Frank Lawrence Owsley make prominent mention of Generals Lee and Jackson, but his tactical maneuvers are studied worldwide in military history classes, and his outrageously bold style of leadership (cavalier in the best sense) is certain to capture Hannah's interest.

4. This concern with the consequence of breaking cultural norms would be, ironically, part of Hannah's inheritance as a southerner, despite the general pattern in the South of honoring community-based codes of behavior. From the work of Edgar Allan Poe through Faulkner's *The Sound and the Fury* and Alice Walker's *The Color Purple*, southerners have manifested an on-going fascination with the aura of incest.

5. It is worth recalling here Kenneth Lynn's portrait of Edmund Ruffin, the hotheaded Virginia planter who virtually raved about the need for the South to be independent and published Byrd's *History of the Dividing Line* in 1841 as an act of insurgence, then as "an aging knight of sixty-seven years with long white hair hanging down to his shoulders, he was permitted the honor of pulling the lanyard on the first gun fired in the Civil War" (22). When the Civil War was done, the South defeated, Ruffin killed himself.

6. Stuart was instrumentally involved in the Confederate invasion of Maryland in September of 1862.

Chapter 6. CIVIL WAR REDUX: Brotherhood or Fratricide?

1. Almost as soon as the staged build-up of American ground forces in Vietnam began in 1965, the idea of the exploitation of minority soldiers began to surface, soon acquiring, in mythic fashion, a life of its own. For example, racial injustice was alleged by the Fort Hood Three, a group of three soldiers (Dennis Mora, James Johnson, and David Samas) who refused in 1966 to go to Vietnam and attempted, unsuccessfully, to file suit in federal court to prevent the army from acting to punish them. Their case, abstracted in Lynd's *We Won't Go: Personal Accounts of War Objectors*, included a joint statement outlining reasons for their taking "a stand against this war" (184), and one paragraph specifically alleged racial discrimination through the draft and conduct of the war, a point of personal relevance to them since Johnson was an African-American and Mora was Puerto

Rican: "We know that Negroes and Puerto Ricans are being drafted and end up in the worst of the fighting all out of proportion to their numbers in the population; and we have firsthand knowledge that these are the ones who have been deprived of decent education and jobs at home" (185). The point about education was particularly relevant during the war years before the draft system was changed to a lottery, for in those years, students in college were allowed a deferral and this happened to favor white males. However, statistics from *The Negro in the Army*, generated by the Department of Defense and republished in the *Statistical Abstract of the United States* by the Department of Commerce (1976), do not show that the proportion of African-American soldiers in the military during the Vietnam War era was out of line with the proportion of African-Americans in the population at large, although by 1973, the last year in which American soldiers were committed to combat in Vietnam, the percentage of African-Americans in the population (11.3%) was exceeded by the percentage of African-Americans in the armed forces (13.2%). Nevertheless, statistics from the same report show convincingly that the proportion of African-American officers (averaging around 2.2% over the course of the war) was much smaller than the percentage of African-American soldiers. Although there were exceptions, minority soldiers were typically led by white officers, hence giving rise to some anxiety—whether it was justified or not—in the African-American community, both at home and in the war zone.

2. Writers of fiction are, by their profession, always a minority. The writers surveyed in this chapter are generally allied in their concern for the nature of race relations in the South; by the very fact that they focus on race relations as a problem, they are implicitly showing commitment to the virtue of a solution: improved relations, black with white. Yet they, as a minority specially given to the task of articulating flash points in the human drama, are not entirely of one mind in their reading of the real direction of their culture vis-à-vis the race issue. In the way their various stories play out, there is ambivalence on how this issue will eventually be resolved—long after the crucibles of the Civil War and Vietnam—and in such ambivalence, they seem to truly represent their culture at large.

Chapter 7. BACK TO ALABAMA, HEART OF DIXIE

1. Southerners—or for that matter, Alabamians—are by no means unique in this pattern of taking some time (and successive books) to bring the war home. Larry Heinemann, for instance, a midwesterner, based his first novel, *Close Quarters*, on combat in Vietnam, and then examined in his second novel, *Paco's Story*, the consequences of return from the war. As noted in chapter 1, Heinemann's returning veteran seems distinctly out of place (and time) in his country, and that is his point, whereas the two writers to be examined in this chapter consider at length the impact of returning to a very specific place—Alabama—and through such a pattern, the ethos of the South is given serious reconsideration.

2. A full report of this atrocity is included in Susan Brownmiller's *Against Our Will: Men, Women, and Rape* (109–10).

3. The idea that the past carries in it the potential—sometimes at least—for one's undoing is not limited to the South. Hawthorne's *The Scarlet Letter* turns on such a point and so does Fitzgerald's *The Great Gatsby*. Yet southerners have been particularly sensitive to the carryover effect of their legacy from the past. In this vein, history haunts the life of Thomas Sutpen in *Absalom, Absalom!*, and although the issues are quite different for Jack Burden of *All the King's Men*, when he starts to dig into the past, the mix of light with darkness in history is mined by Warren for all its tragic potential. Jack has to come to terms with the "burden" of history.

4. Quite a large number of refugees from Southeast Asia, including boat people from Vietnam, eventually found their way to the coastal ports of the Gulf of Mexico, where many went into the shrimping business. Their success has resulted in considerable friction with the Americans of somewhat longer standing whose jobs have been threatened by the influx of a new labor force. Ironically, they have sometimes been at odds with people who once went to the other side of the world to fight on their behalf.

5. The introduction of a "cowboy" automatically links Hasford's work to another genre, the western, which essentially began with Owen Wister's *The Virginian* (1902). Wister was a Philadelphian, but his novel centers upon a man of the South who fought for the Confederacy and then went west, carrying with him the code of honor mentioned elsewhere in this study. The "western" became a popular film genre in the 1940s and 1950s, and many of the soldiers who went to Vietnam were so full of the cowboy/Indian idea that they superimposed their past upon the conditions of Vietnam. Indian country to them was owned by the Viet Cong. Hasford's use of the cowboy motif accurately reflects this sweeping phenomenon.

6. *Full Metal Jacket*, Stanley Kubrick's 1988 film adaptation of Hasford's *The Short-Timers*, brought the story to a close short of the action at the end of the novel, very likely because the image of one good American soldier shooting another good American in order to save his own life would not be acceptable to the movie-going public, even though the scene speaks violently to the kind of horror that was found in Vietnam.

7. Hasford revealed his plans for the future in response to inquiries placed by Frances Carol Locher's *Contemporary Authors*, and his answers appear in Volumes 85–88 of that series, pp. 244–45. Hasford's reputation for arrogance is confirmed by his explanation of how he came to answer the call to the writing profession: "But then I had all these ideas for books which came to me in a vision. Since then, I have been convinced that there is no human problem which could not be solved if people would simply do as I say" (244). Many people would consider his subsequent abuse of library privileges a manifestation of more than just arrogance, something closer to utter contempt for society and its need for order.

8. These details about Hasford's purloined books come from an article, "Police Seek Oscar Nominee over Library Cache in Locker" in *American Libraries*, May 1988, 333–36.

Chapter 9. YOU MUST GO HOME AGAIN, BUT WHAT IS HOME?

1. The "mad minute" was originally service slang for firing the Final Protective Line (FPL), standard procedure as a last recourse in defense of a fixed position, but the phrase soon was used to evoke any incident of unlimited firing of weaponry—the ultimate of giving over to the destructive energy of guns.

2. In the film version of *The Prince of Tides* (1991), directed by Barbra Streisand, Luke's part of the story is cut to a few lines of dialogue and to fleeting images of Luke as a child with his brother and sister. Conroy was involved in writing the screenplay, but the loss of Luke, while necessary to keep the film within reasonable time constraints and to focus on Tom's angry instability, cuts the heart out of the novel, including the title, for Luke, far more than Tom, is the true prince of tides.

Chapter 10. VIETNAM IN THE SOUTH: *Deliverance*

1. It must be noted, however, as a corrective to Hellman's contentious thesis, that in terms of surface motivation, Americans were led, in all sincerity, to conceptualize the Vietnam effort as a necessary, albeit unpleasant task in the containment of communism; a stand had to be taken to keep a set of dominoes (Southeast Asian nations) from falling, one after another, until at last America itself would be toppled. As an exercise in symbolic logic, this reasoning induced considerable support for the American role in Vietnam.

2. As a member of the U.S. Army Air Force in World War II, Dickey flew one hundred combat missions in the 418th Night Fighter Squadron; he also saw service in the Korean War; and he was awarded the Air Medal. Dickey's most aggressive response to his war experience came in "The Firebombing," a poem published in 1965 in *Buckdancer's Choice.* "The Firebombing" represents a backward look at an "anti-morale" air raid on Japan in 1945, with the poet looking back twenty years after the raid. Although there are signs that the persona of the poem is unsettled by the past—as he tries to link the lives of his victims with his own home life in the 1960s—the air raid action, including the horrible burning of people by napalm, is accepted finally as necessary. His pride "as / American as I am" (*Poems, 1957–1967*, 188) is still intact. "The Firebombing" clearly indicates that Dickey would be prepared to justify certain horrors of war, even as they would be part of an engagement that was just commencing on a large scale in 1965.

3. Bly had gone on record with a stinging criticism of Dickey's apparent lack of concern for the victims of the night raid described in "The Firebombing," thus setting himself up as a natural target for Dickey's response a few years later in *Self-Interviews.*

Works Cited

Anderegg, Michael, ed. *Inventing Vietnam: The War in Film and Television*. Philadelphia: Temple University Press, 1991.

Baker, Carlos, ed. *Ernest Hemingway: Selected Letters, 1917–1961*. New York: Scribner, 1981.

Barber, Benjamin. "The Importance of Remembering: The Vietnam Legacy's Challenge to American Democracy." In *The Legacy: The Vietnam War in the American Imagination*, edited by D. Michael Shafer, 3–8. Boston: Beacon Press, 1990.

Beidler, Philip D. *American Literature and the Experience of Vietnam*. Athens: University of Georgia Press, 1982.

———. *Re-Writing America: Vietnam Authors in Their Generation*. Athens: University of Georgia Press, 1991.

———. "Re-Writing America: Literature as Cultural Revision in the New Vietnam Fiction." In *America Rediscovered*, edited by Owen Gilman and Lorrie Smith, 3–9. New York: Garland, 1990.

Bell, Madison Smartt. *Soldier's Joy*. 1989. New York: Penguin Books, 1990.

Blair, Sydney. *Buffalo*. New York: Viking, 1991.

Brinkmeyer, Robert H., Jr. "Finding One's History: Bobbie Ann Mason and Contemporary Southern Literature." *Southern Literary Journal* 19 (1987): 20–33.

Brown, Dee. *Bury My Heart at Wounded Knee: An Indian History of the American West*. New York: Holt, Rinehart and Winston, 1970.

Brown, Larry. *Dirty Work*. Chapel Hill: Algonquin Books, 1989.

Brownmiller, Susan. *Against Our Will: Men, Women, and Rape*. New York: Simon and Schuster, 1975.

Cash, W. J. *The Mind of the South*. New York: Knopf, 1941.

Conroy, Pat. *The Prince of Tides*. Boston: Houghton Mifflin, 1986.

Crane, Stephen. *The Red Badge of Courage*. 1895. New York: Norton, 1976.

Crews, Harry. *Body*. New York: Poseiden Press, 1990.

Davidson, Donald. *Southern Writers in the Modern World*. Athens: University of Georgia Press, 1958.

———. et. al. *I'll Take My Stand*. 1930. Baton Rouge: Louisiana State University Press, 1977.

de Lauretis, Teresa. *Technologies of Gender: Essays on Theory, Film, and Fiction*. Bloomington: Indiana University Press, 1987.

Dickey, James. *Deliverance*. 1970. New York: Dell, 1971.

———. "The Energized Man." In *The Imagination as Glory*, edited by Bruce Weigl and T. R. Hummer, 163–65. Urbana: University of Illinois Press, 1984.

———. "The Imagination as Glory." In *The Imagination as Glory*, edited by Bruce Weigl and T. R. Hummer, 166–73. Urbana: University of Illinois Press, 1984.

———. "Getting to the Gold With Terry Roberts." In *Night Hurdling*, 234–45. Columbia and Bloomfield Hills: Brucolli Clark, 1983.

———. *Poems, 1957–1967*. 1967. New York: Collier, 1972.

———. *Self-Interviews*. Garden City: Doubleday, 1970.

Durham, Sandra Bonilla. "Women and War: Bobbie Ann Mason's *In Country*." *Southern Literary Journal* 22 (1990); 45–52.

Edgerton, Clyde. *The Floatplane Notebooks*. Chapel Hill: Algonquin Books, 1988.

———. *Raney*. Chapel Hill: Algonquin Books, 1985.

———. *Walking Across Egypt*. 1987. New York: Ballantine Books, 1988.

Ellis, Caron Schwartz. "Romancing the Land: American Land-Based Mythology and the Vietnam War." Master's Thesis, University of Colorado, 1990.

Ehrhart, W. D. *Carrying the Darkness—American Indochina: The Poetry of the Vietnam War*. New York: Avon, 1985.

Faulkner, William. *Absalom, Absalom!* 1936. New York: Vintage Books, 1987.

———. *Go Down, Moses*. New York: Modern Library, 1942.

———. *The Sound and the Fury*. 1929. New York: Norton, 1987.

Fitzgerald, F. Scott. *The Great Gatsby*. 1925. New York: Collier, 1986.

Gilman, Owen, and Lorrie Smith, eds. *America Rediscovered: Critical Essays on Literature and Film of the Vietnam War*. New York: Garland, 1990.

Girgus, Sam B. "Religious Freedom or Real Estate: The Problem of Ideology in Interdisciplinary Studies." *American Quarterly* 38 (1986): 299–304.

Gossett, Louise Y. *Violence in Recent Southern Fiction*. Durham: Duke University Press, 1965.

Gotera, Vicente F. "'Depending on the Light': Yusef Komunyakaa's *Dein Cai Dau*." In *America Rediscovered*, edited by Owen Gilman and Lorrie Smith, 282–300. New York: Garland, 1990.

Gray, Richard. *The Literature of Memory: Modern Writers of the American South*. Baltimore: Johns Hopkins University Press, 1976.

Groom, Winston. *As Summers Die*. New York: Summit Books, 1980.

———. *Better Times Than These*. New York: Summit Books, 1978.

———. *Forrest Gump*. New York: Doubleday, 1986.

———. *Gone the Sun*. New York: Doubleday, 1988.

Hall, H. Palmer. "The Helicopter and the Punji Stick: Central Symbols of the Vietnam War." In *America Rediscovered*, edited by Owen Gilman and Lorrie Smith, 150–61. New York: Garland, 1990.

Hannah, Barry. *Airships*. 1978. New York: Vintage Books, 1985.

———. *Geronimo Rex*. 1972. New York: Penguin Books, 1983.

———. *Ray*. 1980. New York: Penguin Books, 1981.

———. *The Tennis Handsome*. 1983. New York: Scribner, 1987.

Hasford, Gustav. *The Phantom Blooper.* New York: Bantam, 1990.

———. *The Short-Timers.* 1979. New York: Bantam, 1980.

Hawthorne, Nathaniel. *The Scarlet Letter.* 1850. New York: Norton, 1988.

Heinemann, Larry. *Paco's Story.* New York: Farrar, Straus & Giroux, 1986.

Hellman, John. *American Myth and the Legacy of Vietnam.* New York: Columbia University Press, 1986.

Hemingway, Ernest. "The Big Two-Hearted River, I & II." *In Our Time.* 1925. New York: Scribner, 1930.

———. *The Sun Also Rises.* New York: Scribner, 1926.

Hendricks, G. C. *The Second War.* New York: Viking, 1990.

Herr, Michael. *Dispatches.* New York: Knopf, 1977.

Hobson, Fred. *The Southern Writer in the Postmodern World.* Athens: University of Georgia Press, 1991.

———. "A South Too Busy To Hate." In *Why the SOUTH Will Survive,* by Fifteen Southerners. Athens: University of Georgia Press, 1981.

———. *Tell About the South: The Southern Rage to Explain.* Baton Rouge: Louisiana State University Press, 1983.

Holman, C. Hugh. *The Immoderate Past: The Southern Writer and History.* Athens: University of Georgia Press, 1977.

Huddle, David. *A Dream with No Stump Roots in It.* Columbia: University of Missouri Press, 1975.

———. *The High Spirits.* Boston: David R. Godine, 1988.

———. *Only the Little Bone.* Boston: David R. Godine, 1986.

———. *Paper boy.* Pittsburg: University of Pittsburg Press, 1979.

———. *Stopping by Home.* Salt Lake City: Gibbs Smith Books, 1988.

Jason, Philip K., ed. *Fourteen Landing Zones: Approaches to Vietnam War Literature.* Iowa City: University of Iowa Press, 1991.

Jeffords, Susan. *The Remasculinization of America: Gender and the Vietnam War.* Bloomington: Indiana University Press, 1989.

Johnson, James Weldon. *The Autobiography of an Ex-Colored Man.* 1912. New York: Penguin Books, 1990.

Just, Ward. *Stringer.* Boston: Little, Brown, 1974.

King, Richard H. *A Southern Renaissance: The Cultural Awakening of the American South, 1930–1955.* New York: Oxford University Press, 1980.

Kinney, Katherine. "'Humping the Boonies': Sex, Combat, and the Female in Bobbie Ann Mason's *In Country.*" In *Fourteen Landing Zones,* edited by Philip K. Jason, 38–48. Iowa City: University of Iowa Press, 1991.

Kizer, Carolyn, and James Boatwright. "A Conversation with James Dickey." In *James Dickey: The Expansive Imagination,* edited by Richard J. Calhoun, 1–33. Deland, Fla.: Everett/Edwards, 1973.

Klein, Julia. "Keeping Tradition, South's Enlistees Abound." *Philadelphia Inquirer* 10 February 1991, 22A.

Komunyakaa, Yusef. *Copacetic.* Middletown: Wesleyan University Press, 1984.

———. *Dien Cai Dau.* Middletown: Wesleyan University Press, 1988.

————. *I Apologize for the Eyes in My Head*. Middletown: Wesleyan University Press, 1986.

Lawson, Jacqueline. "'She's a Pretty Woman . . . for a Gook': The Misogyny of the Vietnam War." In *Fourteen Landing Zones*, edited by Philip K. Jason, 15–37. Iowa City: University of Iowa Press.

Lawson, Lewis A. *Another Generation: Southern Fiction Since World War II*. Jackson: University Press of Mississippi, 1984.

Little, Loyd. *Parthian Shot*. New York: Viking, 1975.

Locher, Frances Carol, ed. "Gustav Hasford." In *Contemporary Authors, Volumes 85–88*, 244–45. Detroit: Gale Research Company, 1980.

Lomperis, Tim. *"Reading the Wind": The Literature of the Vietnam War*. Durham: Duke University Press, 1987.

Lynd, Alice, ed. *We Won't Go: Personal Accounts of War Objectors*. Boston: Beacon Press, 1968.

Lynn, Kenneth S. *Mark Twain and Southwestern Humor*. Boston: Little, Brown, 1959.

McDonald, Walter. *After the Noise of Saigon*. Amherst: University of Massachusetts Press, 1988.

————. *A Band of Brothers: Stories from Vietnam*. Lubbock: Texas Tech University Press, 1989.

————. *Caliban in Blue and Other Poems*. Lubbock: Texas Tech University Press, 1976.

————. *Night Landings: Poems*. New York: Perennial Library, 1989.

Mailer, Norman. *The Naked and the Dead*. 1948. New York: Henry Holt, 1981.

Marx, Leo. *The Machine in the Garden; Technology and the Pastoral Ideal in America*. New York: Oxford University Press, 1964.

Mason, Bobbie Ann. *In Country*. 1985. New York: Perennial Library, 1986.

————. *Shiloh and Other Stories*. New York: Harper & Row, 1982.

Moritz, Charles, ed. "James H. Webb, Jr." In *Current Biography Yearbook*, 590–93. New York: H. W. Wilson, 1987.

Myers, Thomas. *Walking Point: American Narratives of Vietnam*. New York: Oxford University Press, 1988.

Noble, Donald R. "'Tragic and Meaningful to an Insane Degree': Barry Hannah." *Southern Literary Journal* 15 (1982): 37–44.

O'Brien, Michael. *The Idea of the American South, 1920–1941*. Baltimore: Johns Hopkins University Press, 1979.

O'Brien, Tim. *Going After Cacciato*. New York: Delacorte Press/Seymour Lawrence, 1978.

————. *If I Die in a Combat Zone, Box Me Up and Ship Me Home*. New York: Delacorte Press, 1973.

————. *Northern Lights*. New York: Delacorte Press/Seymour Lawrence, 1975.

Phillips, Jayne Anne. *Machine Dreams*. 1984. New York: Pocket Books, 1985.

"Police Seek Oscar Nominee Over Library Cache in Locker." *American Libraries* 19 (1988): 333–36.

Raper, Julius. "Inventing Modern Southern Fiction: A Postmodern View." *Southern Literary Journal* 22 (1990): 3–18.

Ringnalda, Donald. "Unlearning to Remember Vietnam." In *American Rediscovered*, edited by Owen Gilman and Lorrie Smith, 64–74. New York: Garland, 1990.

Rubin, Louis D., Jr. *The Edge of the Swamp: A Study in the Literature and Society of the Old South.* Baton Rouge: Louisiana State University Press, 1989.

———, and Robert D. Jacobs, eds. *Southern Renascence: The Literature of the Modern South.* 1953. Baltimore: Johns Hopkins University Press, 1965.

Searle, William J., ed. *Search and Clear: Critical Responses to Selected Literature and Films of the Vietnam War.* Bowling Green: Bowling Green State University Popular Press, 1988.

Shafer, D. Michael, ed. *The Legacy: The Vietnam War in the American Imagination.* Boston: Beacon Press, 1990.

Shepherd, Allen. "'Firing Two Carbines, One in Each Hand': Barry Hannah's *Hey Jack.*" *Notes on Mississippi Writers* 21 (1989): 37–40.

Simpson, Lewis. *The Dispossessed Garden: Pastoral and History in Southern Society of the Old South.* Athens: University of Georgia Press, 1975.

Sloan, James Park. *War Games.* 1971. New York: Avon, 1973.

Slotkin, Richard. *Regeneration Through Violence: The Mythology of the American Frontier, 1600–1860.* Middletown: Wesleyan University Press, 1973.

Squires, Radcliffe, ed. *Allen Tate and His Work: Critical Evaluations.* Minneapolis: University of Minnesota Press, 1972.

Stewart, Matthew. "Realism, Verisimilitude, and the Depiction of Vietnam Veterans in *In Country.*" In *Fourteen Landing Zones*, edited by Philip K. Jason, 166–79. Iowa City: University of Iowa Press, 1991.

Stone, Robert. *Children of Light.* 1986. New York: Ballantine Books, 1987.

———. *Dog Soldiers.* 1973. New York: Ballantine Books, 1975.

Tate, Allen. *Jefferson Davis: His Rise and Fall.* New York: Minton, 1929.

———. *Poems.* Denver: Swallow Paperbooks, 1961.

———. *The Man of Letters in the Modern World: Selected Essays, 1928–1955.* Cleveland: Meridian Books, 1955.

Taylor, William R. *Cavalier and Yankee: The Old South and American National Character.* New York: George Braziller, 1961.

Thoreau, Henry David. *Walden.* 1854. New York: New American Library, 1980.

Twain, Mark. *The Adventures of Huckleberry Finn.* 1885. New York: New American Library, 1959.

———. *Life on the Mississippi.* 1883. New York: New American Library, 1980.

United States. Department of Commerce. *Statistical Abstract of the United States.* 97th edition. Washington: GPO, 1976.

Walker, Alice. *The Color Purple.* 1982. New York: Pocket Books, 1985.

Warren, Robert Penn. *All the King's Men.* 1946. San Diego: Harcourt Brace Jovanovich, 1982.

Webb, James. *A Country Such As This.* Garden City: Doubleday, 1983.

———. *A Sense of Honor.* Englewood Cliffs: Prentice-Hall, 1981.

———. *Fields of Fire*. 1978. New York: Bantam, 1979.

———. *Something to Die For*. New York: Morrow, 1991.

Weigle, Bruce, and T. R. Hummer, eds. *The Imagination as Glory: The Poetry of James Dickey*. Urbana: University of Illinois Press, 1984.

Welty, Eudora. *The Golden Apples*. 1949. San Diego: Harcourt Brace Jovanovich, 1977.

———. *One Writer's Beginnings*. 1984. New York: Warner Books, 1985.

———. *The Optimist's Daughter*. 1972. Greenwich: Fawcett, 1973.

Westmoreland, William C. *A Soldier Reports*. 1976. New York: Da Capo Press, 1989.

Williams, Raymond Leslie. "The Visual Arts, the Poetization of Space and Writing: An Interview with Gabriel García Márquez." *PMLA* 104 (1989): 131–40.

Wilson, Charles Reagan, and William Ferris, eds. *Encyclopedia of Southern Culture*. Chapel Hill: University of North Carolina Press, 1989.

Wilson, Clyde N., et al. *Why the South Will Survive*. Athens: University of Georgia Press, 1981.

Wilson, James R. *Landing Zones: Southern Veterans Remember Vietnam*. Durham: Duke University Press, 1990.

Wister, Owen. *The Virginian*. 1902. New York: Airmont, 1964.

Wolfe, Thomas. *You Can't Go Home Again*. 1940. New York: Dell, 1960.

Woodward, C. Vann. *The Burden of Southern History*. Baton Rouge: Louisiana State University Press, 1968.

———. *Origins of the New South, 1871–1913*. Baton Rouge: Louisiana State University Press, 1951.

Wyatt-Brown, Bertram. *Southern Honor: Ethics and Behavior in the Old South*. New York: Oxford University Press, 1982.

Index